Engaging Erik Olin Wright

Between Class Analysis and Real Utopias

Edited by Michael Burawoy and Gay Seidman

VERSO

London • New York

For Erik with love from his students, friends, and colleagues

First published by Verso 2024
Contributions © The contributors 2024
The collection © Verso 2024

1 3 5 7 9 10 8 6 4 2

Verso
UK: 6 Meard Street, London W1F 0EG
US: 388 Atlantic Avenue, Brooklyn, NY 11217
versobooks.com

Verso is the imprint of New Left Books

ISBN-13: 978-1-80429-472-7
ISBN-13: 978-1-80429-495-6 (US EBK)
ISBN-13: 978-1-80429-726-1 (UK EBK)

British Library Cataloguing in Publication Data
A catalogue record for this book is available from the British Library

Library of Congress Cataloging-in-Publication Data

Names: Burawoy, Michael, editor. | Seidman, G., editor.
Title: Engaging Erik Olin Wright: connecting class analysis and
    real utopias / [edited by Michael Burawoy, Gay Seidman]
Description: London; New York: Verso, 2024. | Includes bibliographical references.
Identifiers: LCCN 2023051522 (print) | LCCN 2023051523 (ebook) |
    ISBN 9781804294727 (paperback) | ISBN 9781804294956 (ebk)
Subjects: LCSH: Wright, Erik Olin. | Marxian school of sociology.
Classification: LCC HM471 .E64 2024 (print) | LCC HM471
    (ebook) | DDC 305.5—dc23/eng/20231130
LC record available at https://lccn.loc.gov/2023051522
LC ebook record available at https://lccn.loc.gov/2023051523

Typeset in Minion by Hewer Text UK Ltd, Edinburgh
Printed and bound by CPI Group (UK) Ltd, Croydon, CR0 4YY

Contents

Part III
FROM CLASS ANALYSIS TO REAL UTOPIAS

Introduction: Advancing Wright's Unfinished Project
Michael Burawoy and Gay Seidman

Erik Olin Wright, one of the great social scientists of our era, left us with an unfinished project. Sadly, his fifty-year career ended on January 23, 2019, when at the age of seventy-one he succumbed to acute myeloid leukemia, while still at the height of his intellectual powers. There have been a host of tributes to Wright's scholarship, his teaching, his mentorship, his influence, his political engagement, his earnest optimism, his generosity, and his sheer intellectual brilliance, which was always presented with disarming clarity. Accolades poured in from students, colleagues, politicians, from those who knew him personally and those who didn't, and from all corners of the world. There were collective celebrations of his life and work as well, at the University of Wisconsin–Madison, where he taught for forty-three years; at the University of California, Berkeley, where he was a graduate student and frequent visitor; at the New School in New York, where *Politics and Society*, the journal with which he was associated for nearly five decades, hosted a conference in his honor; at the 2020 meetings of the American Sociological Association, where Wright had served as an elected president; and at the University of Coimbra in Portugal and at Barcelona's Catalan Association of Sociology.

We are very grateful to Margaret Eby for her conscientious editing, to Brian Baughan for his meticulous copy-editing, to Tyler Leeds for his expert proofreading, and to the Havens Wright Center for funding that made the publication of this volume possible.

The chapters in this volume are drawn from those events and from two sessions devoted to his work that were held at the International Sociological Association meeting in February 2021. With the exception of a forthcoming book covering the lectures he delivered in his famous course on sociological Marxism, this will be his final book from Verso, Wright's first-choice publisher ever since New Left Books (as Verso was called in those days) issued *Class, Crisis and the State* in 1978.

This volume is no ordinary festschrift. It is explicitly designed to show how generative Wright's ideas have been, and how he nurtured the work of so many students and colleagues. It does what Wright would want us to do: advance and enlarge his ideas. To that end, the contributors held multiple conversations, culminating in a Zoom conference in November 2021, when we agreed to elaborate the connection between the two central projects that preoccupied Wright throughout his academic and political career, and for which he will always be remembered: Class Analysis and Real Utopias.

As a graduate student in the early 1970s, Wright was key to organizing courses on Marxist social science at Berkeley and contributed energetically to the many left journals then flourishing in the San Francisco Bay Area. His own scholarly interventions at that time sprung from the Achilles' heel of Marxist class analysis—the question of the middle classes. He elaborated a theory of "contradictory class locations" situated between capital, working class, and petty bourgeoisie that he would modify over the next thirty years. The evolution of his thinking was informed by the results of carefully designed social surveys conducted in more than fifteen countries, and by his theoretical engagement with colleagues from various disciplines, including many from the formidable "September Group" of Analytical Marxists.[1]

In the wake of the collapse of the Soviet Union and the discrediting of the very notion of socialism, Wright launched a second project, exploring what he called Real Utopias. It tackled another Achilles' heel of Marxism: its failure to give concrete substance to egalitarian and democratic alternatives to capitalism. Cognizant of a state's ability to arbitrarily declare itself "communist," and starting from the defects of capitalism that make the idea of socialism so compelling, he explored institutions

---

1   These included Jerry Cohen, Jon Elster, Adam Przeworski, John Roemer, Philippe Van Parijs, and Sam Bowles.

within the "eco-system" of capitalism that could potentially contribute to a vision of socialism. These included policy proposals such as universal basic income and participatory budgeting, as well as institutions such as Wikipedia and worker cooperatives—but they were not imaginary blueprints.

The Real Utopias Project was "real" in two significant respects: it was grounded in the reality of capitalism, and it documented the existence of feasible strategies for transforming capitalism. Wright understood only too well that these "real utopias" were Janus-faced—simultaneously functional for capitalism but also potentially "eroding" capitalism. In his magnum opus, *Envisioning Real Utopias* (2010), Wright elaborated three political strategies that he thought might help resolve that ambiguity: "interstitial" strategies based on institutions or organizations within the crevices of capitalism that harbored the seeds of socialism; symbiotic strategies that simultaneously advanced the interests of capital and labor; and ruptural strategies that emphasized a break with capitalism. *Envisioning Real Utopias* was anchored in the idea of empowering civil society (where real utopias were nurtured) vis-à-vis the state and the economy—elevating, as Wright would say, the "social" in socialism.

In his last solo-authored book, *How to Be an Anticapitalist in the Twenty-First Century* (published by Verso posthumously in 2019), Wright focused instead on the realization of three sets of values, democracy/freedom, equality/fairness, and community/solidarity. He developed visions of socialism, and strategies for their realization, but he left unresolved the collective actor that might champion those strategies. He broached that question in the very last chapter of *How to Be an Anticapitalist*—a chapter that explicitly decenters the importance of class, turning instead to a broader theorization in which identities are the basis of *interests*, leading to realistic objectives, while *values* forge solidarity across disparate interests and identities. Just as Marx, in his later years, would decenter the working class as *the* agent of history, so Wright would similarly loosen his youthful focus on the working class; just as Marx would come to recognize other dramatis personae on the stage of history, so Wright would embrace a variety of identities and interests that could advance real utopias.

The contributors to this book, colleagues and students of Wright, all address Wright's unfinished task of seeking to bring together his two projects of Class Analysis and Real Utopias. Whether one sees these two projects as distinct and contradictory, or whether one sees an underlying unity, Wright never systematically developed their connection. This was the direction in which he was headed, leaving us to attend to his incomplete work, to the antinomies of science and politics, structure and agency, the actual and the possible.

Part I assesses the relationship between the two projects within Wright's own thinking. We open with Michael Burawoy's association of these two projects with Alvin Gouldner's two Marxisms—the scientific Marxism of the Class Analysis Project and the critical Marxism of the Real Utopias Project.[2] In the beginning, Wright's enthusiasm for science as well as the pressures of academia led him down the path of scientific Marxism. Disillusioned with the political results of class analysis as well as by a wave of conservatism that swept across the world, Wright later turned to a critical Marxism, exploring the meaning of socialism, its viability and its achievability.

Burawoy argues that Wright made a fundamental epistemological break—from class analysis without utopia to utopia without class analysis—a claim that is contested from a variety of standpoints in the rest of Part One. Without denying there are two Marxisms, Gay Seidman proposes a gender explanation of Wright's transition from one to the other. Seidman's chapter explores an anomaly that arose from Wright's research on class analysis: how the class identity of women was forged through different processes from that of men. This inspired Wright to take up a conversation between Marxism and feminism. Struck by the way feminism, without fanfare, contemplates a world that includes men but that seeks to eliminate masculine domination—a notable contrast to Marxism's vision of a seamless shift to a classless society, with too little discussion of what that shift would look like—Wright's engagement with feminism reflected the intersection of his theoretical exploits and his everyday life. Seidman argues that engaging the feminist perspective deepened and perhaps even germinated Wright's interest in exploring real utopias.

If Seidman offers a feminist account of the way Wright's scientific Marxism gave way to his critical Marxism, Greta Krippner contests the very separation of Wright's scientific and critical Marxism. She argues

2 Alvin Gouldner, *The Two Marxisms: Contradictions and Anomalies in the Development of Theory* (New York: Seabury Press, 1980).

that the two were always intertwined and that from the outset a critical moment underlaid Wright's class analysis, namely, that it was premised on a critique of capitalism. Wright's preoccupation with defining and redefining the middle classes derived from a political concern: in a struggle for an egalitarian society, which side would the middle classes take? For Krippner, it is impossible to separate Wright's science from his critique. The concepts he used and the assumptions he made in his class analysis imply a critique of capitalism. The focus on exploitation, and on the antagonistic relations central to that vision, was at the heart of Wright's class analysis—as was a commitment to the possibility, indeed the necessity, of another world.

Kwang-Yeong Shin's chapter criticizes Burawoy's characterization of Wright's work as defined by a fundamental discontinuity, insisting rather that from the beginning until the end, Wright followed a singular emancipatory social science. For Shin, far from being a break from class analysis, *Envisioning Real Utopias* is its logical culmination, working out the implications of class analysis in response to the collapse of state socialism, the spread of neoliberalism, and the appeal of various "post-isms"—post-modernism, post-structuralism, and post-Marxism. Shin argues that socialism, understood as democratic egalitarianism, was an enduring driver of Wright's intellectual trajectory from class analysis to real utopias. Far from negating his class analysis, his Real Utopias Project was its completion, prompted by a new historical context—a "dialectical synthesis" rather than an "epistemological break."

Following the competing interpretations of Wright's oeuvre in Part I, we turn to more specific explorations of the relationship between real utopias and class analysis. Part II begins with Harry Brighouse's chapter, which argues for the logical and political priority of real utopias. Before concerning themselves with class analysis, he suggests, socialists have to worry about the meaning and viability of socialism. If socialism is not a possible form of society, there's no point in worrying about how to get there. One can recognize all the "bad-making features" of capitalism— and, like both Marx and Wright, Brighouse recognizes there are lots of "good-making" features too—but if one cannot make a convincing case for a better alternative, then they cannot claim to be a genuine socialist.

This was the mountain separating Marxism from the great sociologist, Max Weber, and sociology more generally. Weber recognized the "bad-making features" of capitalism, but he considered socialism to be impossible and therefore viewed attempts at its realization as misguided and dangerous. Weber's sociology is distinctive in juxtaposing the good and the bad—efficiency and domination, democracy and bureaucracy, formal equality and substantive inequality—but within capitalism. And yet, even Weber concluded that humanity "would not have attained the possible unless time and again [it] had reached out for the impossible."[3]

Although Brighouse is far more sympathetic to the Marxist project than Weber was, he nonetheless insists that it is not enough to have an appealing "blueprint"; one also has to demonstrate that under reasonably plausible historical conditions, it can actually work. Wright's class analysis postulated an unspecified egalitarian socialism, but did not initially subject that to detailed interrogation. In his Real Utopias Project, however, Wright took on that challenge—which Brighouse suggests is the sine qua non of any socialist project.

Arguing that the viability of any particular real utopia has to be Marxism's first priority, Brighouse says that it is not enough to show that there is a viable alternative to capitalism. That alternative must also exhibit some combination of socialist values: democracy/freedom, equality/fairness, and community/solidarity. Marxism has to be able to challenge spurious claims to socialism, such as those made by the Soviet party-state. In short, Marxism has to be "critical," which for Brighouse means more than simply diagnosing the "bad-making parts" of capitalism. Marxism, he argues, must also offer a convincing alternative that could exist and that embodies agreed-upon socialist values.

The rest of Part II presents a succession of real utopias that can be examined using the Wright-Brighouse criteria—the socialist values they represent and the viability of their institutional form. João Peschanski's analysis of the introduction of free mass transit in seven Brazilian cities rests on the assumption that free public transportation is crucial to any socialist society that relies on the movement of people. Even under capitalism, the benefits of free public transportation are clear relative to the collective costs and externalities of private transportation; moreover, since there already exist free-fare cities, it is obviously viable, and equal access to geographical mobility can facilitate participatory democracy

---

3   Max Weber, "Politics as a Vocation," in *From Max Weber*, ed. H. H. Gerth and C. W. Mills (1919; repr., New York: Oxford University Press, 1994), 128.

and community building. In analyzing why free public transportation is so rare, Peschanski examines the peculiar constellation of social forces that make it both possible and exceptional: the class capacities and class interests within dominant classes, and how they are orchestrated by the municipal state.

Marta Soler-Gallart explores a different real utopia, one that began as a social movement and is now an established institution: the Mondragon Cooperatives, grounded in the working classes of the Basque Country. Soler-Gallart recounts the history of this famous assemblage of cooperatives, describing the source of its democratic and egalitarian principles of operation, as well as its ability to function in the face of crises. Echoing the Brighouse principle of interrogation, she doesn't shy away from the challenges Mondragon faces, both from corporate capital and from its own internationalization. Whether the conditions of its birth in the Basque Country make Mondragon unique, and whether it can be replicated elsewhere remain open questions. Soler-Gallart also asks whether its expansion has been necessary for its survival within capitalism, and whether that expansion might unravel its proto-socialist features. These are among the questions posed by the growing literature on Mondragon and other cooperative ventures.

Jacob Carlson and Gianpaolo Baiocchi turn to a very different real utopia—the decommodification of housing in New York City. They propose the creation of a Social Housing Development Authority, emulating other projects, such as the 1920s Red Vienna. The projected agency would transfer housing out of the open market and into the social housing sector. It would buy up abandoned or foreclosed housing and then redistribute it as subsidized public housing or convert hotels and commercial spaces into residences for the homeless rather than allowing it to fall into the hands of real estate moguls. Three principles guide their proposal: that housing should be sold or rented at subsidized rates, that it should involve collective management by residents, and that it should be publicly backed by some state or parastatal agency.

Having defined this utopia and having made claims to its viability, Carlson and Baiocchi ask whether we can identify class forces that have the interest and capacity to advance such a project. Defining class structure as a matrix of renters and owners operating in a market economy, they identify low-income renters as the potential heart of a coalition for social housing, asking under what circumstances high-income renters and low-income owners might join in. While they acknowledge that racial divisions may render any such coalition fragile, simply making such an "imaginary utopia" seem feasible in the contemporary US is an accomplishment in itself.

In each of these studies of free public transportation, cooperatives, and social housing, the authors distinguish the class basis from the institutions themselves. In his chapter on Brazil's Emancipatory Network, Ruy Braga makes the radical move of collapsing that distinction, arguing that the democratization of access to Brazilian universities simultaneously involves a class agent and a utopia, that is, a class agent reaching for a utopia. There are good reasons for this radical move. Braga argues that the absorption of Wright's Class Analysis Project into mainstream sociology marked the end of class as we knew it, reflecting the fragmentation of a working class once dominated by industrial unionism. The disintegration of the Fordist working class gives rise to a new class made up of interconnected or intersectional movements, each governed by identities and interests whose unity is forged through appeals to common values.

This is, precisely, the political subject Wright outlined in the last chapter of *How to Be an Anticapitalist in the Twenty-First Century*. Brazil's Emancipatory Network, Braga claims, is a social movement with a utopian project: egalitarian access to the university and democratization of education more generally. It is largely focused on giving a poor Black population access to universities, taking advantage of a new, racially defined quota system. The student beneficiaries of the program return to their communities to create schools that, in the spirit of Paulo Freire's legacy, will bring new cohorts of the dispossessed into higher education. The Emancipatory Network is also part of a wider field of interstitial movements—poor people's movements, housing movements, environmental movements, and even Pentecostal movements.

For Braga, the disintegration of the "old" working class requires us to move out of the academy and into society, where the organic intellectual embraces social movements and their emancipatory projects. Wright's original academic Class Analysis Project is transcended and pushed back into history, while the Real Utopias Project invites the continuation of class analysis in a new conjuncture of class fragmentation and burgeoning social movements.

If the chapters in Part II give priority to real utopias and trace their origins and foundations back to class structure, the essays in Part III burn the candle from the other end. Starting from Wright's map of class structure, they reach for an emancipatory politics and the possibility of real utopias. Each begins with a reconstruction of Wright's map to suit a specific historical context. Rina Agarwala's chapter reformulates Wright's theories of contradictory class locations to explore relations among India's subaltern classes, making two crucial modifications. First, she adds a dimension that is somewhat peripheral to Wright's class analysis—the relationship of workers to the state. This divides formal workers—who are recognized by the state and granted rights and privileges—from informal workers, who can only struggle for such recognition. Second, she insists that Wright overlooks the unpaid household labor key to the three fractions of the self-employed, namely, small employers, traditional petty bourgeoisie, and semi-autonomous wage earners. Redrawing the Indian class structure in this way suggests the limits and possibilities of a new politics of real utopias focused on shared appeals to various states within India.

Rodolfo Elbert's analysis of working-class politics in Argentina also contends with expanding armies of informal and self-employed workers alongside the smaller formal, organized sector, exploring the fraught relationship between what are often understood as two different classes. Using survey research, Elbert shows that in terms of their class identification, Argentina's informal and formal workers have more in common with each another than with any other class. But, he points out, this common class identification can give way to divided interests. Focusing on factories where he conducted his field research, Elbert shows how the labor movement shapes the relationship between the formal and the informal, between the organized and the unorganized. The dominant Peronist unions tend to integrate their members vertically, leaving peripheral workers to fend for themselves. However, as Elbert's case studies show, the established unions face challenges from grassroots mobilization whose success depends on building horizontal solidarities between the factory and its neighborhoods. It is from among the latter that a militant, anticapitalist politics might arise, especially from the "recovered" enterprises managed by workers themselves.

Continuing where Agarwala and Elbert leave off, Peter Ramand examines how class locations, as defined by Wright's revised classification, may have influenced participation in the populist politics of the United Kingdom. His chapter highlights a surprising but striking convergence between Wright's *How to Be an Anticapitalist* and Chantal Mouffe and Ernesto Laclau's sweeping hostility to class reductionism in their influential *Hegemony and Socialist Strategy* (1985). In the last chapter of *How to Be an Anticapitalist*, Wright concedes that when it comes to the politics of real utopias and the forging of socialist institutions, class is not enough. Like Mouffe and Laclau (albeit with a different vocabulary), Wright recognizes multiple identities with corresponding interests that can only be brought together into a coherent project through the mobilization of shared values.

But decentering class is one thing; centering discourse and abandoning material constraints, as Mouffe and Laclau propose, is quite another. Ramand rescues Wright from any such radical indeterminacy by showing how class interests influence class participation in populist politics in Scotland. Analyzing five successive waves of public opinion surveys to show how various classes respond differently to the unfolding rhetoric of the Scottish independence campaign, he points to a path forward, tethering class structure to politics, but without sacrificing the relative autonomy of politics.

Also inspired by *How to Be an Anticapitalist*, Stephanie Luce's chapter illustrates the variety of politics that can arise *directly* from working-class struggles. Building on Wright's typology of anticapitalist strategies—from taming and resisting capitalism to dismantling capitalism—her chapter discusses a series of cases, from the collective monitoring and enforcement of progressive labor legislation (taming capitalism) to the radical demands of nurses calling for a genuine national US health system and bank employees calling for publicly accountable banks. These efforts can contribute to "eroding" capitalism if they are linked by a common set of anticapitalist values and if they can forge a collective actor based on intersectional struggles that transcend the workplace. Luce offers us two examples: Bargaining for the Common Good in Minnesota and the class and race struggles organized by the Service Employees International Union (SEIU) in Connecticut. This final essay, appropriately enough, vividly illustrates the continuing importance of working-class politics to the Real Utopias Project.

Just as Marx found himself returning to the vexing question of class at the end of his life, so Wright returned to the agent of transformative politics at the end of his last book. If the chapters in this volume are any indicator, *How to Be an Anticapitalist in the Twenty-First Century* is destined to be an enduring reference point for those committed to an alternative world of equality, democracy, and community. Wright himself was excited by what became a manifesto for real utopias, delivering and defending his ideas not only to academic but also increasingly to activist audiences across the globe. He was only too aware that by themselves, real utopias would as likely as not buttress capitalism by filling its functional gaps, by helping to offset crises, or by offering an escape for dissidents.

Only when real utopias are tied to a common project of "eroding" capitalism can they point to a socialist horizon. Linking them, whether through a political party or social movements, can help to incite submerged classes to join the project and recover their lost energy. But this unity also requires a political ideology—"expressed neither in the form of a cold utopia nor learned theorizing but rather by creation of a concrete phantasy which acts on a dispersed and shattered people to arouse and organize its collective will."[4] Erik Wright was the organic intellectual of such a concrete phantasy, and *How to Be an Anticapitalist in the Twenty-First Century* was its manifesto. It now remains for those he left behind to carry forward what he began.

---

4   Antonio Gramsci, *Selections from the Prison Notebooks*, ed. and trans. Quintin Hoare and Geoffrey Nowell Smith (New York: International Publishers, 1971), 126.

PART I

The Life and Work of Erik Olin Wright

1

A Tale of Two Marxisms
Michael Burawoy

In 1970, Alvin Gouldner could confidently announce that the golden age of Western sociology was over.[1] The civil rights movement, the women's movement, antiwar protests, and a growing antistate radicalism had served to deflate postwar American triumphalism and the sociology it had spawned. The proclaimed "end of ideology"—the notion that the United States had overcome the major challenges of modernity—proved to be the "illusion of the epoch" (a phrase hitherto reserved for Marxism). The shoe was now on the other foot: for the new generation, mainstream sociology was seen as ideology, plastering over the deep pathologies of US society. Demonstrable injustices belied the claims of the dominant "consensus theory."[2]

This contribution was originally prepared for the Erik Olin Wright Festschrift at the University of Wisconsin–Madison, in November 2019. It first appeared in *New Left Review* and then in *Politics and Society*. My thanks to Dylan Riley, Gay Seidman, Greta Krippner, Ivan Ermakoff, and Marcia Kahn Wright for their constructive criticisms.

1 Alvin Gouldner, *The Coming Crisis of Western Sociology* (New York: Basic Books, 1970). For those interested in an assessment of Erik's work as part of the 1970s and 1980s Marxist renaissance in US sociology, see Jeff Manza and Michael McCarthy, "The Neo-Marxist Legacy in American Sociology," *Annual Review of Sociology* 37 (2011): 155–83.

2 The leading exponent of consensus theory—the idea that society is held together by shared values—was Talcott Parsons, the Harvard sociologist whose *The Structure of Social Action* (1937) reinvented sociology through a synthesis of the writings of Weber, Durkheim, Marshall, and Pareto. The research program Parsons spearheaded came to be known as "structural functionalism"; its hypothesis was that the institutions of any

Gouldner was right to identify the crisis of sociology, but he did not anticipate how the social movements of the 1960s and the ideas they generated—feminism, critical race theory, and Marxism—would catalyze a renewal of the discipline. Reflecting on that renewal a decade later in *The Two Marxisms* (1980), Gouldner discerned two opposed but also interdependent tendencies: scientific Marxism and critical Marxism.[3] In brief, scientific Marxism begins from a rational understanding of society that postulates the determinism of objective structures. It uncovers historical tendencies leading to socialism when conditions are ripe. Concepts reflect real mechanisms; politics are epiphenomenal; ideology is distortion of the truth. Critical Marxism, on the other hand, starts out from the ubiquity of alienation obstructing the potential for human self-realization. It highlights human intervention against the obduracy of objective structures—history has no preordained end but is rather the product of collective mobilization. In the view of critical Marxism, concepts exist to interpret social processes; politics is an arena for the realization of ultimate values; ideology is a moral force. In revolutionary times, critical Marxism and scientific Marxism may form a contradictory unity, but in nonrevolutionary times, they more easily go their separate ways.

---

society had to perform four basic functions: adaptation, goal attainment, integration, and latency. This program dominated postwar American sociology and influenced neighboring disciplines in a way sociology never has since. Erik himself had been impressed by Parsons's system analysis, taking his course at Harvard. Structural functionalism was also a Cold War sociology, celebrating the virtues of American capitalist society as against the Soviet Union and its "bankrupt" ideology. But it went into abeyance during the 1970s when Marxism, entirely ignored by Parsons, enjoyed a resurgence alongside burgeoning demands for social justice.

3   Alvin Gouldner, *The Two Marxisms: Contradictions and Anomalies in the Development of Theory* (New York: Seabury Press, 1980). Gouldner (1920–80) came from an older generation of leftists, but he was an instinctive "real utopian," searching for the emancipatory moments in sociology and the world it described. In his first study, *Patterns of Industrial Bureaucracy* (1954), Gouldner interrogated the meaning of "bureaucracy" based on a study of a gypsum plant in upstate New York. Recognizing different types of bureaucracy—"representative" as well as "punishment-centered" and "mock" bureaucracies—he problematized Weber's monolithic view of bureaucracy and the pessimism it entailed—a pessimism that suffused the sociology of organizations at that time. In *The Coming Crisis of Western Sociology* he extended this early critique of the reigning 1950s and 1960s sociology into a systematic sociology of sociology. Just as he tried to recover the liberatory moment of sociology, Gouldner was quick to identify conservative elements within Marxism. In *The Future of Intellectuals and the Rise of the New Class* (1979), Gouldner saw Marxism as an ideology of the intelligentsia, leading him to a theory of intellectuals as a "flawed universal class."

Intended to capture the entangled history of Marxism, these two Marxisms also frame the intellectual biography of Erik Wright. In the 1970s his scientific and critical Marxisms were joined, but later they came apart as each developed its own autonomous trajectory. Erik's scientific Marxism was the program of class analysis that first brought him international fame. Begun in graduate school, it tailed off in the last two decades of his life, when it played second fiddle to the critical Marxism of the Real Utopias Project that he began in the early 1990s. Erik's writings show remarkably little cross-pollination between the two as they each developed independently of the other. *He moves from a class analysis without utopia to utopia without class analysis.* Why did his intellectual life run along these separate tracks, especially given their convergence in the beginning? Are critical Marxism and scientific Marxism ultimately inimical, displaying the binary oppositions identified by Gouldner? Or, as I shall argue, do the reasons for the divergence lie in the political context in which he wrote and his changing relation to sociology? The separation is not inevitable. Indeed, at the end of his life there are intimations of a reconnection of science and critique that call for further elaboration in continuing his legacy.

What follows is therefore divided into four parts: Erik's early Marxism, where science and critique are joined; the scientific Marxism of class analysis; the critical Marxism of real utopias; and my proposals for rejoining science and critique.

Early Marxism

We first have to retrace Erik's path to Marxism. After graduating from Harvard in social studies in 1968, he spent two years at Oxford pursuing a second BA degree, imbibing sociology and politics from Steven Lukes and history from Christopher Hill, respectively. These were turbulent years with Marxism thriving on both sides of the Atlantic, capturing the minds of a new generation of social scientists. In order to avoid the draft, Erik had enrolled in the Unitarian-Universalist seminary at Berkeley. That was even before he went to Oxford, where he would claim to study religion—the Puritan Revolution in England! When he returned to the United States in the fall of 1970, he enrolled as a full-time student at the seminary. As part of his studies, he organized a student-run seminar called "Utopia and Revolution." As he recalled:

> For ten weeks I met with a dozen or so other students from the various seminaries in the Berkeley Graduate Theological Union to discuss the principles and prospects for the revolutionary transformation of American society and the rest of the world. We were young and earnest, animated by the idealism of the civil rights movement and the anti-war movement and by the countercultural currents opposed to competitive individualism and consumerism. We discussed the prospects for the revolutionary overthrow of American capitalism and the ramifications of the "dictatorship of the proletariat," as well as the potential for a countercultural subversion of existing structures of power and domination through living alternative ways of life.[4]

Another part of the seminary program was a field assignment to prepare him for ministerial work. As his site Erik chose San Quentin prison, where he became a student chaplain. Just as he recorded and typed up each session of the "Utopia and Revolution" seminar, so now he assiduously wrote the field notes that he would turn into his first book, *The Politics of Punishment* (1973), with additional contributions from lawyers, prisoners, and journalists. Here he sets out a radical conception of crime and punishment, and a critique of the correctional model as "liberal totalitarianism," with detailed descriptions of conditions in San Quentin. There follows four chapters on the violence, racism, and revolt at Soledad prison in California, co-written by the head psychiatrist, a prisoner, a lawyer representing the Soledad Brothers, and a writer from the Prison Law Collective. The last part of the book has three chapters written by his collaborators on prisoner revolts, legislative changes, and the courts. Erik writes a concluding chapter on prison reform, arguing that any meaningful change would require the transformation of society. *The Politics of Punishment* took a radical stance against prisons and in many ways anticipated the critical standpoint of contemporary incarceration studies. Science and critique were joined in Erik's precocious ethnography of prison life.

---

4   Erik Olin Wright, *Envisioning Real Utopias* (New York: Verso, 2010), ix.

Strange though it may seem, the theological seminary became an incubator for Erik's radicalism, already inflected by an embryonic Marxism suffusing the intellectual worlds through which he traveled. As with so many others, his radicalism found a home in the sociology of the time, leading him to enroll in Berkeley's Sociology Department. He wrote:

> Of all the social sciences, sociology seemed to me to be the least disciplinary: it had the fuzziest boundaries. But even more significantly, sociology has valued its own marginal traditions in a way that other social sciences don't. Even anti-Marxist sociologists recognize the importance of Marx as one of the intellectual founders of what has become sociology.[5]

Once there, he would later state, it was apparent that Marxism was the only game in town. Indeed, Marxism was flourishing in the Bay Area both in Berkeley's sociology department and beyond in various discussion groups, including the editorial collective of the journal *Kapitalistate*, led by James O'Connor; the Bay Area chapter of the Union for Radical Political Economics; the socialist-oriented Union of Marxist Social Scientists; and the *Berkeley Journal of Sociology*. Erik was active in all of these.[6]

---

5   Erik Olin Wright, "Falling into Marxism; Choosing to Stay," in Alan Sica and Stephen Turner, eds., *The Disobedient Generation: Social Theorists in the Sixties* (Chicago: University of Chicago Press, 2005), 338.

6   Sociology attracted Marxists, especially where it was new. Many had a triumphalist vision of taking over the discipline. Writing from Sweden, Göran Therborn concluded: "What the present study indicates, then, is neither convergence nor synthesis, but a *transcendence of sociology*, similar to Marx's transcendence of classical economics, and the development of historical materialism as *the* science of society. To indicate a task, however, is not to accomplish it. The extent to which these possibilities prove capable of realization will not depend on intra-scientific events alone. The rise and formation of the social sciences were determined by the class struggles of particular historical societies, and so, no doubt, will be their further development or arrested development. Thus the question of a future development of social sciences in the direction of historical materialism remains open—above all to those of us who are committed to working for it." See Göran Therborn, *Science, Class and Society: On the Formation of Sociology and Historical Materialism* (London: New Left Books, 1976), 429 (italics in the original). I was in Zambia at the time (1968–72), learning to be a sociologist, where again Marxism was a powerful presence. In those days, in Asia, Latin America, and Africa, Marxism challenged and often swamped all the imported social sciences from the global North.

In those days Berkeley's Sociology Department was in disarray, divided into warring factions by the political dramas on campus.[7] It is difficult now to appreciate the turmoil at Berkeley that began with the Free Speech Movement in 1964 and reached a peak in 1968–70 with the course given by Eldridge Cleaver (which the Board of Regents tried but failed to stop), the Third World Strike that resulted in the formation of the Ethnic Studies Department, the defense of People's Park that led Governor Reagan to call in the National Guard, and antiwar marches that regularly met with police violence. In those years, faculty teaching in the sociology department was in remission, as graduate students organized their own seminars. The most enduring of those courses was "Current Controversies in Marxist Social Science," which Erik would take with him to Wisconsin, where it became the legendary Sociology 621-622—a course he offered every year and later every other year up to 2017. Here he taught graduate students from all over the world his version of Marxism.[8]

While anthropology and political science had their traditions, sociology was a new discipline, vulnerable to invasions from without but also deeply engaged with Marxism.

7   Charles Glock, who chaired the department during those years (1967–68 and 1969–71), wrote: "The Department's outer office resembled a recruiting station for leftist causes. A portrait of Che Guevara was prominently displayed as were other revolutionary posters. Faculty whom staff considered on the wrong side were catered to with the minimum amount of courtesy and respect that staff thought they could get away with." Cited in Michael Burawoy and Jonathan VanAntwerpen, "Berkeley Sociology: Past, Present and Future," unpublished manuscript, 2001, p. 14.

8   The course changed over time. Erik first taught it in his second semester at University of Wisconsin–Madison in spring 1977, when it was based on the original course at Berkeley. In 1979–80 it became Sociology 621-622, a two-semester course— the first semester was called "Introduction to Marxist Social Science" and the second "Methodology of Historical Materialism." The topics were "Classes," "Political Economy of the Capitalist Mode of Production," "Imperialism," "Base and Superstructure," "Ideology and Consciousness," and "State, Socialism, and the Methodology of Historical Materialism." By 1983–84, he had added two topics: "Race and Class," and "Marxism and Feminism." "Base and Superstructure" and "The State" were merged into "The Theory of the State and Politics," while "Imperialism" and "Socialism" disappeared as distinct topics. The syllabus moved from an impressive thirty-eight single-spaced pages in 1979–80 to an even more impressive forty-six pages in 1983–84. By 2017, the syllabus was a whopping eighty-seven pages, but the course had been reduced to a single semester, taught every other year. Now the topics were "Setting the Agenda (Marxism as an Emancipatory Social Science)," "Class Structure," "Class Formation," "The Theory of State and Politics," "Ideology and Consciousness," "Theory of History," and "Socialism and Emancipation." Whereas in 1979 there was no need to justify a

Erik's approach was laid out in his second book, *Class, Crisis and the State* (1978), published by New Left Books, which brought him international attention. It was based on three essays he had written between 1974 and 1976 in *New Left Review*, the *Insurgent Sociologist*, and the *Berkeley Journal of Sociology*. The first essay was his novel and elegant reconstruction of the Marxist conception of class, the second a historicization of the contradictions and crises of capital accumulation, and the third a juxtaposition of the writings of Lenin and Weber on the durability of bureaucracy. This third essay ends with a disquisition on then current debates about the state—whether it was a "state in capitalist society" that if somehow conquered, even through electoral means, could be wielded in the pursuit of socialism, or whether it was a "capitalist state" with its own distinctive "relative autonomy" that inherently reproduced capitalist relations and therefore had to be smashed and replaced by a socialist state. He found both positions wanting, arguing that by conquering the capitalist state with expanding popular support, the state could be transformed from within without any "smashing." This was a position he would hold to the end of his life. Of the three essays, the one on the dynamics of capitalism was never developed; it was notably absent from his class analysis and the strategies of his Real Utopias Project.

Scientific Marxism: Class Analysis

The radicalism of Erik's early writing joined class analysis and the utopian imagination in a singular Marxist project, but what relation did this bear to sociology? "I originally had visions of glorious paradigm battles, with lances drawn and a valiant Marxist knight unseating the bourgeois rival in a dramatic quantitative joust. What is

---

course on Marxism, as its popularity waned Erik introduced rationales: Marxism offers tools for a radical egalitarian project of social change; Marxism offers an exemplary theoretical framework; Marxism offers a powerful explanatory research program. In the heady days of the late 1970s, he had emphasized the "explanatory" aspect, but by 2017 the emphasis was on Marxism as an "emancipatory" social science. The title of the course moved from "Marxist Social Science" to "Sociological Marxism." Throughout, Erik didn't discard older readings but added new ones as his own perspective changed, hence the encyclopedic syllabus. While he set class analysis and real utopias side by side, I do not believe he married them.

more, the fantasy saw the vanquished admitting defeat and changing horses as a result," he wrote in 1987.[9] Of the three essays in *Class, Crisis and the State*, it would be the one on class that tangled with sociologists.

Marxism, Erik argued, had never successfully wrestled with the limits of Marx's original theory of class polarization. Time and again sociologists emphasized that the signal feature of modern class structures is the rise of the "middle classes." It was the most common criticism sociology leveled against Marxism. A common Marxist response was to argue that the rise of the middle classes was an illusion, marking the effectiveness of bourgeois ideology—the majority of the middle class were wage laborers and should be lumped in with the proletariat. Other Marxists refused such subterfuge, instead referring to the middle class as a new class—a new petty bourgeoisie, a service class, a professional managerial class—but few built their arguments systematically into a broader theory of class structure.

Enter Erik Wright. He argued that there are essentially three fundamental classes under capitalism: capitalists (employers), laborers (wage earners), and petty bourgeoisie (self-employed). But there also emerged three intermediary positions situated between the fundamental classes: managers and supervisors (between capital and labor); small employers (between the petty bourgeoisie and capital); and semi-autonomous employees (between the working class and the petty bourgeoisie). These intermediary positions became his famous "contradictory class locations," positions that shared features of both the adjacent classes. He showed how, using these measures, the size of the working class far exceeds that entailed by competing definitions, especially the one developed by Nicos Poulantzas in *Classes in Contemporary Capitalism* (1975). He asked under what conditions those in contradictory class locations adjacent to wage laborers—supervisors, managers, and semi-autonomous employees—would join the working class in the pursuit of socialism.

---

9   Erik Olin Wright, "Reflections on *Classes*," *Berkeley Journal of Sociology* 32 (1987): 44. Erik would cite these two sentences repeatedly and at different moments in his career. For example, "Falling into Marxism; Choosing to Stay," 338; *Understanding Class* (London: Verso, 2015), 1. Each time it was to suggest how far he had come from his original vision of a valiant struggle. It turned out that his debates with mainstream sociologists were less frequent and less intense than those with other Marxists.

Erik argued that the pursuit of the *immediate* interests of those in contradictory class locations might hinder the advance of common *fundamental* class interests, but he never put the occupants of those contradictory class locations into motion as a historical force, even an ambiguous one. Instead, for his PhD dissertation, he set his portrait of class structure against sociologists' status-attainment theory and economists' human-capital theory in explaining income inequality.[10] Using existing data, he was able to sustain the view that his novel Marxist model of classes did at least as well as competing models in sociology and economics. Why had he chosen the terrain of quantitative research as a means of adjudicating between Marxism and sociology? First, and most obviously, at that time stratification was at the heart of sociological theory and research. It was argued that stratification as measured in terms of the prestige ranking of occupations or later socioeconomic status reflected an underlying value consensus about social hierarchy. It was also the area of a major methodological advance in statistical models, known as "path analysis," pioneered by Peter Blau and Otis Dudley Duncan's *The American Occupational Structure* (1967). Erik considered quantitative work to be a way of legitimating Marxism within sociology, even demonstrating the superiority of Marxism as a science. At the same time, he conceded, it would also be a way of advancing his career within academia.[11]

Erik's model of class structure became widely known in both Marxist and sociological circles, but it hardly led to gladiatorial battles; in sociology, it was not perceived as threatening and was instead easily absorbed into the discipline. With disarming honesty, typical of his approach to scholarship, he confessed in 1987:

---

10   His dissertation was soon published as *Class Structure and Income Determination* (New York: Academic Press, 1979).

11   Erik wrote: "I was very ambitious as a young scholar—ambitious in my search for what I considered to be the 'truth,' but also ambitious for status, recognition, influence, world travel. Embarking on a line of research anchored in conventional survey research thus offered tangible rewards." ("Falling into Marxism; Choosing to Stay," 339.) But really he never got the recognition from the academic establishment that his international reputation, his extraordinary scholarly record, and his brilliant teaching deserved. I never heard him complain about this, and I doubt it even crossed his mind. He considered himself excessively privileged, and he was, but his self-assured Marxism still rankled many. He was never fully assimilated.

What has been striking over the past decade is how little serious debate by mainstream sociology there has been in response to the outpouring of neo-Marxist research. I have generally been unable to provoke systematic responses to my research among mainstream sociologists, of either a theoretical or empirical kind ... The main effect of my research on the mainstream, as far as I can tell, is that certain "variables" are now more likely to be included in regression equations. What I envisioned as a broad theoretical challenge to "bourgeois sociology" backed up by systematic empirical research has resulted in the pragmatic appropriation of certain isolated elements of the operationalized conceptual framework with little attention to abstract theoretical issues.[12]

Having stripped the politics out of Marxism, having left behind the contradictions of capitalism, having abandoned history—especially history as the history of class struggle—and having reduced class analysis to another set of independent variables, mainstream sociologists were quite at home with Erik's multivariate Marxism. If this was Marxism, then bring it on.

Quantitative work may not have delivered remarkable new findings, but it did have the effect of forcing him to develop clearer definitions of his class categories. In having to "operationalize" class, the contradictory class location he had called "semi-autonomous employees" proved especially difficult to define in a consistent manner. Indeed, wrestling with this ambiguity stimulated him to revamp the basis of his class structure, following the theory of exploitation developed by the budding economist John Roemer.[13] Erik now reconstructed his own theory of exploitation around the distribution of different assets: labor power, means of production, organization, and skills, or credentials. Feudalism centered on the control over labor power, capitalism on the control of means of production, statism on the control of organizations, socialism on the control of skills or credentials, while communism allowed for collective control of all assets and elimination of exploitation. An evolutionary history was built into the successive elimination of exploitations, giving

---

12   Wright, "Reflections on *Classes*," 44–45.
13   John Roemer, *A General Theory of Exploitation and Class* (Cambridge, MA: Harvard University Press, 1982).

rise to a new map of classes under capitalism, now defined by the assets held by employers, petty bourgeoisie, managers, supervisors, nonmanagement experts, and workers. This was elaborated in detail in Erik's 1985 book, *Classes*.[14]

While Erik disagreed with Roemer that you could define class exploitation without relations of domination,[15] he wanted to emphasize the centrality of exploitation (as opposed to domination, which had been central to the definition of contradictory class locations). Henceforth, he would presume those relations of domination rather than observing, measuring, or mapping them. His revamping of class structure in terms of assets held by individuals brought Erik a step closer to sociology. Just as his earlier formulations may have indirectly contributed to the atrophy of the status-attainment model, his new scheme prepared the way for the popularity of new notions of class, such as the one based on different "capitals"—social, economic, and cultural—pioneered by Pierre Bourdieu, a notion of class in which, ironically, exploitation disappears.[16]

Erik became a victim of his own success. In a period of Marxist renaissance, his work attracted a lot of attention. Here was a Marxist of unquestionable integrity who combined empirical sophistication,

---

14 Subsequently, Erik further revised his scheme of exploitation, pointing to its limitations and extending the framework to include the temporal dimension of class (class mobility) and the way the effects of class are mediated by such institutions as the family and the state. See "Rethinking Once Again the Concept of Class Structure," in Erik Olin Wright, ed., *The Debate on Classes* (New York: Verso, 1989), 269–348. It was all part of an endeavor to demonstrate the importance of class as an "independent variable" that could explain variation in "dependent variables" (attitudes, behaviors, nonclass relations). He was still trying to demonstrate the explanatory power of class, once it was correctly defined and its effects contextualized. In his final accounting, *Class Counts* (1997), he melded the old contradictory class locations approach and the newer asset-based approach to exploitation in order to increase the explanatory power of "class"—the permeability of class boundaries, the effects of class on gender relations in the home and at work, and the effects of class on class consciousness.

15 Erik Olin Wright, "The Status of the Political in the Concept of Class Structure," *Politics and Society* 19, no. 3 (1982): 321–41.

16 There is a paradox here. While in *Distinction* (1979) Bourdieu defines classes by positions in social space determined by the addition of economic and cultural capital, elsewhere he rails against the idea of "classes on paper," class categories invented by the theorist, classes given by objective attributes. See, for example, the widely cited article "Social Space and the Genesis of 'Classes,'" in Pierre Bourdieu, *Language and Symbolic Power* (1982; repr., Cambridge, MA: Harvard University Press, 1991), 229–51.

analytical rigor, and theoretical innovation. There was nothing quite like it in the world of sociology, although John Goldthorpe became an ardent anti-Marxist competitor. Erik was able to secure funding to conduct national social surveys designed to identify the distinctive dimensions of class structure, based on a combination of exploitation and domination, and measures of class consciousness intended to map out possible class alliances. His fame spread beyond national borders, as country after country fielded surveys based on his design.[17] Within ten years some fifteen countries had collected data on class structure and class consciousness. For Erik this involved an enormous amount of work—advising, consulting, collaborating, and coauthoring papers on comparative class analysis. The final product was a bulky volume, *Class Counts*. It is not clear there was a memorable empirical result, and in the preface he admits that he is not sure that "the results were worth the effort"—two decades of strenuous work.[18] Again with characteristic honesty, Erik wrote:

> Mostly, the data analysis has served to lend moderate support to particular theoretical arguments about the class structure and its effects, but frequently—as chronically occurs in this game—the results are ambiguous, troubled by noise and weak correlations and thus fail to provide compelling adjudications between rival arguments. There have, of course, been some interesting surprises. I had not expected, for example, to find such pervasive and often dramatic interactions between class and gender. My expectation had always been that class mechanisms would more or less have the same

17   Even Soviet sociologists wanted to get in on the act. I went to Moscow with Erik in 1986—the beginning of perestroika—to develop a survey that could be administered in both the United States and the Soviet Union. At the end of a very frustrating—but revealing—ten days, Erik was asked to deliver a lecture to the Academy of Sciences. The room was packed, and the audience was curious to hear this strange animal—a renowned Marxist scientist from the West. In a beautifully crafted talk he argued that exploitation on the basis of private property may have been abolished in the Soviet Union, but exploitation based on unequal access to organizational resources remained. The audience became increasingly tense as he unfolded an implicit critique of the Soviet order. Suddenly and awkwardly the talk was shut down, and we were ushered out of the room. Erik had clearly run afoul of the powers that be.

18   Erik Olin Wright, *Class Counts: Comparative Studies in Class Analysis* (Cambridge, MA: Cambridge University Press, 1997), xxx.

empirical effects for women as for men, but this is simply not the case. But overall it remains the case that direct empirical payoffs of the research have, so far at least, not been spectacular.[19]

I don't think Erik ever changed his mind about this.

The upshot was that he lost interest in opposing Marxism to sociology and instead focused on linking dependent variables and independent variables in a massive research program that reached its climax when Marxism was already in retreat within sociology.[20] Accordingly, he began to take a more conciliatory approach to sociology, and a more modest positioning of his own work. In the 2005 collection he edited, *Approaches to Class Analysis*, Marxist class analysis was presented as but one approach among many, including neo-Weberian, neo-Durkheimian, Bourdieusian, rent-based, and post-class analysis. From his early enthusiasm for adjudication among competing theories, he became more ecumenical. Erik assumed a more defensive posture, upholding a Marxist concept of class alongside and complementary to other approaches to class—which, ironically, had arisen in part out of the space he had created by criticizing the old models of status attainment.

In his last book dealing with class, *Understanding Class* (2015), he introduced a collection of essays written between 1995 and 2015 with an attempt to revitalize class analysis, not through adjudication or pluralism, but through synthesis. He tried to bring together three approaches: class as exploitation, as opportunity hoarding, and as individual attributes. Broadly speaking, these were, respectively, Marxist, Weberian, and status-attainment approaches, each dealing with a distinct set of problems. He wrote:

---

19   Wright, "Reflections on *Classes*," 42.

20   As a scientific research program, his class analysis was able to absorb anomalies and resolve contradictions but at the expense of parsimony, and it may be said to have failed the ultimate test, the prediction of novel facts. See Imre Lakatos, *The Methodology of Scientific Research Programmes* (Cambridge: Cambridge University Press, 1978). Undoubtedly, part of the problem is that he developed his research program as a brilliant but lone scholar; he did not cultivate acolytes or disciples, although he would write numerous articles with his students, helping launch their careers. The Real Utopias Project, on the other hand, was a more collaborative venture disseminated through conferences and his students, but also through political architects and activists around the world. It has, therefore, had more staying power as a research program.

A fully elaborated class analysis, then, combines this kind of dynamic macro model of conflict and transformation with the macro-micro multilevel model of class processes and individual lives. In such a model the key insights of stratification approaches, Weberian approaches, and Marxist approaches are combined.[21]

This move toward a synthetic model—"grand paradigm battles" to "pragmatic realism," as he would call it—might be seen as a reflection of Erik's rise to prominence within sociology: he could now afford to accept the validity of other models of class, incorporating them within a Marxist frame. But I do not believe that was the only factor at play. As Marxism became more marginal within sociology, so Erik took a more conciliatory stance, trying to uphold the idea of class by embracing sociological visions that he had hitherto criticized. He was transitioning from what he called a "flaw-centered" critique of sociology to a "virtue-centered" critique, recognizing the explanatory role of each within a broader frame.[22] But in the end it meant his class analysis lost its distinctiveness as it was integrated into sociology, alongside perspectives that often did not rely on a notion of capitalism, let alone the transcendence of capitalism. What began as a Marxist challenge to sociology turned into one particular sociology, a *Marxist sociology* that coexisted with other sociologies.[23]

Erik's class analysis was undoubtedly a major intervention—not only his reconceptualization but, even more novel, the dedicated empirical measurement and mapping of class structures that followed. Such an

---

21   *Understanding Class*, 14.

22   Ibid., vii.

23   It should be said that in the beginning, Erik and I thought our approaches were complementary—he focusing more on the relations *of* production and I on the relations *in* production; he the quantitative analyst and I the ethnographer. But I became more critical of the operationalization of his conceptual scheme through survey data rather than through historical analysis. He was always honest about the limitations of the path he had taken and tolerated my critical stance toward his spurious "objectivism" and distance from the world he theorized. At the provocation of Jeff Manza, we debated our different perspectives in the *Berkeley Journal of Sociology*. See Wright, "Reflections on *Classes*"; Wright, "Reply to Burawoy's Comments on 'Reflections on *Classes*,'" *Berkeley Journal of Sociology* 32 (1987): 73–8; Burawoy, "The Limits of Wright's Analytical Marxism and an Alternative," *Berkeley Journal of Sociology* 32 (1987): 51–72; Burawoy, "Marxism, Philosophy and Science," *Berkeley Journal of Sociology* 34 (1989): 223–49. The wider debate about Erik's class analysis appeared in *The Debate on Classes*.

ambitious and successful project gave unprecedented legitimacy to Marxism within sociology. Still, it came at a cost. Rather than questioning the foundations of sociology, he competed with existing sociological models on their own terms. He used standard techniques (social surveys and statistical analysis) to demonstrate that his class categories best captured the "underlying mechanisms" that explain a variety of phenomena, from income inequality to different dimensions of class consciousness. In reality the battle of paradigms became an adjudication between models, dragging him onto the terrain of sociology. His scientific Marxism turned into a Marxist sociology. During the last two decades his most successful empirical research was no longer specifically Marxist—the work with Rachel Dwyer on the changing mix of good and bad jobs in the US occupational structure, debunking the 1990s euphoria of a "rising tide lifts all boats."[24]

At this point Erik could have left Marxism, like so many others. He would have won accolades for seeing the light, for recognizing the error of his youthful ways. That was not Erik. Instead he reinvented Marxism, suited to the times. Breaking from his class analysis, he recovered his old interest in utopian thinking. His relation to sociology changed: rather than drawing on its positivist tradition he appealed, implicitly if not explicitly, to its emancipatory tradition. From his "pragmatic" scientific Marxism—a *Marxist sociology*, a variant of sociology—he

---

24   Erik's analysis of changes in the US class structure itself shifted over time. In 1982, writing with Joachim Singelmann, using the scheme of contradictory class locations, they show that for 1940–70 there is "proletarianization" within sectors, but it is obscured by the movement of people into sectors with lower levels of proletarianization. Erik then shifted from class analysis to a study of employment quality. Stimulated by an optimistic report on job creation by Joseph Stiglitz, written in 1997 when he was chairman of Clinton's Council of Economic Advisers, Erik and Rachel Dwyer reexamined and extended the data to show that although there were many newly created "good" jobs, there were also lots of "bad" jobs, and moreover, the latter were disproportionately occupied by African Americans and Hispanics—a story of a polarizing, racialized division of labor. They continued to work together on the transformation of the job structure, extending the analysis to other countries. Although these were very important accounts of the transformation of the occupational structure and tied into an important policy debate, this research nonetheless displaced the concept of class, now present only notionally. See, respectively, Erik Olin Wright and Joachim Singelmann, "Proletarianization in the Changing American Class Structure," *American Journal of Sociology* 88, Supplement; Erik Olin Wright and Rachel Dwyer, "The American Jobs Machine: Is the New Economy Creating Good Jobs?," *Boston Review* 25, no. 6 (2000).

would turn to a critical Marxism: a *sociological Marxism*, a variant of Marxism.

Critical Marxism: Real Utopias

The project on real utopias represents an epistemological break akin to the one Louis Althusser identified in Marx.[25] However, where Althusser saw Marx's transition as being from a critical or humanist philosophy to a truly scientific theory of capitalism, Erik's epistemological break was in the opposite direction: from science to critique; from a mapping of social structure to the project of social transformation; from the study of real mechanisms to the study of possible futures; from scientific neutrality to explicit value foundations; from measurement at a distance to engagement at close quarters; from ideology as distortion to ideology as a moral force; from politics as epiphenomenal to politics as integral to the advance of real utopias; from the determinism of objective structures to the erosion of capitalism.

To be sure, as with Marx, so with Wright, there are transitional texts. Perhaps the most important was the one Erik would later title "Marxism after Communism," in which he defined Marxism by three interconnected nodes: class analysis, class emancipation, and a theory of history.[26] When neither historical trajectory nor class analysis seemed to indicate that capitalism was abolishing itself, the choice was either to abandon Marxism or to consider the project of emancipation on its own terms. He drew the same conclusion when he compared the emancipatory projects of Marxism and feminism: in feminism the idea of gender

---

25   Louis Althusser, *For Marx* (London: Verso, 1977).

26   See "Class Analysis, History and Emancipation," *New Left Review* 1, no. 202 (November–December 1993): 15–35, which later appeared in revised form as "Marxism after Communism" in *Interrogating Inequality* (New York: Verso, 1994), chap. 11. The most clearly "transitional" piece may be the one we wrote together, in which the importance of real utopias stems from the durability of capitalism and the social reproduction of class relations. Class is no longer a transformative force and, *therefore*, the construction of real utopias is necessary. This portended the *disconnection* of class analysis and real utopias. See Michael Burawoy and Erik Olin Wright, "Sociological Marxism," in Jonathan Turner, ed., *The Handbook of Sociological Theory* (New York: Springer, 2002), 459–86. Thanks to Greta Krippner and Ivan Ermakoff for pointing to continuities, notwithstanding the break between Erik's scientific and critical Marxisms.

equality was seen to be unproblematic, whereas Marxism had to confront challenges to the very possibility of a classless society.[27] Classical Marxism tried to resolve the problem by demonstrating capitalism's long-term non-sustainability, thereby displacing the question of socialism; yet given the justifiable skepticism about such law-like claims for capitalism's future, Marxists would do well to focus more on the emancipatory project itself. Here lay the beginning of Erik's Real Utopias Project.

The turn to utopian thinking was not entirely new. Erik had run the seminary course on "Utopia and Revolution" in the early 1970s. In 1979, he had joined a group of "Analytical Marxists," sometimes self-described as the "No-Bullshit Marxist Group," which set about hacking the living body of Marxism to death. When asked why he quit, Adam Przeworski, one of its leading members, responded: "Because I thought we had accomplished our intellectual programme . . . We ultimately found that not much of Marxism was left and there really wasn't much more to learn."[28] It was a testament to Erik's formidable intellectual resilience that he could withstand the onslaught of these brilliant scholars against his Marxism.[29] Yet the group did sensitize him to the importance of

---

27 Wright, "Explanation and Emancipation in Marxism and Feminism." Note the shift from the statistical analysis of the noneffects of class on gender relations to the comparison of gender and class emancipation. Erik was deeply devoted to egalitarian relations in his personal life, not least in his family, and this inspired a long-standing interest in feminism. Gay Seidman, who knew him as a close friend, colleague, and neighbor, has written eloquently of the evolution of his thinking on gender emancipation. See "Class, Gender and Utopian Community: In Memory of his Olin Wright," presented at the conference "Transforming Capitalism through Real Utopias: Featuring Erik Olin Wright's Legacy," Coimbra University, January 23–24, 2020. Reprinted in this volume as chapter 2.

28 Erik Olin Wright, "Adam Przeworski: Capitalism, Democracy, and Science," in Gerardo L. Munck and Richard Snyder, eds., *Passion, Craft, and Method in Comparative Politics* (Baltimore, MD: Johns Hopkins University Press, 2007), 490.

29 Erik and I diverged over the significance of Analytical Marxism. To be sure, some of the early works remain Marxist classics such as G. A. Cohen's *Karl Marx's Theory of History: A Defence* (1978) and Przeworski's *Capitalism and Social Democracy* (1985), but the group soon lost interest in Marxism. Only Erik sustained a commitment to Marxism and still remained a key figure in the "September Group," as it came to be renamed, relishing the intellectual exchange. From the beginning I was skeptical of Analytical Marxism's adoption of methodological individualism and rational-choice theory—and criticized the work of Jon Elster, Sam Bowles, Herb Gintis, and Przeworski for forcing Marxism into a methodological straitjacket based on spurious microfoundations and mythological individualism. This was not the way to reconstruct Marxism, I

moral foundations, a driver for the "utopian" side of his real utopias. On the "real" side, Erik was influenced by his colleague and friend Joel Rogers, who arrived in Madison in 1987. They would take walks together almost every Sunday. Joel was an indefatigable propagator of progressive social change at the state and national level, a powerful inspiration and a reality check on Erik's utopias. Joel and Erik brought the real and the utopian together in *American Society: How It Really Works* (2010), the basis of a course they designed that asked to what extent the United States realized five "key values" of American society—freedom, prosperity, economic efficiency, fairness, and democracy—and how it might do a better job.

A broader influence on the Real Utopias Project was the political conjuncture of the time. In 1991 the Soviet Union dissolved, two years after the collapse of state socialism in Eastern Europe. The disappearance of an existing alternative to capitalism, no matter how problematic, would inevitably have consequences for politics in the West; capitalism would no longer need to make political concessions with an eye to "Cold War" competition from the Soviet Union. The unqualified rejection of the Soviet past by the Yeltsin leadership and its equally resolute adoption of a market economy, while it spelled disaster for the majority of Russians, was an enormous fillip for neoliberalism and the proponents of "the end of history." In this context, for those who maintained the possibility of an alternative to capitalism that would guarantee a better life for the majority, it became imperative to discover—or rediscover— imaginations of socialism.

This is where Erik introduced his Real Utopias Project. Classical Marxism had an allergy to utopian thinking. In *Socialism: Utopian and Scientific*, Engels subjected the former variant to withering critique as the projection of a blueprint without warrant in reality, endowed with a miraculous power of self-realization. Instead Engels insisted on attending to the ways capitalism sows the seeds of its own destruction,

---

argued, but to end it. See Michael Burawoy, "Making Nonsense of Marx," *Contemporary Sociology* 15, no. 5 (1986): 704–7; "Should We Give Up on Socialism? Reflections on *Capitalism and Democracy*," *Socialist Review* 89, no. 1 (1989): 57–74.; "Marxism without Micro-foundations: Przeworski's Critique of Social Democracy," *Socialist Review* 89, no. 2 (1989): 53–86; "Analytical Marxism—A Metaphysical Marxism," *Häften för kritiska studier* 22, no. 2 (1989); "Mythological Individualism," in Terrell Carver and Paul Thomas, eds., *Rational Choice Marxism* (London: Macmillan, 1995).

outlining the Marxian argument of intensifying crises of overproduction coinciding with deepening class struggle. It was a compelling theory
that nonetheless proved to be wrong, not least due to its undeveloped
understanding of the state, its flawed concept of class struggle, and its
absent or naive notion of transition. Erik's real utopias were not based
on the laws of capitalist development, but on the discovery of socialist
prefigurations within capitalist society. Classical Marxism had underes-
timated the durability of capitalism. If its collapse was not imminent,
then developing a credible imagination of socialism became all the more
difficult—but all the more important. The viability of Marxism would
hang on sustaining the idea of a "socialist" alternative to capitalism. But
what would it comprise?

Blueprints for a future socialist society were either too remote or
risked leading to "totalitarianism" if realized. So Erik coined the phrase
"real utopia" to refer to actually existing organizations, institutions, and
social movements that operated within capitalist society, but followed
anticapitalist principles. Four favorite examples were participatory
budgeting, originally developed in Porto Alegre, Brazil; universal basic
income; Wikipedia; and Mondragon's worker-owned cooperatives. In
each case Erik explored the functioning of the real utopia, outlined its
principles, and examined its dynamics and internal contradictions, as
well as its conditions of possibility and dissemination.[30]

Starting in 1992, Erik organized a series of conferences at the
University of Wisconsin–Madison's Havens Center (today the Havens
Wright Center for Social Justice) in which an analytical position paper,
focused on a particular real utopia, was circulated to a select group of

---

30   The distinction between real and imaginary utopias is admirably illustrated in
the debate between Erik and Robin Hahnel, proponent of the "participatory economy"
based on democratic participation in a planned economy. As ever, Erik sought out the
best in Hahnel's design for a socialist future, but the difference is clear: Erik started from
existing institutions and organizations and examined how they could be extended and
expanded, whereas Hahnel was in the business of perfecting a blueprint. See Robin
Hahnel and Erik Wright, *Alternatives to Capitalism: Proposals for a Democratic Economy*
(New York: Verso, 2016). Erik thought of utopias very much in the way that Ruth Levitas
saw them—flexible, open-ended, provisional, and above all subject to public debate and
democratic decision-making. See Ruth Levitas, *Utopia as Method: The Imaginary
Reconstruction of Society* (London: Palgrave Macmillan, 2013). I'm reminded of Erik's
unpublished manuscript, "Chess Perversions and Other Diversions" (1974), where the
idea is not to imagine a new game, but to give an old one new meaning by tinkering with
its rules.

participants who each wrote and presented commentaries. There have been six volumes that Erik formally oversaw: on associative democracy, led by Josh Cohen and Joel Rogers; on a particular version of market socialism, led by John Roemer; new forms of egalitarianism, led by Sam Bowles and Herb Gintis; participatory governance, led by Archon Fung and Erik; redesigning redistribution, led by Bruce Ackerman, Anne Alstott, and Philippe Van Parijs; and gender equality, led by Janet Gornick and Marcia Meyers. A seventh volume, published in 2022, three years after Erik's death, on democratizing finance, was led by Fred Block and Robert Hockett.

Erik was actively involved in all the conferences and the publication of the papers, first in *Politics and Society* and then in extended book form with Verso. It was not until 2010 that Erik published his own magnum opus, *Envisioning Real Utopias*, originating in a paper we wrote together. *Envisioning Real Utopias* begins with "diagnosis and critique," a catalog of the ailments of capitalism that call for "alternatives."[31]

But what alternatives? Classical Marxists focused on the self-destruction of the capitalist economy—leaving the working class and its representatives to seize power and run the new society in their own image. No need for any utopia. In a second period, the debate around socialism was influenced by the unanticipated constitution of the Soviet Union. The state now figured centrally—you might say this was socialism on earth.[32] Our claim was that in the third period, socialism should be

---

31   Burawoy and Wright, "Sociological Marxism." From the beginning I was enthusiastic about Erik's Real Utopias Project, and we discussed it at length through the 1990s as I was trying to come to terms with the fall of the Soviet Union and the destruction of the Soviet working class (see Burawoy, "Marxism after Communism," *Theory and Society* 29, no. 2 [2000]: 151–74). On one of Erik's visits to Berkeley, we set about drafting a theoretical framework that brought together his work on real utopias and my view of the history of Marxism in the light of the collapse of communism. This was to have been the basis of a jointly authored book on sociological Marxism, but I got diverted into a project on public sociology. Erik went on to develop our early formulation in *Envisioning Real Utopias*, with me kibitzing on the side.

32   One of our biggest disagreements revolved around the status of the Soviet Union. Erik tended to dismiss this as a form of "statism" of little relevance to the socialist project, whereas I saw it, with all its warts, as a form of socialism—state socialism—of inescapable relevance. The centrality of democracy to the Real Utopias Project was an implicit reaction to the Soviet Behemoth, but it never led Erik to examine the latter's form or its source. The Soviet Union was a great and tragic experiment that defined the contours of the twentieth century; we ignore it at our peril. Marxists have much to learn

defined as the collective self-regulation of civil society, expanded in two dimensions: empowerment of the social in relation to the state—deepening democracy through participatory budgeting, citizens' assemblies, associative democracy—and in relation to the economy through initiatives like Wikipedia, the solidarity economy, the Mondragon Cooperative, universal basic income.[33]

The third part of *Envisioning Real Utopias* developed a theory of transformation. Erik considered three strategies: ruptural transformation, about which he was skeptical (as he always had been); interstitial transformation, involving the development of autonomous institutions within capitalism; and symbiotic transformation, which returned us to ways in which the state can be used to promote transformative struggles against itself. Here Erik developed the idea of class compromise as a way in which both capital and labor could benefit from struggle—though whether those benefits could ever stimulate struggles that led beyond capitalism was unclear. This was, indeed, a crossover from the class analysis, but where the latter was intensely empirical and definitive, class compromise was highly abstract and conjectural. Class was now a possible strategy of social transformation rather than a meticulous analysis of social structure; this was an entirely different understanding of the term.

In the twenty years that Erik worked on this book, he traveled the face of the earth talking about real utopias to scholars, activists, and

---

from this attempt to put socialism into practice, not least the limits and possibilities of a socialism based on planning, as well as the subaltern struggles for alternative democratic socialisms that opposition to state socialism inspired. Nor can we ignore Soviet Marxism, degenerate though it was, as if the history of Marxism were a supermarket from which you pick out whatever you like. We have to live with the good and the bad— they fortunately and unfortunately shape each other. Erik was never keen on examining the dark side of utopia. See Burawoy and János Lukács, *The Radiant Past: Ideology and Reality in Hungary's Road to Capitalism* (Chicago: University of Chicago Press, 1992).

33   I traced the argument for socialism as the collective self-organization of civil society to the complementary convergence of Polanyi and Gramsci: in the former, from the reaction to the economy; in the latter, from the reaction to the state. See Burawoy, "For a Sociological Marxism: The Complementary Convergence of Antonio Gramsci and Karl Polanyi," *Politics and Society* 31, no. 2 (2004): 193–261. Erik, meanwhile, was working on elaborating and systematizing the relations between state, economy, and civil society—or, as he put it, taking the social in socialism seriously. See Wright, "Compass Points: Towards a Socialist Alternative," *New Left Review* 41 (Sept.–Oct. 2006): 93–124.

politicians. The eloquence and optimism that he exuded drew enthusiastic supporters; *Envisioning Real Utopias*, bulky though it is, was translated into many languages. But he knew it might be more effective if there was a shorter, popular version, more like a manifesto. He managed to complete *How to Be an Anticapitalist in the Twenty-First Century* in 2019, before he died. No sooner was it published in English than there were ten translations of the book underway or already completed.

A more straightforward account of the Real Utopias Project, *How to Be an Anticapitalist* shifted the argument and its emphases. Instead of the long and perhaps rather arbitrary list of capitalism's discontents, it built on three normative foundations for opposing capitalism: equality/fairness, democracy/freedom, and community/solidarity. Formulating the project in this way had the advantage of appealing to values that are at the foundation of liberal democracies—values that capitalism violates or realizes in only a limited way. Erik now considered five strategies for achieving democratic socialism. He was critical of the first, "smashing capitalism"—how could one build a new order out of the ruins of the old?—and instead concentrated on *dismantling* capitalism from above, *taming* capitalism (containing its worst effects), *resisting* capitalism, and *escaping* capitalism. He envisioned these strategies working in combination to *erode* capitalism and build a future socialism based on the ideas of economic democracy. He offered the familiar set of real utopias that could contribute to that end, building an alternative economy and a more democratic order.

By the time he was diagnosed with acute myeloid leukemia in April 2018, Erik was near to completing this book, but he had still to write the most challenging last chapter: who would be the agents of such a transformation? For the first time he tackled the question of the collective actors necessary for eroding capitalism. While clear that democratic socialism would not arise without collective struggle, he didn't come down on any one particular agent or combination of agents. Instead he examined the conditions for such a struggle—the importance of *identities* that can forge solidarities, *interests* that lead to realistic objectives, and *values* that can create political unity across diverse identities and interests.

Here Erik came to terms with the conundrum of his oeuvre—his move from class analysis without utopias, to utopias without class analysis. In *How to Be an Anticapitalist*, he argued that it is one thing to be an

anticapitalist, but quite another to be a democratic socialist. Class struggle can contribute to the former, but it is inadequate to the latter. Where
Marx considered an inevitable class polarization would lead to the
magical coincidence of the demise of capitalism and the building of
socialism, he drew the conclusion that, by itself, class was too fragmented and limited a social force to build something new. If "eroding"
capitalism was not to lead to barbarism but to democratic socialism, the
transformation would require a moral vision to propel struggles for a
better world—the troika of equality, democracy, and solidarity.

There was no singular, pregiven actor, impelled by their social or
economic location to engage in class struggle. Erik wrote: "I won't be
able to provide a real answer to the question of where these collective
actors are to be found, but I hope to clarify the task we confront in creating them."[34] To use Bourdieu's language, Erik broke with this earlier
"theoretical" notion of class: class on paper.

> This "class on paper" has the *theoretical* existence that belongs to all
> theories: as the product of an explanatory classification, one which is
> altogether similar to that of zoologists and botanists, it allows one to
> *explain* and predict the practices and properties of the things classi-
> fied—including their propensity to constitute groups. It is not really a
> class, an actual class, in the sense of being a group, a group mobilized
> for struggle.[35]

The actor or actors, if they are to appear, are constituted by their adher-
ence to a binding ideology that brings unity to scattered struggles. If
before, class preexisted struggle, now struggle preexists class.

This suggests a radical contingency in class formation, occurring
through political practice and ideology of which Marxism was one
expression.[36] Here Erik exemplified a Gramscian vision of political

---

34 Erik Olin Wright, *How to Be an Anticapitalist in the Twenty-First Century* (New
York: Verso, 2019), 119.

35 Bourdieu, "Social Space and the Genesis of 'Classes,'" 231–2.

36 Apart from Bourdieu there are many other thinkers who start from "class for
itself" rather than "class in itself." See, for example, E. P. Thompson, *The Making of the
English Working Class* (1963), who sees class as present in the making of its own history,
although still rooted in objective conditions of exploitation. Or Nicos Poulantzas,
Political Power and Social Classes (1973), where class is an effect rather than a cause, an
idea that is elaborated by Adam Przeworski in *Capitalism and Social Democracy* (1985),

ideology: "expressed neither in the form of a cold utopia nor as learned theorizing, but rather by the creation of a concrete phantasy which acts on a dispersed and shattered people to arouse and organize its collective will."[37] He left behind the "learned theorizing" of the classroom, and he was not dreaming up some "cold utopia" detached from the real world, but created a "concrete phantasy" developed in close connection to the practitioners of real utopias working in the trenches of civil society. He spent time with the grassroots organizers of the participatory budget in Porto Alegre, the cooperatives of Mondragon, the social economy of Quebec.[38] From the analyst of survey data, Erik became the ethnographer, coproducing an understanding of the principles of real utopias, and the conditions of their existence and dissemination. Over the last two decades his major audience increasingly became political activists around the world. Giving voice to their latent aspirations, he connected them to one another, articulating the elements of a collective socialist project. He effectively became a Modern Prince, a permanent persuader that another world was possible.

Joining Science and Critique

Erik was elected president of the American Sociological Association, and for the 2011 annual meeting in Denver we were treated to a cornucopia of real utopias—three plenary sessions and seventy thematic panels. Sociology itself became a real utopia as Erik moved it away—perhaps

---

for whom classes are treated, in part, as the contingent outcomes of electoral strategies of political parties. Instead of the conventional political sociology that groups have pregiven interests dependent on their place in the class structure and will vote accordingly, Przeworski argues that the very meaning of class is constituted in and through politics. As with Bourdieu, classification struggles precede class struggles. In the last chapter of his last book, I believe Erik was moving in that direction, leaving behind his earlier ideas of class.

37   Antonio Gramsci, *Selections from the Prison Notebooks*, ed. and trans. Quintin Hoare and Geoffrey Nowell Smith (New York: International Publishers, 1971), 125–6.

38   This brings to mind Alain Touraine, for whom the role of the sociologist is to "conscientize" militants in social movements, that is, help them develop a wider and deeper vision of their project. See Touraine, *The Self-Production of Society* (Chicago: University of Chicago Press, 1977); *Return of the Actor* (Minneapolis: University of Minnesota Press, 1988); Touraine et al., *Solidarity: The Analysis of a Movement; Poland, 1980–81* (Cambridge: Cambridge University Press, 1983).

only temporarily—from a value-free, objectivist, technocratic discipline toward an engaged, emancipatory science. Influenced as much by philosophers as by sociologists, his turn to value commitments had an elective affinity to classical sociology's foundations. His emphasis on equality, freedom, and solidarity recalls the work of Durkheim, especially *The Division of Labour in Society* (1893), which built a vision of guild socialism based on occupational groups that would assume ownership of the means of production and the economic direction of society. Durkheim's socialism required equality of opportunity so each had the freedom to find their true place in the division of labor that, in turn, required power equality between functional groups and the elimination of the inheritance of wealth. Durkheim considered the perfection of the division of labor and, thus, the realization of organic solidarity to be immanent to modern society. He did not think in terms of the obstacles posed by capitalism. Capitalism was not even a category in his analysis.

Even though Erik became more Durkheimian as he advanced his Real Utopias Project—that is, more interested in solidarity and shared values—it was always Weber who absorbed his attention. His 1974 study of the state in Lenin and Weber, chapter 4 in *Class, Crisis and the State*, was complemented by repeated engagements with Weber's notion of social stratification. Under Roemer's influence, Erik also flirted with the methodological individualism at the core of Weber's sociology; and then there was Weber's passion for classification. Later, Erik became fascinated by Weber's "Marxist" exploration of the slave mode of production.[39] As compared to Durkheim, Weber was more influenced, if negatively, by Marx and Marxists. He saw capitalism—along with its necessary accompaniment, bureaucracy—as an insuperable obstacle to socialism; but that didn't mean his sociology was bereft of values. Weber has been widely misunderstood as the prophet of value-free sociology, for he was anything but; he, too, saw the sociologist's claim to neutrality as bogus. Indeed, he considered his fundamental methodological unit, the ideal type, as a utopia, a one-sided, value-based construction of the real world.[40] Conservative liberal though he was, even Weber based his

39   Erik Olin Wright, "The Shadow of Exploitation in Weber's Class Analysis," *American Sociological Review* 67, no. 6 (2002).

40   Max Weber, "'Objectivity' in Social Science and Social Policy," in *The Methodology of the Social Sciences*, trans. Edward Shils and Henry Finch (1904; repr., New York: Free Press, 1949), 90.

sociology on the idea of individual freedom and autonomy, wrestling with the juggernaut of rationalization. This made him suspicious of socialist projects, predicting that a dictatorship of the proletariat would become a dictatorship of officials. In as much as he, too, insisted on value foundations, His real utopias reconnect to the normative bases of classical sociology.

If Erik's class analysis—following a realist, objectivist methodology—was absorbed into mainstream sociology, his real utopias recovered a lost dimension of the sociological tradition, the idea of a moral science built on the institutional realization of declared value commitments. More than that, he was engaged in a dialogue with the practitioners of real utopias. The subjects of his science were no longer anonymous respondents to prepackaged survey questions, but activists badly in need of a sustaining ideology.

If real utopias drew on the critical potential rooted in the sociological tradition, what had happened to Erik's Marxism? His Real Utopias Project allies itself with a vision of socialism, but—as with the account of changes in class structure—there was still no theory of the dynamics of capitalism. Doubts about capitalism's inevitable demise led him away from the study of capitalist tendencies *tout court*. Instead, *Envisioning Real Utopias* listed the *defects* of capitalism, which in *How to Be an Anticapitalist* changed into a set of "socialist" values that cannot be fully realized under capitalism. But real utopias cannot be driven just by an anticapitalist imagination of a future; they are driven by grievances generated by capitalism. In a scientific enterprise, utopias have to emerge from the logic of capitalist development.

Where shall we look for a theory that connects the rise of real utopias to capitalism? One place to begin is chapter 3 of Erik's *Class, Crisis and the State*, "Historical Transformations of Capitalist Crisis Tendencies." In this abandoned chapter he did advance a theory of capital accumulation: the contradictions of capitalism lead to economic crises of overproduction and declining profits, calling for "solutions" or temporary "fixes" that engender new crises, all of which involve the restructuring, expansion, and deepening of the market—by extending credit, or seeking out cheaper inputs of raw materials or human labor. How can we connect his early theory of capitalist development to real utopias?

One answer, I believe, lies in the canonical work of Karl Polanyi, *The Great Transformation* (1944). If Erik's theory focused on capitalist crises as the driving force behind marketization, Polanyi looked at the—catastrophic—*consequences* of marketization. Having traced the origins of the political crises of the 1930s to the relentless expansion of the market, Polanyi believed that humanity would never again experiment with market fundamentalism. He was wrong, because he thought market fundamentalism was an irrational policy under human control. He didn't see the expansion of markets as a response to the crises of capitalism—it was a temporary fix, but a fix nonetheless. As long as there is capitalism, there will be crises; and the crises will be contained by markets that, in turn, propel the development of capitalism and new crises.

Polanyi saw one long wave of marketization, from the 1790s to the 1930s, when reaction set in—taking the form of Stalinism, social democracy, the New Deal, or, what he most feared, fascism. But once we recognize another wave of marketization beginning in the 1970s, it is possible to discern at least two previous waves, one in the nineteenth century and the other in the first part of the twentieth century. Each long wave of capitalist development engenders its own crisis that calls forth a corresponding wave of marketization, characterized by the *articulation of the commodification of factors of production*, namely, Polanyi's fictitious commodities: nature, labor power, money, and, today, knowledge. If the commodification of labor power dominated the first wave, and the commodification of money (finance capital) dominated the second, then the commodification of nature and knowledge may be said to dominate the third wave, though not to the exclusion of the (re)commodification of the others.

Each of the three waves of marketization calls forth a Polanyian "countermovement" to defend "society": the first wave led to movements of a local character; the second led to regulatory states; the third wave, so-called neoliberalism, has generated countermovements at local and national levels, including both leftist and rightist nationalist regimes. So far there have been only weak efforts to regulate commodification where it is most needed, namely on a global scale—that is, to regulate international finance, climate change, the transnational movement of labor, and the global flows of knowledge.[41] Today countermovements

---

41 See Michael Burawoy, "Marxism after Polanyi," in Michelle Williams and Vishwas Satgar, eds., *Approaches to Marxism in the Twenty-First Century* (Johannesburg: Wits University Press, 2013), chap. 2.

may include local and national reactions, but patterns of commodification under third-wave marketization actually call for an effective global countermovement, something Polanyi never seriously considered.

How are we to connect these countermovements to real utopias? In brief, real utopias can be viewed as partial countermovements to the commodification of these four fictitious commodities. But this requires us to examine the meaning of "fictitiousness" and how it can lead to countermovements. Here, I believe, there are three answers. First, Polanyi argues that nature, labor, money, and now knowledge were never *intended* to be commodified. Labor is about who we are, nature is about how we exist, money is a means of exchange, knowledge is to improve life. In other words, the commodification of these entities disturbs our *moral compass* for it violates the essence of their existence. Second, commodification is economically dysfunctional: when fictitious commodities are subjected to unregulated market exchange, they lose their use value, even to the point of being unusable, becoming waste—that is, ex-commodified. This, too, leads to collective protest. But "fictitiousness" has a third significance, underemphasized by Polanyi. It is not just the *consequences* of commodification that are so destructive, but also the very *production* of a fictitious commodity, that is, the process of disembedding nature, labor, money, and knowledge from their social integument—a process that others have called "dispossession."[42] The countermovement is then collective action inspired by some combination of moral opprobrium, the production of waste, and dispossession.

Here lies the significance of real utopias. They are an index of Polanyi's countermovement to commodification, or, to put it more positively, an index of processes of decommodification. Universal basic income—or, better, universal provision of social services to meet basic needs—is a response to the commodification of labor power, which involves the subjugation of women and the crisis of care, just as unregulated commodification generates high levels of precarity.[43] Public banks and

---

42 See, for example, David Harvey, *The New Imperialism* (New York: Oxford University Press, 2003); Michael Levien, *Dispossession without Development: Landgrabs in Neoliberal India* (New York: Oxford University Press, 2018); Klaus Dörre, Stephan Lessenich, and Hartmut Rosa, *Sociology, Capitalism, Critique* (London: Verso, 2015).

43 See Nancy Fraser, "A Triple Movement? Parsing the Politics of Crisis after Polanyi," *New Left Review* 81 (May–June 2013); Silvia Federici, *Revolution at Point Zero:*

participatory budgeting are a reaction against the commodification of money, of making money from money, of finance capital. Agricultural and housing co-ops are a response to the commodification of land and water, while environmental-justice groups organize against the plundering of the atmosphere on the way to its commodification through carbon trading. Wikipedia and peer-to-peer collaboration are a counterpoint to the commodification of knowledge through surveillance capitalism. The institute that Erik developed over thirty years—the Havens Wright Center for Social Justice—with its collective form of organization, can be seen as a counterpoint to the commodification of knowledge in the university. This appropriation and reconstruction of *The Great Transformation* is one way to recover the contradictory unity of critical and scientific Marxism that appeared so spontaneously at the beginning of Erik's career, a half-century ago.

Real utopias cannot stop the expansion and deepening of the market, but they can provide the basis of a countermovement to the commodification of everything—a commodification that is neither conjunctural nor contingent but systematically generated by capitalism—so as to contain the crises of accumulation. Erik's real utopias thus signify something organic to capitalism, namely the reaction to commodification. If capitalism depends on deepening commodification, a move toward decommodification conducted across all fictitious commodities has the *potential* to be anticapitalist—but there are no guarantees. First, a countermovement to commodification is as likely to save capitalism from itself as to abolish it. Second, a Polanyian countermovement can easily assume an authoritarian form, as in the right-wing populism of today and the fascism of yesterday. That's the rub—how to turn a Polanyian "countermovement" into a Gramscian "counter-hegemony." For decommodification can only lead beyond capitalism if it inspires a socialist movement. Hence the importance of Erik's engagement with particular real utopias and their practitioners, linking them together in an anticapitalist movement that gives direction to a democratic-socialist project.[44]

Housework, Reproduction, and Feminist Struggle (New York: PM Press, 2012); Guy Standing, *The Precariat: The New Dangerous Class* (New York: Bloomsbury, 2011).

44   An interesting contrast to Erik's approach is Wolfgang Streeck's *How Will Capitalism End?* (2016), which sees falling growth, rising debt, and increasing inequality resulting in chronic decay and anomie—whereas Erik, focusing on the durability of capitalism, conjured up real utopias.

This would be my response to critics who label Erik's project "neoliberal socialism" or "neo-Tocquevillian Marxism," or who call for an "intermittent revolution."[45] Real utopias have to become part of a Gramscian "war of position" in civil society. The key premise is that struggles no longer revolve around "exploitation" but around "commodification."[46] Who will be the agents in such struggles? Clearly class, however defined, is a likely candidate, for the moral outrage and destructive material effects of commodification are skewed against lower classes, be they peasants or wage laborers. But alliances across classes are also possible, since the commodification of nature, money, labor, and knowledge affects everyone; no less important are the different and unequal effects of racialization and gender. There are many potential movements and alliances, but it is also likely that struggles against commodification will tend toward fragmentation and localization. Only a powerful "counter-hegemonic" ideology can make the market an object of socialist struggle, given its capacity to naturalize its own working. Erik not only provided the basis for such an ideology; he was also its charismatic propagator.

The Real Utopias Project demands that we return to Erik's early Marxism, in which science and critique were joined. It cries out for a scientific basis to identify the forces behind real utopias, as well as the possibilities for successful political engagement. His trajectory took him from scientific to critical Marxism, but now the latter requires an infusion of science—a theory of the dynamics of

---

45 Marion Fourcade, "On Erik Wright, *Envisioning Real Utopias*," *Socio-Economic Review* 10, no. 2 (2012): 369–402; Dylan Riley, "Neo-Tocquevillian Marxism: Erik Olin Wright's *Real Utopias*," *Socio-Economic Review* 10, no. 2 (2012) 136–50; Cihan Tuğal, "Intermittent Revolution: The Road to a Hybrid Socialism," *Socio-Economic Review* 10, no. 2 (2012): 382–6.

46 I'm using the word "exploitation" in the technical sense used by Marx: the extraction of surplus value in production. Marx himself said that it was hidden from both labor and capital, as workers appear to be paid for all the labor they expend. Following Przeworski, Erik advanced a theory of class compromise based on the capacity of capitalism to grant economic concessions that turned struggles around exploitation into struggles for reform. Finally, third-wave marketization has stripped the working class not only of the interest but also the capacity to effectively challenge capital. Whether commodification offers greater opportunities to challenge capitalism is still an open question. My argument rests on the claim that commodification, rather than exploitation, corresponds to the discontent of the majority of the world's population.

capitalism and how they are experienced—as well as a more elaborated ideology to unify fragmented struggles. This is the problem Erik left us with—a problem I would tackle by linking real utopias to decommodification, and analyzing decommodification as a reaction to marketization, which is itself impelled by successive crises of overproduction and profitability.

Coda: Sociological Marxism

In *Reconstructing Marxism* (1992), Erik and his coauthors, Andrew Levine and Elliott Sober, set out to clarify the foundations of Marxism—addressing its theory of history and related issues in the philosophy of science. Their idea of "reconstruction" was analytical rather than historical. Applying conventional positivist views of objectivist science, they dispensed with the history of Marxism, the examination of iconic texts, and the political and economic context of their authorship. To Erik, such a historical view smacked of religion and dogma. Unencumbered by the heavy weight of the Marxist tradition, Analytical Marxism offered a new beginning. Yet it also threatened to mark the end of Marxism. Indeed, Erik was the only Analytical Marxist to maintain an identification with Marxism. Why? No doubt there are different answers to this question; here I emphasize one—his connection to sociology.

Analytical Marxism was dominated by philosophers, economists, and political scientists. Erik was the only representative from sociology, which, I believe, sustained his commitment to Marxism. To be sure, he used to say he was not particularly interested in professional sociology, but spending forty years in a leading sociology department, reading the work of students and colleagues, reviewing for sociology journals, directing sociological dissertations, teaching sociology to undergraduates, locked in arguments with sociologists—with all these engagements he could not but absorb sociology's distinctive worldview. In the last decade of his life his engagement with sociology became more self-conscious and deliberate, especially after he was elected president of the American Sociological Association. He may not have married class analysis and real utopias, but he did marry sociology and Marxism—an unequal marriage dominated by Marxism.

In the final analysis, that's why his legacy is a sociological Marxism rather than a Marxist sociology.[47]

As we have seen, there were three borrowings from sociology. His first was methodological, turning the tools of survey analysis and statistics against the theoretical framework of sociology. He had to confront the challenge, famously defined by Audre Lorde, that the master's tools "may allow us temporarily to beat him at his own game, but they will never enable us to bring about genuine change."[48] Addressing this very issue, Erik wrote in my copy of *Class Counts*—the culmination of his comparative class analysis—"Alas, see what has become of revolutionary dialectics . . ." His second borrowing was from sociology's standpoint of civil society, a borrowing elaborated in *Envisioning Real Utopias*, where the struggle for socialism is based on the collective reorganization of civil society. Real utopias were to empower the social, restore the social to socialism. His third borrowing was from sociology's moral foundations, its commitment to universal values: equality/fairness, democracy/ freedom, community/solidarity. Already present in *Envisioning Real Utopias*, they became central to *How to Be an Anticapitalist*. Real utopias were not only about the empowerment of the social but the institutional realization of shared values that could never be realized in their full

---

47 My own approach to "reconstruction" was rather different. In wrestling with the fate of Marxism in the post-Soviet period, I had to confront the history of Marxism found in Perry Anderson's *Considerations on Western Marxism* (1976), which sought to recover revolutionary theory from the political retreat of Western Marxism; in George Lichtheim's *Marxism* (1961), a pessimistic history which saw Marxism dissolving with the Russian Revolution, and petrifying as soon as it becomes academically respectable; and in Leszek Kolakowski's *Main Currents of Marxism* (1978), a three-volume history that degenerates into an assault on the New Left when it comes to the contemporary period. Perhaps the most significant contribution to the Marxism of Marxism remains the *Prison Notebooks* of Antonio Gramsci. Unique among classical Marxists, he was concerned to develop a theory of intellectuals and thus the political and economic context for a flourishing Marxism. Inspired by Gramsci, I have tried to combine the historical and the scientific by regarding Marxism as an evolving scientific research program, following Lakatos's "post-positivist" philosophy of science. The taken-for-granted "hard core" assumptions are rooted in the writings of Marx and Engels, out of which evolve successive belts of auxiliary theories, responding to the contradictions and anomalies that arose in particular historical conjunctures. I used the metaphor of a tree with roots, a trunk, and progressive and degenerate branches. See Burawoy, "Marxism as Science: Historical Challenges and Theoretical Growth," *American Sociological Review* 55 (1990): 775–93.

48 "The Master's Tools Will Never Dismantle the Master's House," in Audre Lorde, *Sister Outsider: Essays and Speeches* (Berkeley, CA: Crossing Press, 1984), 112.

form under capitalism. It was a curious, critical, but unconscious return to where Erik began, with the work of Talcott Parsons; only now Parsons's euphoria about US society was projected onto a future, so far unrealized, socialism.

Threading through Erik's work, therefore, is not just a bifurcation between scientific and critical Marxism, but a productive engagement of Marxism with sociology. As Gouldner wrote, however much they are engaged in mutual polemic, Marxism and sociology are like Siamese twins: "The demise of one presages the demise of the other. They have a common destiny not *despite* the fact that they have developed in dialectical opposition, but precisely *because* of it."[49] Sociologists have every reason to keep the Marxist flame alive, as a large part of their raison d'être lies in opposing Marxism. By the same token, as Erik showed, Marxists can also borrow, fruitfully, from sociology. Marxism has a special place in the history of sociology and, I wager, in its future.[50]

The balance between sociology and Marxism shifts with the political context, reflecting the ebb and flow of the times. Throughout all this, Erik stood firm. Even when Marxism was in retreat, he never wavered. He did not passively wait for its renaissance but actively reconstructed Marxism, turning from his class analysis to his project on real utopias, eagerly appealing both to a new generation of socialists entering the academy and to a growing community of activists across the planet. Behind Erik's reconstruction of Marxism lay his abiding commitment to truth, clarity, dialogue, community, and social justice. In his dying days he elevated a fourth dimension of human flourishing: to equality, democracy, and solidarity he added love, an intense emotion of mutual recognition and interdependence.[51]

---

49 "Sociology and Marxism," in Alvin Gouldner, *For Sociology: Renewal and Critique in Sociology Today* (New York: Basic Books, 1973), 401.

50 This view of sociology is not the conventional Marxist perspective. Writing in 1976, Perry Anderson tracked the displacement of revolutionary Marxism by a Western Marxism that had been diluted by bourgeois thought, including sociology. In this rendition, sociology is an ideology that hides or justifies bourgeois rule. It has no emancipatory moment. Ironically, Anderson's *Considerations on Western Marxism* won the distinguished book award of the American Sociological Association—indicating, perhaps, sociology's antagonistic attachment to Marxism.

51 During the last ten months of his life, liberated from writing for a professional or political audience, Erik recorded his reflections on life and death, based on daily events in the cancer ward—his multiple relations with others, his hopes and despairs for

Erik was not just an architect of the theory of real utopias; he also put that theory into practice. Possessed of rich and varied abilities himself, he orchestrated participatory communities wherever he went, whether with children, family, friends, neighbors, students, or colleagues, thereby empowering others to realize their own distinct potentialities. In practice as well as in theory he was committed to a future in which everyone would have access to the conditions of their flourishing—conditions that his privileged existence allowed him to enjoy. He lived under capitalism as though he were in socialism, setting an often impossible example to follow, but always instilling an imagination of what could be. Two Marxisms, yes; but only one Erik Olin Wright.

---

humanity, even as the disease consumed his body. Made available as a blog on the website for CaringBridge, it was read, discussed, and admired across the globe. A condensed version was published by Haymarket Books, *Stardust to Stardust* (Chicago: 2020).

2

Class, Gender, and Utopian Community
Gay Seidman

Most sociologists try to understand society as it is in the present, not ponder how we might want to organize it in some far-off future. What prompted Erik Wright's shift from his decades-long effort to map class structures in industrial societies to a search for paths to a more egalitarian future?

Like many sociologists, I found this turn to "real utopias" puzzling—especially coming from Erik, a scholar who took such pride in his early work combining Marxist concepts with rigorous social science methods. By the late 1990s, Erik's focus seemed almost diametrically opposed to that earlier project. Instead of mapping complicated capitalist employment relations, he began looking for new social arrangements that might encourage egalitarianism, seeking organizational patterns that might produce communities shaped by fairness and generosity rather than by exploitation and competition.

That shift intrigued me. I first met Erik in the late 1980s, when his work on "contradictory class locations" had already established him as a

This essay was originally presented as prepared remarks at the conference "Transforming Capitalism through Real Utopias: Featuring Erik Olin Wright's Legacy," Coimbra University, Portugal, January 23–4, 2020, and an earlier version, illustrated with photos from Erik's poster collection, was included in a special issue of *Politics and Society* (vol. 48, issue 4). For comments and suggestions, I am indebted to Boaventura de Sousa Santos, Michael Burawoy, Inés Campillo Poza, Greta Krippner, Heinz Klug, Sara Trongone, and especially Marcia Kahn Wright.

leading Marxist sociologist. In 1990, largely because of Erik, I joined the University of Wisconsin–Madison faculty, where I had a front-row seat as Erik embarked on what Michael Burawoy calls a "tale of two Marxisms."[1] Yet even from the office next door, Erik's transformation seemed surprising. What prompted his turn away from his early "scientific Marxism"—that careful, data-based, analytic mapping of capitalist class structures and class locations—and why did he shift to searching for alternative social organizations and a new emancipatory project?

A few months after Erik passed, a question from Boaventura de Sousa Santos about how Erik approached gender issues pushed me to think in new ways about his intellectual trajectory—especially about what propelled that extraordinary intellectual shift. Erik's turn to searching for real utopias stemmed from a very sociological perspective, one informed by classic sociologists, deep egalitarian ideals, and above all by his endless intellectual curiosity. But on rereading Erik's work, I am increasingly impressed by how much that new direction was shaped by a profound engagement with feminist concerns, by how his interactions with feminists, and feminist thinking, reshaped his vision of how we might construct a better world.

But before turning to the role feminism played in Erik's surprising shift to the study of real utopias, I want to say a little more about Erik—who was my colleague, neighbor, and dear friend for thirty years, for literally half my life. As a mutual friend at Berkeley, Carol Hatch, often said, Erik had the personality of a summer camp director—someone who pulled everyone around him into joyous, productive games, who could see the bright side of anything, who kept us going when things got rough. More than four years after his passing, his absence still leaves a gaping hole.

Erik brought his energetic warmth to our community, as well as to his intellectual work, pulling friends, students, and colleagues into activities like canoeing on the Wisconsin River or cross-country skiing across an icy lake, year-end retreats, helping those who might be struggling with personal issues, giving generous advice to graduate students. Sadly, I

---

1   Michael Burawoy, "A Tale of Two Marxisms: Remembering Erik Olin Wright (1947–2019)," *New Left Review* 121 (January–February 2020): 67–98. Reprinted in this volume as chapter 1.

never did go on any of the sociocultural bike tours he offered every year to members of the UW–Madison sociology department, but I will always miss the dinners he organized for visiting scholars, Thanksgiving feasts with Erik playing fiddle while we danced Virginia reels, baby showers for pregnant colleagues, graduation celebrations for our students. Erik and Marcia's home became the heart of a global community of scholars and activists, simultaneously close-knit and limitless—a community those of us who were lucky enough to have been in will cherish forever.

Of course, very few camp directors have ever come close to Erik's brilliance, or his intellectual rigor and insight, but Carol's description also captures the spirit that infused Erik's intellectual work, as well as his face-to-face interactions: his infectious energy and enthusiasm, his ability to point out new directions, to pull us into new collective adventures, to build a better community. Those who have read his work know how brilliant his insights could be—and how clearly he could spell out complicated issues or interrogate simple ones. In person, you could always count on him for thoughtful, reasonable responses, even to ideas that challenged his basic beliefs—responses that were rooted in his deep generosity, his commitment to social justice, and his egalitarian universalism. He could always find the gem in a student's dissertation proposal, acknowledge a reasonable insight even in arguments with which he completely disagreed, or offer a way out of an intellectual dead end.

But back to my initial question. What prompted that search for "real utopias," that direction that seemed more idealistic than empirical, more philosophic than pragmatic? Indeed, skeptical colleagues in our department sometimes wondered aloud whether Erik's Real Utopias Project might reflect a return to his past—pointing out that after graduating from Harvard, he attended a liberal religious seminary and served as a student chaplain in California's notorious San Quentin prison. Although he moved to a doctoral program in sociology at Berkeley just a year or two later, perhaps the shift in the 1990s, to a search for a new emancipatory vision, simply marked a return to his more religious, philosophical beginnings?

Of course, no one could deny that his initial turn was initially prompted by real-world events: Erik was quite clear that the collapse of the Soviet Union in 1991 posed new theoretical challenges, for Marxist theory and for sociology more broadly. When the only historical example of Marx's "dictatorship of the proletariat" fell apart, he argued,

Marxists confronted a theoretical vacuum. Without an acceptable vision of what a more inclusive society might look like, what kind of society should leftists aspire to? If "actually existing socialism" offered no guide to a better future, how should activists think about their goals?

That question certainly nagged at Erik—who, although he did not consider himself a committed Weberian, always insisted on confronting "inconvenient facts" when they contradicted his theoretical assumptions. For decades, Erik participated actively in a group of social scientists who called themselves "Analytical Marxists" (or, as he often called them, informally, the "No-Bullshit Marxists")—a group of leftist scholars who prided themselves on a direct engagement with mainstream economic and "rational choice" theories, trying to develop an intellectually rigorous "scientific Marxism." For many of those scholars, and certainly for Erik, the collapse of the Soviet Union raised serious questions about what Marxists should be focusing on and whether Marxism's long-term vision of a classless society really promised a desirable or attainable future—questions that are likely to be debated for years to come.[2]

But interpreting Erik's intellectual shift as stemming simply from the Soviet Union's collapse may lead us to overlook the extent to which, by the early 1990s, feminist perspectives had already begun to push him to rethink some of his assumptions about social relations. Rereading his work, I think it becomes clear that questions raised by feminists—about what social relations matter to individuals, about what emancipation means, and about how to get there—shaped his vision of real utopias and prompted a reexamination of how we might reach them.

As anyone who knew his personal history will recognize, Erik's understanding of gender dynamics was shaped by his personal experience, at home and at work. He grew up in a household marked by domestic egalitarianism: in contrast to gender stereotypes of the 1950s, both his father and his mother were highly regarded professors of psychology. Later, as an undergraduate at Harvard, he met his life partner, Marcia; in fact, they both took an undergraduate sociology course with Talcott Parsons. I don't think anyone who knows the family could doubt that Erik's domestic life, with Marcia and their daughters Jenny

2   See Burawoy, "Tale of Two Marxisms"; Dylan Riley, "Reply to Burawoy," *New Left Review* 121 (January 2020): 99–107.

and Rebecca, strengthened his faith that a better world is possible and that gender inequalities would have no place in a real utopia.

That conviction was also influenced by Erik's interactions at work, especially with feminist graduate students and colleagues. Soon after he arrived in Madison in the late 1970s, Cindy Costello and other graduate students pushed him to include feminist theorists in his graduate seminars on sociological theory. Always open to suggestions, Erik asked his feminist graduate students to design an entire section of the course, and he incorporated the readings they proposed into his syllabus. In the process, several graduate students formed what became an ongoing women's group—one that was still meeting in 2020, some forty years later.

That openness to others' ideas was evident throughout Erik's career. Some extraordinary graduate students came to Madison to work with him, including socialist feminists, like Janeen Baxter, Raka Ray, Greta Krippner, Elizabeth Wrigley-Fields, Julia Adams, and many, many others. Working with these students pushed Erik to ask new questions, as did his broader collaborations with leading feminist scholars such as Nancy Folbre, Juliet Schor, Janet Gornick, Marcia K. Meyers, Debra Satz—the list goes on and on.

Boa Santos's question pushed me to think about the influence of feminist colleagues and graduate students on Erik's daily life, but even more, it prompted me to ask how Erik's growing appreciation of gender inequality coincided with—or even shaped—his efforts to rethink scientific Marxism in the early 1990s. As I reread his work from that period, it seems clear that a growing awareness of the social dynamics that produce gender inequality, at home as well as at work, pushed him to think differently about the way all identities are embedded within, and shaped by, social relations—and to ask how those social relations might be changed. Over time, Erik began to ask how household dynamics, as well as the workplace, would have to change if humans were ever going to live in the kind of ideal community that Marxists hoped for—and to argue that our vision of an emancipatory future would have to be "genderless" as well as "classless."

In retrospect, it seems clear that even before the collapse of the Soviet Union, Erik was beginning to wonder what acknowledging inequalities beyond class might mean for Marxist dreams. Of course, as we all know, he spent the first twenty years of his career carefully analyzing large data sets, insisting that a fuller understanding of class location in complex industrial societies required going beyond Marx's focus on wages and ownership. Class location—especially for workers in the rather fuzzily defined "middle class"—had become more complicated than a simple dichotomy between proletarian and bourgeoisie suggested: Erik's term "contradictory class location" was used to describe a shift in workplace realities. As workers were increasingly spread across very different positions within the production process, very different degrees of autonomy, control, and exploitation experienced by individuals would complicate the seamless "class consciousness" assumed by most classical Marxists.

Although that concept is what Erik's early work is known for, by the late 1980s he realized that his findings involved unanticipated complications for Marxist assumptions, especially as more and more women worked outside the home, even in upper- and middle-class families. How might an increasing number of two-income households complicate the class structure of industrial society? How would a growing percentage of married women working outside the household affect our understanding of the relationship between individual work experience and class identity?

At first, Erik focused on questions related to his work on class dynamics: How did these new social patterns complicate class consciousness or reshape individuals' identities? Husbands and wives may hold jobs that confer very different statuses—for example, when one partner in a couple works in a full-time managerial job and the other works in a part-time, flexible job. Working women, even in upper-class families, often hold part-time jobs, often with less autonomy or control—a nurse married to a doctor, an administrator married to a tenured professor. When there are two workers in the household, each theoretically occupying a different "class location," what shapes individual class identity?

More questions quickly followed. If there are two earners in the family, what determines the class location of the entire household? If a single male breadwinner no longer provides all the household's income, why would the husband's job alone define the household's class location? If a lower-status worker's sense of her social standing is shaped by her husband's status, how will that worker understand her own class position? As women's own identities became increasingly shaped by their work status, would their husbands' professional status prevent working women from developing the kind of class consciousness that Marxist theorists saw as critical for radical social change?

In his early work on gender, Erik focused on how two-income households might complicate conventional thinking about class, which generally assumed that household members' class status would be defined by shared property and wealth and by the male's occupation. But as he began to compare data from Sweden and the United States, Erik realized that national context was also critical to shaping class consciousness—in large part because national redistributive policies play a key role in allocating, or alleviating, household burdens.

In the United States, he found "the class character of the wife's job seemed to have no effect on the class identification of either men or women"; respondents defined their class position largely by household consumption levels, not by employment status. This finding led Erik to offer another new concept, "mediated class location"—class location viewed as shaped by property and social relations, as well as by employment status. "Since families are units of consumption," he wrote, "the class interests of actors are derived in part from the total material resources controlled by the members of a family and not simply by themselves."[3]

In Sweden, by contrast, Erik found "consistent effects of both husband's and wife's job-class on the subjective class identification of respondents." Swedish wives tended to contribute more to household income overall than American wives; but even more significant, Sweden's welfare and redistributive policies allowed married women to feel "less dependent on their husbands"—which Erik suggested meant that wives were able to construct their own class identities, independent of household status and perhaps more aligned with their experiences at work.[4]

In that first discussion of how gender relations might affect class identity, Erik acknowledged that this inquiry had produced some of the

---

3   Erik Olin Wright, "Women in the Class Structure," *Politics and Society* 17, no. 1 (1989): 35–66.
4   Wright, "Women in the Class Structure," 58. See also Erik Olin Wright et al., "The Non-effects of Class on the Gender Division of Labor in the Home: A Comparative Study of Sweden and the United States," *Gender and Society* 6, no. 2 (1992): 252–82; and Erik Olin Wright, Janeen Baxter, and Gunn Elisabeth Birkelund, "The Gender Gap in Workplace Authority: A Cross-National Study," *American Sociological Review* 60, no. 3 (1995): 407–35.

few real surprises that came out of the large, cross-national comparative studies that defined the first half of his career. "I had not expected to find such pervasive and often dramatic interactions between class and gender," he wrote in a different article. "My expectation had always been that class mechanisms would more or less have the same empirical effects for women as for men, but this is simply not the case"—especially, he noted, because gendered stereotypes often led sociologists as well as employers to overlook and underestimate the skills that are required for "women's work," such as childcare or nursing.[5]

Even before the collapse of the Soviet Union, then, Erik's recognition that people understand their relationship to the larger class structure not simply through their personal jobs and property, but also through a "variety of other kinds of social relations"—such as households—began to shift his thinking about class, and especially about class consciousness, profoundly. Adding gender to our understanding of class location, he wrote, complicates the "simple, polarized image of class structure contained in Marx's theoretical writings."[6]

That realization, I would argue, gradually produced an understated shift in the way Erik thought about individual identities and class consciousness—and, by extension, about the dynamics that would likely produce radical transformation in society at large. By 1993, instead of viewing family relations through the lens of property ownership and consumption, as he once had, Erik began to recognize that individuals experience life through a lens of networks and social relations—and he began to see those relations, especially family relations, as central to people's lived experiences, shaping an individual's relationship to the larger class structure.

In a 1993 article in *New Left Review*, Erik suggested that Marxists needed to recognize that

> people are linked to the class structure through social relations other than their immediate People live in families, and via their social relations to spouses, parents and other family members, they may be linked to different class interests and capacities. This problem is particularly salient in households within which both husbands and wives are in the

---

5   Erik Olin Wright, "Reflections on Classes," in Erik Olin Wright, ed., *The Debate on Classes* (1989; repr., London: Verso, 1998), 74.

6   Wright, "Women in the Class Structure," 62.

labour force but may occupy different job-classes. A schoolteacher married to a business executive has a different class location than a schoolteacher married to a factory worker. For certain categories of people—housewives and children, for example—"mediated" class locations may be the decisive way in which their lives are linked to class.[7]

This new concept—what Erik called "mediated class location"— reflected a fundamental rethinking of his basic theoretical categories. Rooted in the recognition that class location is shaped by, and shapes, gendered family and household relations as well as by work relations, the concept also prompted him to ask much larger questions about dynamics of social change, and ultimately led to a reexamination of emancipatory goals and the paths through which those goals might be reached.

Of course, those questions about what radical change might look like were especially relevant in the 1990s, an historical moment when, as Erik put it, many Marxists had "come to doubt the feasibility of the most egalitarian forms of their historic emancipatory class project, partially as a result of the failures of authoritarian state socialist systems and partially as a result of theoretical developments within Marxism itself."[8]

But as we reread his work, it becomes clear that these new questions also stemmed from a theoretical insight, one that involved a rather dramatic revision of the starting points of Erik's earliest work. As Greta Krippner put it, "An ever more complicated map of class structure made Erik less confident that class, alone, could provide the foundation for the emancipatory working-class revolt envisaged by Marx, [or] even the emancipatory promise of a 'classless' future."[9]

Erik had always been critical of authoritarianism, but in the 1990s he was also increasingly uncertain about how we might organize future "classless" societies. In a global economy dependent on complex industries and massive amounts of information, how could a truly classless society organize investment, production, or distribution without some kind of market-like mechanism? "Today," Erik wrote in 1994,

7   Erik Olin Wright, "Class Analysis, History and Emancipation," *New Left Review* 20 (November–December 1993): 31–2.

8   Erik Olin Wright, "Explanation and Emancipation in Marxism and Feminism," *Sociological Theory* 11, no. 1 (1993): 45.

9   Greta Krippner, "Love and Marxism," *Politics and Society* 48, no. 4 (2020): 495–504. Reprinted in this volume as chapter 3.

relatively few Marxists still believe that class analysis alone provides a
sufficient set of causes for understanding the historical trajectory of
capitalism, and even fewer feel that this historical trajectory is such
that the likelihood of socialism has an inherent tendency to increase
with capitalist development.[10]

Feminism, as he pointed out in 1993, offered a somewhat different route
to emancipation and a different approach to organizing a more cooperative and egalitarian society. Although Marxists might be increasingly
skeptical about how to attain a society without exploitation, or even
what that society might look like, Erik wrote, "no feminists imagine that
male *domination* in even vestigial form is essential for social life."[11]
Moreover, although feminists might disagree about whether gender
inequality stems primarily from cultural or sexual practices, or whether
inequality is rooted in economic and political institutions of power and
privilege, he noted that among feminists there is virtual unanimity
about "the possibility of eventually eliminating differences in welfare
and power based on gender."[12]
As he would write repeatedly over the subsequent decades, any
biological differences between sexes are far less influential than the
sociological mechanisms that create and reinforce gender inequality.
And, indeed, he would come to argue by the 2000s that men would
benefit as much as women from a society that was free of pressure to
perform roles shaped by classic stereotypes of masculinity and femi-
ninity. By contrast, Marxist visions of utopia were based on simply
abolishing the capitalist class, by upending property relations. At a
moment when Marxist thinkers were beginning to doubt that socialism would be an inevitable result of capitalist class conflict, or even
whether a classless society could sustain twenty-first-century industrial production, feminists were far more confident that egalitarianism
would benefit everyone.
Feminists' unanimous agreement that society without gender oppression would be better for everyone was, Erik argued, rooted in lived

---

10   Erik Olin Wright, *Interrogating Inequality: Essays on Class Analysis, Socialism
and Marxism* (London: Verso, 1994), 242.
11   Wright, "Explanation and Emancipation," 45.
12   Ibid., 43.

experience—a sharp contrast to Marxist visions of a postcapitalist utopia. Under capitalism,

> prefigurative emancipatory experiences are not between workers and capitalists, but exclusively among workers. [The] solidarities experienced in the interpersonal practices of class struggle and in the micro settings of the labor process do not translate in any simple way into the institutional mechanisms of planning, information flows, allocation of capital, or price setting.[13]

Militant workers have no experience of close collaborations with managers or engineers—yet, equally problematic, they might not be confident that a revolutionary working class could keep factories running without them.

By contrast, most feminists have experienced solidarity and cooperation in their daily lives, in the real world, with women—and crucially, sometimes with men. As Erik wrote, the "women's movement itself generates a range of solidarities among women, which prefigure a society in which women are not dominated by men." Equally important, "women have male children, whom they nurture; boys have mothers, whom they love. Even between husbands and wives within traditional 'patriarchal' relations . . . there are elements of reciprocity and companionship which prefigure the potential for egalitarian relations."[14] In other words, whereas Marxist theorists and militant workers could only imagine classlessness, feminists' daily experiences offer obvious evidence that "another world is possible."

Feminists' lived experiences of solidarity, Erik argued, gave them faith that an egalitarian future is a realistic vision as well as the confidence that they could build on existing relationships to get there. Could sociologists draw on analyses of real utopias to offer new hope to activists and scholars trying to address other kinds of social and economic inequality? It was that question, of course, that prompted Erik's turn to real utopias: his attempt to identify lived experiences of egalitarian community stemmed from his effort to figure out how we might get there. His recognition that women assumed that men would also be

---

13   Ibid., 47.
14   Ibid., 46.

present in an emancipated future inspired his interest in finding a way to imagine a world beyond capitalism.

But, at the personal level, it is worth emphasizing what would be obvious to anyone who knew him: Erik's description of feminist solidarity says a great deal about his own values and experiences. By the early twenty-first century—not coincidentally, as he became a doting grandfather to his daughters' children, but also at a time of widespread acceptance of nontraditional families—his vision of what a real utopia would look like, or how it might take shape, was quintessentially defined by his sense of the strength and importance of family ties.

Most obviously in his posthumous *How to Be an Anticapitalist in the Twenty-First Century* (2019), Erik would repeatedly hold family relationships up as a central example of community solidarity: "The value of community applies to any social unit in which people interact and cooperate. The family, in this sense, is a particularly salient community, and in a healthy family one certainly expects cooperation to be rooted in both love and moral concern"—prefiguring the "strong concern and moral obligation" that he believed shapes most religions, vibrant communities, and democratic social movements.[15]

It is also worth noting that Erik's shift to what he began to call his Real Utopias Project in the late 1990s went through two phases—both informed by a comparison between "classlessness" and "genderlessness"—in which Erik repeatedly offered policies aimed at changing gender relations as a model for rethinking other kinds of emancipatory paths.

First, Erik began to think more critically about the dynamics of social change—especially about Marxist assumptions that class consciousness would produce a revolutionary proletariat that would overturn all relations of production. In a widely cited article published in 2000 in the *American Journal of Sociology*, he explicitly acknowledged the limits to labor's demands in capitalist societies—building on his earlier questions about the realities of capitalist production in an integrated global economy and the key role of managers in organizing and managing complex production processes. While he acknowledged that workers in large

---

15 Erik Olin Wright, *How to Be an Anti capitalist in the Twenty-First Century* (London: Verso, 2019), 18–19.

industries can, and do, disrupt production when they want to demand higher wages or benefits, he also recognized that even militant union members generally see their livelihood as dependent on keeping their employers afloat—and that this dependency could limit workers' willingness to pursue what "scientific Marxists" would consider their "true" class interests.[16]

On the other hand—perhaps reflecting an increasing acknowledgment that cross-class relations shape most people's lives—Erik acknowledged that progressive labor movements often go beyond the "disruptive power" of the workplace, to build what he called "associational power." Increasingly, he recognized that successful struggles invariably involve community support as activists seek to mobilize their neighbors, building solidarity across lines of class, gender, and race to demand far-reaching change. "Structural power," as he called the ability to stop production or trade, may give workers' organizations tactical strength; but associational power offers a much broader promise, by expanding activists' demands and their vision of social change beyond a limited group of employees, offering a better world for an entire community and building alliances far beyond the workplace.

Thus, much as he had previously recognized that class location is mediated through individuals' social relations at home and in communities, Erik began to view social relations beyond the workplace as crucial to constructing a more emancipatory movement. But what would that emancipatory project look like, and how could activists persuade their communities that their demands are possible or realistic?

Here, again, feminism offered a model. Just as women's experiences of living, and cooperating, with men helped strengthen their faith in egalitarian ideals, Erik noted that feminists' careful analyses of the specific, day-to-day mechanisms that reinforce gender inequality allowed them to imagine and propose "a wide range of social changes . . . necessary to give men and women equal real power"—from public provision of childcare to labor market equality to a more equitable distribution of childcare.[17]

16   Erik Olin Wright, "Working-Class Power, Capitalist-Class Interests, and Class Compromise," *American Journal of Sociology* 104, no. 4 (2000): 957–1002.
17   Wright, "Explanation and Emancipation," 41.

In the 1990s, when he first discussed feminist policy proposals that aimed to address gender inequalities at home and at work, Erik sounded slightly dismissive of what he considered a tendency among feminists to focus on pragmatic reforms rather than seek revolutionary change.[18] But as he became attentive to the value most people place on their communities and existing day-to-day relationships, he became increasingly interested in exploring new ways to advance egalitarian ideals—strategies that might remove political and economic mechanisms that create or reinforce inequality, or selfishness, but also strategies that could create an emancipatory future without destroying the positive social relationships we treasure in the present.

By the early 2000s, one could argue that Erik's growing awareness of the value of existing day-to-day relationships—his awareness that individuals' identity and happiness are shaped by the social ties that support them—led him away from his earlier insistence on a path of radical, total social transformation. Instead, he became intrigued with exploring mechanisms that might impel people toward more egalitarian practices, providing both carrots and sticks to make us more cooperative, more generous, and more empathetic.

Although Erik continued to reject mild reformism, he grew increasingly concerned with finding a path to utopia that would bring everyone along on the journey—a path that would not cause chaos but would change our behaviors enough to "erode capitalism from within." That question—could social change come through a conscious effort to redesign economic and social dynamics, aiming to support more cooperative, more egalitarian relationships in the here and now, rather than through revolutionary change?—was at the core of his later work, and I would argue it was at least partly inspired by his interaction with feminist scholarship.

Although many of the reforms he discussed focused on economic and political institutions, Erik paid close attention to how emancipatory projects might reshape family dynamics, often through pushing fathers to participate actively in childcare.[19] In the late 1990s, he went even further, suggesting that state policies should push fathers to participate

---

18   Wright et al., "Non-effects of Class on the Gender Division of Labor"; Wright, Baxter, and Birkelund, "Gender Gap in Workplace Authority."

19   Wright, "Explanation and Emancipation."

in childcare and housework, both to promote equity at work and in the home and to create the healthy family bonds that he considered so critical.

One of Erik's earliest workshops on real utopias focused on policies designed to address gender inequality; famously, he seemed to support policies that granted more days of parental leave to households where fathers participated actively in childcare, a step that some feminists argue risks punishing women, because if a partner refused to take days off work to help with childcare, the family as a whole would lose those paid days of parental leave.[20]

But a more sympathetic reading of his work makes it clear that Erik viewed those policies not as punitive but as attempts to redefine childcare as a collective responsibility rather than primarily a female burden. Perhaps based on his own experience, he assumed that fathers would quickly learn to revel in increased engagement with their children and that the entire family would benefit from the shift. In a 2008 article, Erik and his close collaborator Harry Brighouse suggested that state policies should be designed explicitly to reward families in which both parents took family leave. True, the proposal can be interpreted as threatening to reduce the days of leave available to mothers whose partners refuse to cooperate, but Erik and Brighouse saw that as a rather unlikely outcome.[21] Instead, they described the policy as a nudge that would prompt households to adapt to new norms of sharing household labor, a shift that they believed most people would welcome. And, they suggested, the policy could also reduce gender inequalities at work by changing employers' expectations, undermining gender stereotypes of mothers as less reliable workers—an argument that seems borne out by Sweden's experience, where a gradually extended "take it or lose it" approach has produced a measurable shift in Swedish parenting and in women's experiences at work.[22]

---

20   Inéz Campillo Poza, "Género, clase y emancipación: Una lectura feminista de Erik O. Wright" (paper presented at the Universidad Complutense de Madrid, January 30–1, 2020).

21   Harry Brighouse and Erik Olin Wright, "Strong Gender Egalitarianism," *Politics and Society* 36, no. 3 (2008): 360–72.

22   Emily Hagkvist et al., "Parental Leave Policies and Time Use for Mothers and Fathers: A Case Study of Spain and Sweden," *Society, Health and Vulnerability* 8, no. 1 (2017).

Along the way, I think, Erik's theoretical understanding of what real utopias might look like began to change. By 2011, his vision of a truly egalitarian society suggested that a true utopia would have to be genderless as well as classless; "gender equality" risked leaving in place gender stereotypes that "impose socially enforced constraints on the choices and practices of men and women." "Such constraints," he argued, would "thwart egalitarian ideals of a world in which all people have equal access to the social and material means necessary to live a flourishing life."[23]

"A full degendering of family life," he wrote, "would not mean removing all traits or behaviors considered 'masculine' or 'feminine'; rather, it would mean removing any systematic expectations that those traits would correspond to physical characteristics." In a genderless community, "norms around family roles would be connected to parenthood, rather than to specific gender roles. In any [family] there might well be difference in the extent to which [an individual] took on particular responsibilities, but there would be no *normatively backed expectations* about who should do what." A community that embraced caregiving across gendered lines, he argued, would produce "strong positive norms about the general desirability of nurturance for everyone."[24]

As a sociologist, it is hard to disagree with Burawoy's observation that Erik's genderless, anticapitalist vision of utopia is as Durkheimian as it is Marxist, emphasizing the importance of community ties and social relations in shaping individuals and in creating happiness.[25] Erik was a sociologist, of course, and Durkheim's recognition of the importance of social bonds is central to our discipline. But perhaps, in the end, my colleagues who pointed to Erik's early career as a seminarian were also right: perhaps he was always a faith leader at heart, a spiritually inclined camp director, offering a vision of a better world to inspire us in the present.

But I think Erik's perspective is equally a reflection of his own lived experiences—as a husband and father, as a member of the global community that he built, nurtured, and enjoyed. A day or two before he

---

23   Erik Olin Wright, "In Defense of Genderlessness," in Axel Gosseries and Yannick Vanderborght, eds., *Arguing about Justice: Essays for Philippe Van Parijs* (Louvain-la-Neuve, France: Presses Universitaires de Louvain, 2011), 403–14.

24   Wright, "In Defense of Genderlessness."

25   Burawoy, "A Tale of Two Marxisms."

died, he wrote that in his late teens or early twenties, he decided he wanted to "create meaning ... by trying to make the world a better place." I think all of us who knew him would agree that, over the course of his life, he did exactly that. Typical of Erik, his final words underscore how much his love for family and community shaped his intellectual journey; and typical of Erik, he rejoiced in those warm and loving ties. In his last few days, he wrote,

> Without being embedded in a social milieu where those ideas were debated and linked [to] social movements, I would never have been able to pursue this particular set of ideas. But I was enabled, and it's made for an incredibly meaningful and intellectually exciting personal life. So no complaints. I will die in a few weeks, fulfilled. Not happy that I'm dying, but deeply happy with the life I've lived, and the life I've been able to share with all of you.

In the end, Erik's real utopia was the world in which he actually lived, as a loving father, generous adviser and mentor, a dear friend. He will always be with us.

3

Love and Marxism
Greta R. Krippner

A common theme in retrospective analyses of Erik Olin Wright's scholarship is the distinct nature of the two main projects that make up his intellectual journey through Marxism. Through the early to middle years of his career, Erik was the hard-hitting empiricist, puzzling through the conundrums presented by class structure in advanced industrial capitalism. In his middle to later years, his emphasis changed, and he embraced a normative project that sought to elucidate (and through his various engagements with scholars and activists, actively promote) the principles by which "real utopias" could be carved out from actually existing capitalist societies. Different interlocutors of his work might weight these two projects differently, giving greater priority to one or the other in understanding the whole, but there seems to be little question of a fundamental divide in his work.[1]

Among observers of Erik's long career, perhaps none is better positioned to characterize its broad trajectory than Michael Burawoy, his lifelong friend and collaborator, who in 2020 published an illuminating appreciation of Erik's scholarship in the *New Left Review*, reprinted in

---

1   I base this conclusion in part on the views expressed by former colleagues, collaborators, and students at a conference honoring the life and legacy of Erik Olin Wright, held at the Havens Wright Center for Social Justice at the University of Wisconsin–Madison on November 1–2, 2019. This paper was originally prepared as a contribution to the festschrift.

this volume as chapter 1.[2] In his essay, Burawoy leans hard on this "two Marxisms" formulation, observing a schism between Erik's early empirical work on class analysis, in which broader "utopian" strivings are suppressed, and Erik's later utopian project, in which class analysis falls out. Borrowing from Alvin Gouldner, Burawoy names the first of these projects Erik's "scientific" Marxism, and the second Erik's "critical" Marxism.[3] Burawoy further suggests that these two projects are fully disjointed—Erik, in other words, experienced something akin to what Louis Althusser described as Marx's "epistemological break."[4] Here is how Burawoy describes the transformation in Erik's work: "From science to critique; from a mapping of social structure to the project of social transformation; from the study of real mechanisms to the study of possible futures; from scientific neutrality to explicit value foundations; from measurement at a distance to engagement at close quarters; from ideology as distortion to ideology as a moral force; from politics as epiphenomenal to politics as integral to the advance of real utopias; from the determinism of objective structures to the erosion of capitalism."[5]

At one level, there is little to take issue with in this characterization of Erik's work. There are certainly different stages in his career, and the work on class structure undeniably has a different flavor—and perhaps a different set of objectives, although that point is more open to interpretation—than does the work on real utopias. At the same time, I find myself resisting Burawoy's characterization of Erik's "two Marxisms." I think the reason for my resistance to Burawoy's formulation is that, just as with the claim that there is a "critical" Marx and a "scientific" Marx,

2   Michael Burawoy, "A Tale of Two Marxisms: Remembering Erik Olin Wright (1947–2019)," *New Left Review* 121 (January–February 2020): 67–98, reprinted here as chapter 1. Given Burawoy's unique relationship to Erik, it feels somewhat presumptuous to take a different view of Erik's scholarship, as I do in this essay. My own perspective on Erik's work is not based on the same sort of deep and sustained dialogue that he shared with Burawoy over many decades. Instead, my perspective is shaped by the experience of having been a student of Erik's during the period in the mid-to-late 1990s in which he was transitioning from his work on class analysis to his work on real utopias.

3   Alvin Gouldner, *The Two Marxisms: Contradictions and Anomalies in the Development of Theory* (New York: Seabury Press, 1980).

4   Louis Althusser, *For Marx* (London: Verso, 2006). The analogy doesn't fit perfectly, as Erik traversed these stages in the opposite order as is alleged to be the case for Marx, from a scientific to a critical Marxism rather than from a critical to a scientific Marxism.

5   Burawoy, Chapter 1 of this volume, "A Tale of Two Marxisms," p. 30 in this volume.

this is not simply a descriptive claim but an evaluative one: if one is an enthusiast of the early Marx, this is usually at the expense of the Marx of *Capital*, and vice versa. While Burawoy's contrast of Erik's "two Marxisms" is not quite as stark as this, I discern a clear valuing in Burawoy's formulation of the Marxism of real utopias over the Marxism of Erik's work on class structure. While appreciating the analytical rigor and precision of the early work, Burawoy suggested that Erik in his "scientific Marxism" succumbs to professional pressures, the political impetus behind the work blunted by the methodological imperatives of what over time becomes a fairly conventional stratification analysis. After a long period lost in the wilderness of professional sociology, Burawoy's narrative had Erik finding his way home to sociological Marxism when he embarked on the investigation of real utopias. This is the culmination of Erik's expansive body of work, where his early prom-ise as a radical thinker reached its full realization.

Now it is of course Burawoy's prerogative to prefer the Erik of real utopias to the Erik of class analysis—with this, I have no argument. And in fact, I suspect that Erik's own self-assessment—to judge from the scattered comments he left in his writings—might be similar. Nor does Burawoy's narrative taken on its own terms strike me as inaccurate; Erik himself was honest (and to my mind, admirably self-reflexive) about the role that the desire for professional recognition and status had in shap-ing his early work and career, as well as the way that the methodological tools he was working with constrained the kinds of questions he could ask and answer.[6] Nevertheless, I do want to suggest that something is

---

6   "Adopting the scientific practices of conventional social science risks neutralizing the revolutionary aspirations of Marxism. Above all, there is the risk of narrowing the field of legitimate questions to those that are tractable with these sophisticated tools. Statistically rigorous data analysis tends to restrict investigations to problems that are easily quantifi-able; rational choice theory tends to direct attention to those problems of strategic inter-action that can be formally modeled within the repertoire of game theory models. Such potential restriction on the domain of inquiry imposed by the choice of scientifically rigorous methods poses serious threats to the political vitality of radical thought . . . These risks need to be acknowledged and resisted. But to respond to them by refusing to build enclaves of radical scholarship within leading universities robs Marxism of the capacity to play an effective role in the academy; and to cope with these risks by rejecting these analytical and scientific methods altogether undermines the ability of Marxism to enhance its theoretical understandings of the world in ways which will enable it, once again, to play an effective role in politics as well." Erik Olin Wright, *Interrogating Inequality: Essays on Class Analysis, Socialism and Marxism* (London: Verso, 1994), 197–9.

lost from our understanding of both of the projects that make up Erik's unique contribution to Marxism and to social science by pulling them so far apart. Just as reading the late Marx is enriched, I believe, by an engagement with the early Marx, so I think "scientific" and "critical" elements are more fully intertwined in *all* of Erik's work than Burawoy's formulation allows.

Accordingly, I want to re-narrate Erik's intellectual biography using Burawoy's essay as a foil, emphasizing points of connection between the two strands of Erik's work rather than the disjunctures that Burawoy's account highlights. In the following discussion, I will highlight the continuities between Erik's work on class analysis and his work on real utopias by suggesting that the "critical" elements of the latter were never as foreign to Erik's "scientific" Marxism as Burawoy suggests is the case. It might be more difficult to argue for continuities in the other direction—that is, by demonstrating that Erik's early "empiricism" pervades the normative project he embraced more fully in his later work. I do not attempt to make that argument here, but I would merely suggest that the Real Utopias Project was not devoid of empirics (as Burawoy himself notes when he suggests that Erik reinvented himself as an ethnographer late in his career), but it was empirical work that rested on very different methodological and epistemological premises than Erik's early "multi-variate Marxism."[7]

Let me start with the formulation of the problem of the middle classes—the signature contribution of Erik's "scientific" Marxism, to adopt Burawoy's terminology. As early as graduate school, Erik was aware that the simple, polarized model of the class structure derived from Marx's writings was inadequate to grasp the complexity of advanced industrial capitalism, and accordingly, he sought to generate a more complex mapping of the class structure by exploring the problem of the middle classes—individuals who were neither fully capitalist nor worker, but occupied what he called "contradictory class locations."[8] Erik's original attempt to deal with the problem of the middle classes melded Marxian concepts of domination and exploitation, although in a manner that gave top billing to domination: to be in a contradictory

---

7   Burawoy, "A Tale of Two Marxisms," p. 24 in this volume.

8   The original phrase was more cumbersome: "contradictory locations within class relations." See Erik Olin Wright, *Class, Crisis and the State* (London: Verso, 1978).

location was simultaneously to exercise *and* experience domination in different relations.[9] Erik soon became disenchanted with this approach precisely because he felt it privileged domination over exploitation; accordingly, a later formulation of the problem of the middle classes— the one he elaborated in his 1985 book *Classes*—was conceptualized solely in terms of exploitation.[10] Now, on its face, this shift from domination to exploitation in Erik's conception of class appears to provide strong evidence for Burawoy's "two Marxisms" formulation. Domination is closely associated with Marx's concept of alienation, especially as elaborated in the *Economic and Philosophical Manuscripts*, in which the early Marx railed against a system in which the capitalist is empowered to order the worker at her task. Here is where the direct experience of the worker in production potentially generates possibilities for class formation and class struggle—precisely the sort of issues that have been at the heart of Burawoy's own ethnographic investigations of *relations in production* (as opposed to relations of production).[11] Does the pivot here from domination to exploitation not put politics and struggle at one remove?

Perhaps it does. But here I think it's important to be clear on Erik's reasons for making this maneuver. Erik preferred an elaboration of class that was centered on exploitation precisely because the concept of exploitation implies a set of material interests that can be mapped onto concrete class locations. By contrast, while domination is an integral part of the lived experience of class relations, he suggested that it is a more abstract concept that cannot be specified with the same level of concreteness. Here was Erik's legendary empiricism on full display! But note how he explained this development in his work, writing: "The new class concept [based on exploitation] provided a particularly nuanced empirical map for studying the relationship between class structure and class formation . . . By introducing three distinct dimensions [of exploi- tation]—dimensions based on [control of] capital assets, organization

---

9   Erik Olin Wright, *Classes* (London: Verso, 1985), 56.

10   Ever one to revise and update his thinking, Erik's mature class analysis rejoined domination and exploitation, elaborating a more sophisticated version of contradictory class locations. See Erik Olin Wright, *Class Counts: Comparative Studies in Class Analysis* (New York: Cambridge University Press, 1997).

11   Michael Burawoy, *The Politics of Production: Factory Regimes under Capitalism and Socialism* (London: Verso, 1985).

assets, and skill assets—the picture of class structure can become quite differentiated. The proliferation of concrete structural 'locations' within the map allows for much more subtle empirical investigation of the ways in which people in these locations become collectively organized into class formations."[12] This passage makes clear that the motivation behind Erik's extensive and detailed empirical investigations into class structure reflected his firm belief that solving the problem of the middle class was key to creating a viable socialist politics. I do not see a hard separation between Erik's "scientific" and "critical" Marxism here.

It is possible to make this point even more directly. Erik's preference for exploitation not only reflected the utility of the concept for mapping the class structure in ways that could inform socialist strategy, but also the manner in which the concept of exploitation itself expressed a deep normative commitment to human liberation. As Erik wrote,

> An emancipatory normative theory is directly implicated in [the concept of] exploitation . . . As an explanatory concept, exploitation is meant to identify one of the central mechanisms through which class structure explains class conflict. Class relations are thought to explain conflict in part because classes do not simply have *different* material interests which are contingently conflictual; their material interests are *intrinsically antagonistic* by virtue of being based on exploitation. Identifying such class relations as exploitative . . . implies a moral judgment about the inequalities generated within those relations . . . The emancipatory ideal of radical egalitarianism—ending class exploitation—is thus implicated in the very conceptualization of class itself.[13]

It is true that as Erik's empirical project became more ambitious and his map of class locations more elaborate, he became increasingly doubtful that the work would yield the political gains he had initially anticipated. As early as 1989, when *The Debate on Classes* was first published, he was already harboring doubts. A footnote in that text read, "While I continue to believe that solving the conceptual problems in class structure analysis is important, I no longer feel that it provides the key to

---

12   Erik Olin Wright et al., ed., *The Debate on Classes* (London: Verso, 1989), 307.
13   Wright, *Interrogating Inequality*, 239.

understanding the more general problem of variations in class formation and possibilities for the creation of radical coalitions."[14] We see the
beginnings here of a shift in Erik's preoccupations that ultimately seeds
the Real Utopias Project. Here I disagree with Burawoy's suggestion that
that there was "remarkably little cross-pollination" between Erik's work
on class structure and his investigation of real utopias and that "each
developed independently of the other."[15] On the contrary, I detect a clear
lineage from the first project to the second—we might even say that the
new grew up in the bosom of the old!

The best evidence for this interpretation, I think, is Erik's essay
"Marxism after Communism," first published in 1993 just as Erik was
pivoting to the Real Utopias Project.[16] In this essay, Erik considered the
fate of Marxism in light of the historic defeat of communism—the context
in which the essay was written lends credence to Burawoy's contention
that the shift he detects in Erik's work reflected, at least in part, the changing political context in which Erik was carrying out his research program.
After first considering the challenges to Marxism presented by the fall of
communism, Erik's essay then suggested that Marxism involves three
distinct "nodes": a class analysis, a theory of a historical trajectory, and an
emancipatory project. These nodes, Erik observed, were seamlessly integrated in classical Marxism: Marx's account of a polarized class structure
gave rise to a theory of a historical trajectory toward an emancipatory
future. In more recent times, however, the unity of the three nodes has
eroded: "Today," Erik wrote, "relatively few Marxists still believe that class
analysis alone provides a sufficient set of causes for understanding the
historical trajectory of capitalism, and even fewer feel that this historical
trajectory is such that the likelihood of socialism has an inherent tendency
to increase with capitalist development."[17] Erik signaled a further problem: while classical Marxism established the viability of socialism simply
by demonstrating the *non-viability* of capitalism, this strategy is no longer
workable in a context in which the failure of capitalism cannot be
assumed. Two conclusions followed from this analysis: First, radicals
have to think not in terms of deterministic historical trajectories but

14   Wright, *Debate on Classes*, 273.
15   Burawoy, "A Tale of Two Marxisms," p.17 in this volume.
16   The article was originally published in *New Left Review*, but later reprinted in
revised form in *Interrogating Inequality*, which is the version of the essay I refer to here.
17   Wright, *Interrogating Inequality*, 240.

rather in terms of contingent historical possibilities; and second, it is necessary to make the positive case for socialism on its own terms, not simply as the negation of capitalism.

Both of these points are picked up and elaborated more fully in the 2002 article, "Sociological Marxism," that Erik coauthored with Burawoy.[18] But rather than seeing these insights as representing a departure from Erik's class analysis, as Burawoy does, I see them as growing directly out of Erik's earlier research program: it is the complexity of the terrain of social class that lies behind Erik's skepticism about the possibilities for a "ruptural" transformation in the mode of production, redirecting his attention instead toward the search for democratic, egalitarian, and participatory alternatives within the cracks and crevices of the existing economic system that could potentially erode its capitalist logic. Relatedly, in a context in which many individuals have class interests that are fundamentally ambiguous, neither "capitalist" nor "worker," the case for socialism must be made not on the basis of material interests but on explicit normative criteria. Notably, both of these elements are foundational to the Real Utopias Project in its mature form: The first finds expression in Erik's explorations of institutional design principles laid out in *Envisioning Real Utopias*; and the second is most fully developed in *How to Be an Anticapitalist in the Twenty-First Century*, a work in which Erik explored the values—equality/fairness, democracy/freedom, community/solidarity—that undergird real utopias.[19] Thus, rather than leaving Erik's class analysis behind, I think it is more accurate to see his elaboration of real utopias as grounded firmly in it.[20]

I want to close on a more personal note. Burawoy wrote in the final section of his essay that while Erik developed "two Marxisms," there was really only "one Erik Wright"—a man who will be remembered, Burawoy wrote, for "his abiding commitment to truth, clarity, dialogue, community, and social justice."[21] I am in full accord with Burawoy's characterization of "one Erik" here, although as Burawoy also notes, Erik was in

---

18   See Burawoy and Wright, "Sociological Marxism," in Jonathan H. Turner, ed., *The Handbook of Sociological Theory* (New York: Springer, 2002), 459–86.

19   See Erik Olin Wright, *Envisioning Real Utopias* (London: Verso, 2010); Wright, *How to Be an Anticapitalist in the Twenty-First Century* (London: Verso 2019).

20   Burawoy acknowledges these same connections (see "A Tale of Two Marxisms," pp. 30–1 in this volume) but seems to draw a different lesson from them than I do.

21   Burawoy, "A Tale of Two Marxisms," p.47 in this volume.

his final months moving toward a different formulation that wove together the strands of his work and life—one that he expressed in terms of love. Erik seemed at least a little surprised to discover that it was love that undergirded his intellectual and political commitments, in exactly the same way that love drew him into an enriching and sustaining community of family, friends, and students. I, for one, was not surprised; Erik's epiphany seemed totally in keeping with what I had always intuited about him as a sociologist, as a Marxist, and as a human being.

I learned of Erik's cancer shortly after it was diagnosed in April of 2018. Paradoxically, this devastating news came as I was working on a paper for a conference to mark the 200th anniversary of Marx's birth and 150th anniversary of the publication of *Capital*. In preparation for this meeting, I had been spending the semester delving into texts that I first read twenty-four years earlier in my first year of graduate school at the University of Wisconsin—texts, which outside of the "greatest hits" that I now teach in my graduate and undergraduate social theory courses, I had not revisited in all the years since. Erik was very much on my mind that spring as I worked my way through Marx's early writings, the *Grundrisse* and *Capital*—although not because I had studied these texts with him. Erik was wary of what he referred to as "Marxology," and accordingly, he included very few, if any, original texts from Marx in his teaching. If Marxism was truly a social science, I remember him telling me, the knowledge it produced was cumulative. It would be a sad statement on the enterprise of Marxism if the best we could offer was a text written in 1867! Notwithstanding this assessment, Erik tolerated our youthful indulgences, and there was a large group of students in the spring semester of 1995 who took Erik's "Marxism and Social Science" course in the morning and then marched across campus to study the Marxist classics in Jess Gilbert's seminar in the afternoon. The combination was intoxicating; I have rarely felt so intellectually alive as I did that semester. Rereading those works in the spring of 2018, I traveled back in time and felt Erik's presence strongly, just as I learned that his life circumstances had suddenly become tenuous.

I recovered something else other than these vivid memories in my reading that spring when I came across a little-known gem in the Marx canon—Marx's 1844 essay on James Mill's *Elements of Political Economy*. As Erik frequently observed, Marxist theory (and Marx himself) thought about emancipation largely in terms of the negation of the ills of capitalism.[22] Communism was characterized as the *absence* of alienation, the *absence* of exploitation, the *absence* of inequality, and so on. But how could we characterize communism when viewed in more positive terms? Here Marx, and for the most part Marxist theory too, fell silent. As Erik noted, as long as the expectation was that capitalism was doomed to fail, there wasn't much need to dwell on such matters. Once it became clear, however, that capitalism's demise was neither imminent nor inevitable, characterizing utopia in more positive terms became necessary to securing it—a task Erik embraced with vigor in his later work.

Notably, in the essay on James Mill, Marx does offer a more positive characterization of what it would mean to live free of capitalism, describing the experience of producing directly as a human being without having one's labor "mediated" through the exchange of an external object. Interestingly enough, Marx expressed this utopian idea, as Erik also did in his final months, in terms of love. I cannot think of anything that better expresses who Erik was as a scholar and a teacher than Marx's description of production without alienation; and it makes me realize that the most real utopia of all was the one Erik's students got to experience in the lecture halls and classrooms of the University of Wisconsin. So, with apologies to Erik for indulging in what he would likely consider "Marxology," I would like to conclude with a passage from Marx's essay that, I believe, encapsulates Erik's spirit exceedingly well:

> Let us suppose that we had produced as human beings. In that event each of us would have *doubly affirmed* himself and his neighbor in his production. (1) In my *production* I would have objectified the *specific character* of my *individuality* and for that reason I would both have enjoyed the *expression* of my own individual *life* during my activity and also, in contemplating the object, I would experience an individual pleasure, I would experience my personality as an *objective sensuously perceptible* power *beyond all shadow of doubt*. (2) In your use or enjoyment of my product I would have the *immediate* satisfaction and knowledge that in my labour I had gratified a *human* need, i.e., that I had objectified *human* *nature* and hence had procured an object

22 This idea is expressed especially eloquently in "Marxism after Communism" and "Sociological Marxism."

corresponding to the needs of another *human being*. (3) I would have acted for you as the *mediator* between you and the species, thus I would be acknowledged by you as the complement of your own being, as an essential part of yourself. I would thus know myself to be confirmed both in your thoughts and your love. (4) In the individual expression of my own life I would have brought about the immediate expression of your life, and so in my individual activity I would have directly *confirmed* and *realised* my authentic nature, my *human, communal* nature.[23]

One Erik, indeed.

---

23   Karl Marx, "Excerpts from James Mill's *Elements of Political Economy*," in *Karl Marx's Early Writings*, with an introduction by Lucio Colletti (New York: Penguin, 1975), 277–8, emphasis in original.

4

Wright's Emancipatory Theory and Practice
Kwang-Yeong Shin

More than four years have passed since Erik Olin Wright passed away, and it is time for us to consider his contribution to sociological Marxism and the emancipatory social sciences in general. It is also a moment to reflect on the current theoretical and practical perspectives in the contemporary critical social sciences as we discuss Wright's *Envisioning Real Utopias*, published in 2010. As Göran Therborn says, *Envisioning Real Utopias* became a benchmark for rethinking the world's progressive forces.[1] Over the last ten years, the global financial crisis and the upsurge of rightist populism have emerged as a response to neoliberal globalization. Though Wright was unable to complete the Real Utopias Project in his lifetime, his work offers a good foundation for further development of the leftist project and the emancipatory social sciences at a time when the current political chaos threatens our alternative vision.

Wright's intellectual trajectory in Marxism and Marxist sociology started from his engagement in the 1968 antiwar protest movement in the United States. The anti–Vietnam War movement triggered the revival of Marxism and critical theories in advanced societies. It also contributed to the rise of anti-imperialist movements in the Third

I thank Gay Seidman and Michael Burawoy for their wonderful comments on an earlier draft of this essay.

1   See Göran Therborn's endorsement on the cover of Erik Olin Wright's *Envisioning Real Utopias* (London: Verso, 2010).

World, promoting critical perspectives such as dependency theory and liberation theology in Latin America. In the 1960s and the 1970s, the idea that alternatives were needed circulated across university campuses in the global North and the global South.

Envisioning Real Utopias extends theoretical interests that were present at the beginning of Wright's work as a Marxist sociologist. His theory of social transformation, developed later in his life, reflects the recession of the working-class movement, the demise of state socialism in Eastern Europe, and the rise of various social movements with social- ist ideals that were not necessarily framed in classical Marxist terms. His Real Utopias Project published six books that explore alternatives to democratic capitalism in the West, dealing with such issues as "associa- tions and democracy," "market socialism," "recasting egalitarianism," "empowered participatory governance," "basic income grants," and "gender equality."[2] We might say that *Envisioning Real Utopias* repre- sents Wright's enduring preoccupation with the socialist transformation of capitalism, reflecting the changing tide of transformative movements in the twenty-first century and the reconceptualization of socialism as social empowerment.

I argue that the Real Utopias Project is not a complete departure from Wright's earlier engagement in reconstructing the Marxist theory of social class—the project he was focused on when I worked with him in Madison, as his advisee in the doctoral program. Socialism as demo- cratic egalitarianism is an enduring theoretical thread running through Wright's intellectual trajectory, ranging from structural Marxism to analytical Marxism, from interests in macro-social structure to micro- transformative practices, and from social class to civil society. His theo- retical development did not negate his earlier theoretical framework,

---

2   Here are the first six volumes in the Real Utopias series, all edited and introduced by Erik Wright: Joshua Cohen and Joel Rogers, *Associations and Democracy: The Real Utopias Project, Vol. 1* (London: Verso, 1995); John Roemer, *Equal Shares: Making Market Socialism Work* (London: Verso, 1996); Samuel Bowles and Herbert Gintis, *Recasting Egalitarianism: New Rules for Communities, States and Markets* (London: Verso, 1999); Archon Fung and Erik Olin Wright, *Deepening Democracy: Institutional Innovations in Empowered Participatory Governance* (London: Verso, 2003); Bruce Ackerman, Ann Alstott, and Philippe van Parijs, *Redesigning Distribution: Basic Income and Stakeholder Grants as Cornerstones for a More Egalitarian Capitalism* (London: Verso, 2005); Janet Gornick and Marcia Meyers, *Gender Equality: Transforming Family Divisions of Labor* (London: Verso, 2009).

but showed a dialectical synthesis, resolving theoretical dilemmas associated with social transformation and incorporating historical changes. Wright's ceaseless mission was to rehabilitate Marxism as a scientific and critical theory of contemporary capitalism at a time when Marxism had been severely tarnished by state socialism in Eastern Europe and completely pushed aside by postmodernism and post-structuralism in the West. *Envisioning Real Utopias* exemplifies the contemporary Marxist social scientist's work of searching for ways to transform contemporary capitalism by combining analytical dissection with emancipatory goals.

Three Historical Conjunctures

Social sciences are neither speculative philosophy nor political doctrine in that social theories do not seek eternal truth but change with the dynamics of society. At the same time, social theories also transform social reality, diagnosing and providing directions for alternative worlds. According to Wright, Marxist social science is not a political ideology but a critical social science that attempts to analyze the reality of capitalism in order to offer guidelines for egalitarian social transformation.

Wright's reformulation of the leftist project took place when Marxism and alternative political movements had rapidly declined, due to three historical conjunctures in the late twentieth century. The first was the sudden collapse of state socialism in Eastern Europe between 1989 and 1991. While the transition from state socialism to liberal capitalism in Eastern Europe began in 1989, the crisis of state socialism had already become noticeable in the 1980s, when the Polish Solidarity workers went on strike at Gdańsk. Though the declaration of the end of history by Francis Fukuyama turned out to be premature, state socialism's demise contributed significantly to the crisis of anti-systemic movements.[3]

The second conjuncture was the rise of neoliberalism advocated in the 1980s by the global capitalist class and by conservative politicians such as Margaret Thatcher in Britain and Ronald Reagan in the United

---

3 Francis Fukuyama, *The End of History and the Last Man* (New York: Free Press, 1992).

States. The core tenets of neoliberalism attacked Keynesian economic ideas and welfare states, promoting the logic of an unregulated market as a cure for state failure. It negated "the social," as epitomized in Margaret Thatcher's 1987 statement in an interview with *Women's Own* magazine that "there is no such thing as society. There are individual men and women, and there are families."[4] Neoliberal economists and politicians revived the market as a savior of capitalism in crisis. The specter of neoliberalism haunted the globe in the late twentieth century. It became a global ideology integrating East and West, North and South. The global market formation, accompanied by global value chains, accelerated the race to the bottom in search of cheap labor and cheap resources.

The third conjuncture was the rise of various post-theories, such as post-modernism,[5] post-structuralism,[6] and post-Marxism.[7] As Wright points out, postmodernism reflects "cynicism about the human capacity to realize those [emancipatory] values on a substantial scale."[8] In the late twentieth century, postmodernism's upsurge discouraged and demoralized leftists, denying reason and progress, disseminating agnostic epistemology, and downplaying social theories on a grand scale. Social constructivism played a significant role in undermining mainstream sociology and emasculating radical social critiques as the discursive or cultural formations of meaning and difference replaced structural approaches based on foundationalism.[9]

In the late twentieth and early twenty-first century, neoliberal globalization has accelerated with a series of scientific and technological innovations. The formation of a global market has obscured national boundaries, integrated local markets, and created global value chains, resulting in de-industrialization in the industrialized West and industrialization in the Third World (particularly in China and India). Neoliberal

---

4   Quoted in Chris Moncrieff, "Margaret Thatcher: In Her Own Words," *Independent*, April 8, 2013.

5   Fredrik Jameson, *Postmodernism, or, the Cultural Logic of Late Capitalism* (Durham, NC: Duke University Press, 1992).

6   Jacques Derrida, *Of Grammatology*, trans. Gayatri Chakravorty Spivak (Baltimore, MD: Johns Hopkins University Press, 1974).

7   Ernesto Laclau and Chantal Mouffe, *Hegemony and Socialist Strategy: Towards a Radical Democratic Politics* (London: Verso, 1985).

8   Erik Olin Wright, *Envisioning Real Utopias* (London: Verso, 2010), 10.

9   Terry Eagleton, *Ideology: An Introduction* (London: Verso, 1991); Fredric Jameson, "Marxism and Postmodernism," *New Left Review* 176 (1989).

globalization has weakened labor unions across whole countries, generating massive precarity for workers and their households. Labor unions failed to build solidarity with precarious workers, concentrating instead on defending members' job security and employment benefits. The division between secured workers and precarious workers deepened as neoliberal globalization expanded after the collapse of state socialism in the Soviet Union and Eastern Europe.

Analytical Marxism and Class Analysis

In this turbulent period, Wright engaged with an Analytical Marxism group known as the "September Group," which sought to resuscitate a Marxism different from Western Marxism, imbued with philosophy and metaphysics. Committed to conventional scientific norms, it emphasized systematic conceptualization, elaborating detailed theoretical arguments and focusing on individuals' intentional actions.[10] In short, the group attempted to revive Marxist social theory using methodologies developed in mainstream academia, such as analytical philosophy, rational choice theory in economics, and theory construction in sociology.

In the 1980s, Wright's commitment to Analytical Marxism directly affected his reformulation of the Marxist class analysis that he had begun in graduate school at University of California–Berkeley in the early 1970s. He engaged in the debate on working-class boundaries with Nicos Poulantzas, criticizing the latter's concept of the new petty bourgeoisie in a famous 1976 *New Left Review* article, a critique based on Althusser's structural Marxism.[11] "Contradictory class locations," the term Wright coined in that period and later redefined twice, refers to ambiguous class locations within the social division of labor as shaped by capitalist development. Control over economic resources, the physical means of production, and the labor power of others have been transformed by the evolution of capitalism. As monopoly capitalism emerged,

---

10   Erik Olin Wright, *Interrogating Inequality: Essays on Class Analysis, Socialism and Marxism* (London: Verso, 1994), 181–2.

11   Louis Althusser, Étienne Balibar, Roger Establet, Pierre Macherey, and Jacques Rancière, *Reading Capital: The Complete Edition,* trans. Ben Brewster and David Fernbach (London: Verso, 1986).

organizational hierarchies and labor processes within capitalist enterprises were reshaped, generating "contradictory" class locations between the capitalist class and the working class and between the capitalist mode of production and simple commodity production.[12]

Proposing the concept of contradictory class locations marked the beginning of Wright's long journey, reconstructing Marxist class analysis over the next two decades. His work on class analysis focused on the theoretical reformulation of the meaning of "contradiction" in his concept of the contradictory class location, stemming from his engagement with Structural Marxism and Analytical Marxism. After he joined the September Group, he began to incorporate John Roemer's new conceptualization of exploitation, a conceptualization he elaborated in *Classes*.[13] Applying game theory, Roemer, an American Marxian economist and a member of the September Group, proposed the "class exploitation correspondence principle" in his 1982 book *A General Theory of Exploitation and Class*. Though Wright did not accept Roemer's concept of exploitation as based solely on property relations, he found the concept useful in redefining contradictory class locations based on material relations, asymmetrical power, and appropriation of effort.[14]

Wright's class analysis project was brought to fruition in his seminal work *Class Counts*, where he created a complex exploitation and inequality matrix for contemporary capitalism. He defined contradictory class locations as those class locations which allowed an individual to be simultaneously an exploiter in one dimension and exploited in another. For example, managers are exploited by capitalists because they do not own productive assets; but they exploit unskilled workers because they have organizational assets. In late capitalism, Wright suggested, three assets generate exploitation: ownership of means of production, organizational assets (authority), and skills and expertise (credentials).[15]

12   Erik Olin Wright, *Class, Crisis and the State* (London: New Left Books, 1978), 61–91.

13   John E. Roemer, *A General Theory of Exploitation and Class* (Cambridge, MA: Harvard University Press, 1982); Erik Olin Wright, *Classes* (London: Verso, 1985), 86–92.

14   Erik Olin Wright, *Class Counts* (Cambridge: Cambridge University Press, 1997), 10–13.

15   Wright, *Class Counts*, 15–25.

The reformulation of contradictory class locations allowed Wright to argue that other classes beside the proletariat could challenge capitalist rule: "There are other class forces within capitalism that have the potential to pose an alternative to capitalism."[16] In particular, he identified the potential of the middle class to oppose the class power of the bourgeoisie under certain political and ideological conditions, such as permanent economic stagnation. This matrix of complex exploitation relations, he argued, allows us to better understand the process of class formation and class struggle in contemporary capitalism.

Wright frequently argued that class analysis consists of three dimensions: class structure, class formation, and class struggle.[17] However, he spent much time and energy in reformulating a theory of class structure, taking twenty years to complete *Class Counts* in 1997. As he emphasized, Marxist class analysis, unlike stratification research and neo-Weberian class analysis, has to include the examination of class formation and class struggle as well as class structure. After completing a theory of class structure, Wright began to elaborate a theory of social transformation, rather than class formation and class struggle, in the 2000s.

Wright's second project to renovate Marxism was his Real Utopias Project. It began in 1992 when the perception that "there is no alternative" (also known as TINA) prevailed with the downfall of countries in the Soviet bloc and as neoliberalism reigned over the globe. The trajectory of the working class, particularly organized workers and working-class parties in the West, had been rather disappointing in the postwar period. According to Wright, the working class, as a major agent for social transformation, had been losing its "system-challenging capacity" as a result of its ever-increasing heterogeneity and the pervasiveness of "class compromise" in the West.[18]

Thus, before completing *Class Counts*, Wright launched the Real Utopias Project in the early 1990s to envision emancipatory alternatives to democratic capitalism in the West, hoping to figure out desirable,

---

16 Wright, *Classes*, 89.

17 Erik Olin Wright, *Class, Crisis and the State* (London: Verso, 1978), 102–8; Wright, *Classes*, 27–31; Wright, "A Framework of Class Analysis in the Marxist Tradition," chap. 1 in *Approach to Class Analysis*, ed. Erik Olin Wright (Cambridge: Cambridge University Press, 2005).

18 Wright, *Envisioning Real Utopias*, 195.

viable, and achievable alternatives.[19] It dealt with much broader theoretical and political issues than social class, embracing participatory
democracy as an alternative to representative democracy, egalitarianism
as an alternative distributive principle, and gender equality as an alternative to patriarchy. During the 1990s, Wright engaged in the double
projects of the reconstruction of Marxist class analysis and reconstruction of emancipatory social theory and practice.

Eventually, Wright's engagement with the Real Utopias Project
resulted in *Envisioning Real Utopias*, which provides a theory of social
transformation encompassing diverse critical theories and emancipatory social practices across countries. It is the culmination of Wright's
dual projects in one book: the Class Analysis Project and the Real Utopia
Project. It is not based on an epistemological break, as Michael Burawoy
claims in this volume, but rather, on a synthesis of his interests in social
transformation of capitalism as a Marxist sociologist. The more simpli-
fied, but more refined, discussion of his lifelong project appeared as a
short book titled *How to Be an Anticapitalist in the Twenty-First Century*,
published posthumously in 2019.

Envisioning Real Utopias as a Theory of Social Transformation

Envisioning Real Utopias, which appeared in 2010, continued Wright's
notion of scientific Marxism, reflecting his interest in social transformation beyond capitalism via structural contradiction and collective
action. Within Marxism, the dualism of structure and agency requires
an account of how the formation of a collectivity ends with the breakdown of an existing social system and the generation of an alternative
social system to replace it.

There are two approaches to bridging structure and agency in contemporary sociology. One is the theory of structuration developed by
Anthony Giddens in The *Constitution of Society*, which proposes the
concept of the duality of structure. Giddens emphasizes the structure
itself as both the medium and the outcome of the reproduction of practices: structure constitutes social practices that reproduce structure.
Giddens uses language as an example of structuration in which language

---

19   Ibid., 20–5.

is a rule and a resource for social interaction. Each individual's speech act uses words and grammar, reproducing a particular form of language itself. Similarly, Giddens distinguishes structure from social systems, arguing that structure is outside time and space and marked by an "absence of the subject"; social systems, by contrast, are social outcomes of a situated agent's action, adapting rules and resources in historical contexts.[20] Thus the structure is real but invisible, like a generative rule in linguistics, whereas a social system can be observed in social relations and social practices. The social system is an outcome of daily individual and collective actions constrained and enabled by the structure.

While Giddens's theory of structuration provides a novel understanding of the problem of structure and agency, it mostly focuses on reproductive actions rather than transformative actions. It postulates action and interaction between structure and agency in shaping and reshaping the social system. However, it falls short of theorizing the transformation of social systems by actors' purposeful actions that challenge and replace the existing structure with a radically new one. We might call Giddens's theory of structuration a reproduction-oriented social theory.

Another reproduction-oriented social theory is the theory of practice articulated by Pierre Bourdieu in his *Outline of a Theory of Practice*, postulating "habitus" as a new concept linking objective structure and subjective disposition. Bourdieu reconsidered structure and agency from the French intellectual context—a debate between Jean-Paul Sartre, an existentialist philosopher, and Claude Lévi-Strauss, a structural anthropologist, in the 1950s. Like Giddens, Bourdieu postulates the structure as structured by social practice but simultaneously structuring actors' practices. The habitus is a structured disposition formed as a cumulative product of the social life of actors. It enables social actors to act and react in social interactions. Habitus is a source of actions "organized as strategies without being the production of a genuine strategic intention."[21] Social practice is not a translated practice from the social structure but mediated by habitus. Thus habitus is key to the

20   Anthony Giddens, *The Constitution of Society* (Berkeley: University of California Press, 1984), 25–6.

21   Pierre Bourdieu, *Outline of a Theory of Practice*, trans. Richard Nice (Cambridge: Cambridge University Press, 1976), 73.

connection between structure and practice, "functioning at every moment as a matrix of perceptions, appreciations, and actions."[22]

While Bourdieu's theory of practice derives from a different intellectual context than that of Giddens and proposes the concept of habitus to link structure and practice, it also falls short of providing a theory of social transformation. It is also a reproductive theory of action enhanced by the addition of cultural dimensions. Consider his explanation of the student movement in the 1960s that relies on the mismatch between the rapid expansion of universities, occupational aspiration, and limited opportunities.[23] The temporary breakdown of reproduction comes from the functional mismatch between the different fields of education and labor market, but it does not lead to social transformation.

According to Wright, Giddens and Bourdieu only offer "a theory of social reproduction" that attempts to explain the continuity of social institutions and practices in everyday life.[24] While Giddens and Bourdieu attempt to explain social practices that contribute to maintaining social structure and social life, they fail to recognize the importance of institutional mechanisms that discourage and halt collective challenges to the capitalist social order. Wright views some of these as obstacles to emancipatory transformation, arguing that the continuation of domination, oppression, and exploitation has been possible because of varieties of state regulation of physical and ideational power. Focusing on a theoretical dualism of structure and agency fails to capture the varieties of institutional mechanisms that act as protective shields for the capitalist social order.

Wright distinguished two types of social reproduction. One is passive social reproduction, by which everyday social life is maintained with a sense of naturalness by socialization. "Ingrained habits and dispositions" are the core elements in passive social reproduction. Another is active social reproduction, orchestrated by social institutions such as "the police, the courts, the state administration, education, the media, and churches."[25] Four social mechanisms work to generate the stability

22   Ibid., 83.

23   Pierre Bourdieu, *Distinction: A Social Critique of the Judgment of Taste,* trans. Richard Nice (Cambridge, MA: Harvard University Press, 1983), 151–3.

24   Wright, *Envisioning Real Utopias,* 273–7.

25   Ibid., 275.

of the capitalist social system: coercion, institutional rules, ideology, and material interests.[26]

Thus Wright's main concern is quite different from that of Giddens and Bourdieu in that he focuses on transformative practices—that is, social practices that aim to turn existing institutions in a democratic and egalitarian direction. Whereas Giddens and Bourdieu direct their attention to "mundane and routine activities," Wright seeks out transformative social practices that will create a new order.

While Wright focused on class structure, he also sought forms of class politics that could transform capitalism. He was all too aware of rising class inequality (recorded by many researchers since the late 1970s), the weakening of working-class capacity, and the diminishing anti-systemic labor movement. As neoliberal globalization engulfed the world partly in response to the 1970s crisis of capitalism, class inequality exploded, and the concentration of wealth in the top 1 percent accelerated in the late twentieth century.[27] Nevertheless, working-class politics continued to dwindle in the West after the 1970s, and the associational power of working-class organizations was substantially diminished. It seemed an unrealistic expectation for the left to think of the working class as a historical agent for transforming capitalism in the near future.

State socialism in Eastern Europe was also in crisis, with workers subordinated to state cadres in politics and, in the workplace, to managers appointed by the Communist Party.[28] The transition from state socialism to market capitalism occurred between 1989 and 1991, breaking the socialist countries up into religious-ethnic nation-states. The sudden demise of state socialism made leftist discourse less appealing than ever before, and contributed to a rising perception that "there is no alternative." Instead, a liberal discourse about "the end of history" prevailed among conservative academics and politicians, exemplified by Francis Fukuyama's *The End of History and the Last Man*. The optimism for progress that flourished after World War II had exhausted itself by the late twentieth century as neoliberal globalization dominated the global economy.

---

26 Ibid., 279.

27 Thomas Piketty, *Capital in the Twenty-First Century* (Cambridge, MA: Harvard University Press, 2014).

28 Michael Burawoy and Janos Lukács, *The Radiant Past: Ideology and Reality in Hungary's Road to Capitalism* (Chicago: University of Chicago Press, 1992).

Envisioning Real Utopias was published amid the chaotic and murky situation politics that progressive intellectuals face in the twenty-first century. It provides a new theorization and new insights for rethinking emancipatory social sciences. First, Wright found Marx's theory of social transformation inadequate to explain the future of contemporary capitalism. He argued that, based on capitalism's history, major theses suggested by Marx—regarding immiseration, anti-systemic challenges led by the proletariat, the ever-deepening crisis of capitalism and its eventual ruptural transformation—are not justifiable. Accepting that those prophecies turned out to be untenable, Wright instead proposed an alternative theory of emancipatory social transformation. If emancipatory social transformation by the working class is not plausible in contemporary capitalism in the West, he argued, new pathways are needed.

Wright's new theorization of socialism is built around three related concepts: "the social," civil society, and social power (empowerment). He argues that the social has received less attention and is not adequately clarified in the theory of social democracy and socialism. Instead, Wright proposes that the social should be a basis of a new theorization of socialism, using a triad similar to Antonio Gramsci's— the state, economy, and civil society—to formulate a new concept of socialism.[29] The social refers to the social units engaging in independent economic activity, not reducible to private ownership or state ownership. Civil society refers to the "sphere of social interactions in which people voluntarily form associations of different sorts for various purposes."[30] Then Wright proposes a different form of power corresponding to each sphere: state power, economic power, and social power. Socialism is an economic structure within which economic activity is controlled through social power, a power rooted in civil society, and thus economic power is subordinate to social power. Differentiating socialism from statism, in which the means of production are owned and controlled by the state—as was the case in the former Soviet-type economic system—Wright elaborated the concept of social power and distinguished socialism from statism in order to resuscitate the concept

29   Antonio Gramsci, *Selections from the Prison Notebooks*, ed. and trans. Quintin Hoare and Geoffrey Nowell Smith (New York: International Publishers, 1971).

30   Wright, *Envisioning Real Utopias*, 119.

of socialism. In *Envisioning Real Utopias*, Wright found emancipatory potential not in the production site but in civil society. He considered civil society as "the site of a form of power with emancipatory potential rooted in the capacity of the people to form an association to advance their collective goals."[31]

The notable elements in Wright's theory of transformation include his theoretical discussion about already-existing transformative social practices and his new ideas based on theoretical projections, suggesting visionary trajectories of systemic transformations beyond capitalism. He conceptualizes three modes of transformation—ruptural, interstitial, and symbiotic—and proposes corresponding political strategies. This is a new theoretical discussion completely absent in previous research on social movements and Marxist discussions about practices. In principle, "ruptural" transformation refers to the type of revolutionary social transformation imagined and attempted by the communist parties to the end of World War II, characterized by the breakdown of existing institutions and the introduction of new ones. "Interstitial" transformation refers to the building of new social institutions "in the niches and margins of capitalist society."[32] Wright argues that while leftists downplay interstitial transformation, it might be important for expanding *its* transformative potential over time. "Symbiotic" transformation refers to transformative practices contributing to the growth of social empowerment, while at the same time strengthening existing institutions by reducing social problems within them. Traditionally, the latter two transformative practices were not considered effective strategies by those who wanted a ruptural transformation, but they have been common among community activists and NGOs.

The emancipatory social practices described in Wright's *Envisioning Real Utopias* are neither specific to the working class nor to any other social group. Some real utopias are comprehensive and universal programs or institutions, such as Wikipedia or universal basic income, while others are confined to specific regions, such as Mondragon in the Basque region of Spain or specific social groups such as worker-owned cooperatives. He maps each real utopia within his triumvirate of transformative practices—ruptural, interstitial, and symbiotic.

---

31 Ibid., 145.
32 Ibid., 303.

Envisioning Real Utopias does not reveal a fundamental shift, some-times called an epistemological break, in Wright's theory. Instead, it displays his deepening understanding of the evolution of capitalism in the context of the discrediting of "communism" and the evolution of global capitalism. In *Class Counts*, Wright focused on one dimension of capitalism—class relations. In *Envisioning Real Utopias*, however, he discusses an additional dimension of capitalism—economic coordina-tion—to discuss the types of power that shape the economic system's nature, namely state power, economic power, and social power. Thus he uses social power to redefine a socialism in which the working class is a key agent, but not the sole agent. This is a reformulation, not a complete break from the theory he had previously elaborated in *Class Counts*.

Marxist social sciences incessantly promote dialectical processes in theory and empirical reality. When empirical reality changes, and when it does not confirm theoretical conjecture or predictions, theory should be transformed, discarded, or reformulated as a research program, in Lakatos's sense of the term.[33] However, Marxist social sciences are unusual in that they pursue emancipatory social transformation through scientific endeavors and through exploring social practices associated with emancipatory values such as democracy and egalitarianism.

From the beginning, Wright considered transformative social prac-tices (class formation and class struggle) a core part of class analysis. He might have developed a theory of transformative social practices based on social classes if he had attempted to complete it in the 1960s or 1970s, when the labor movement revived and union density increased in most European countries.[34] However, neoliberal politicians, including Margaret Thatcher and Ronald Reagan, were hostile to labor unions and, together with the prolonged economic crisis in the 1980s, contrib-uted to the overall decline of unions.

Wright had also observed the rise of various social movements in civil society, including the student movement, the environmental move-ment, the feminist movement, workers' self-management, civil rights

---

33   Imre Lakatos, *The Methodology of Scientific Research Programmes Volume 1*, ed. Hohn Worrall and Gregory Currie (Cambridge: Cambridge University Press, 1978).

34   Colin Crouch and Alessandro Pizzorno, *The Resurgence of Class Conflicts in Europe since 1968* (Teaneck, NJ: Holmes and Meier, 1978); Walter Korpi and Michael Shalev, "Strikes, Power, and Politics in the Western Nations," in *Political Power and Social Theory*, vol. 1, ed. Maurice Zeitlin (Boulder, CO: JAI Press, 1980), 301–4.

movement, the anti-nuclear movement, and the antiwar movement after the student upsurge of 1968. This wave of new social movements was distinguished from that "old social movement": the labor movement.[35] While some Marxists, like Ellen Meiksins Wood, did not consider the new social movements significantly transformative, Wright recognized their potentiality for enhancing democracy and egalitarianism, transforming capitalism by taming and resisting it.[36] He still considered class-based transformative social practice to be important, but not the only agent capable of transforming capitalism. Thus, Wright did not retreat from class to civil society since, in his conceptual map, the labor union is a part of civil society. The only thing that changed was the weight of the working class in his theory of transformative social practices. If in his major work, *Class Counts*, the working class was the single most important agent for social transformation, in *Envisioning Real Utopias*, the working class is only one of multiple collective actors.

A theoretical issue unanswered by Wright in *Envisioning Real Utopias* is the origin of his three transformative social practices. Wright argues that a "vital utopian ideal may be necessary to motivate people to set off on a journey from the status quo in the first place."[37] From where does the utopian ideal come? One of the challenges of structural approaches is that the existence of classes does not imply class consciousness. The lived experience in the labor process or in communal life can promote shared feelings and the culture of solidarity among coworkers, but Althusser's over-simplified version of interpellation cannot explain the formation of the ideals of transformative social practices.[38] As Paul Willis notes, work ideology might be formed in school culture and peer groups.[39] There are

---

35   Alberto Melucci, "The New Social Movements: A Theoretical Approach," *Social Science Information* 19, no. 2 (1980): 199–226; Nelson A. Pichardo, "New Social Movements: A Critical Review," *Annual Review of Sociology* 23, no. 1 (1997): 411–30.

36   Christopher Phelps, "An Interview with Ellen Meiksins Wood," *Monthly Review* 51, no. 1 (1999).

37   Wright, *Envisioning Real Utopias*, 6.

38   Michael Burawoy, *Manufacturing Consent: Changes in the Labor Process under Monopoly Capitalism* (Chicago: University of Chicago Press, 1979); E. P. Thompson, *The Making of the English Working Class* (Harmondsworth, UK: Penguin, 1963); Louis Althusser, *Lenin and Philosophy and Other Essays*, trans. Ben Brewster (London: New Left Books, 1971).

39   Paul E. Willis, *Learning to Labour: How Working Class Kids Get Working Class Jobs* (London: Saxon House, 1977).

diverse pathways to the formation of anticapitalist consciousness through articulating counter-hegemonic discourses.[40]

The formation of consciousness behind transformative social practices is not fully elaborated in Wright's *Envisioning Real Utopias*, but he did devote the last chapter of his last book, *How to Be an Anticapitalist in the Twenty-First Century*, to issues of identity, interests, and values. The title of the book's last chapter is "Agents of Transformation," a chapter dealing with the formation of collective actors challenging capitalism. Here Wright directly raises the question, "Where are these collective actors?" Resisting capitalism, escaping capitalism, taming capitalism, and dismantling capitalism, which together might erode capitalism, are propelled by different types of political actors. Wright argues that even though identities and interests might vary, "values, then, constitute a potential basis for constructing political unity across diverse identities."[41] From the perspective of values, Wright could argue that collective actors in civil society (including unions) could contribute to the transformation of capitalism if they were welded together by common values such as democracy and egalitarianism in spite of different identities and interests. Values provide an essential bridge between class politics and identity politics, although some "new social movement" theorists consider them opposed. Forming the values needed for transformative social practices has been a challenging issue for most civil society organizations, but as the last sentence of Wright's work makes clear, many anticapitalist movements have resulted from "the contingencies of historical events and the creative agency of activists and collective actors."

Conclusion

Envisioning Real Utopias provides a new vision for emancipatory social sciences in the midst of chaotic political and academic conditions. While the current situation can be characterized as a crisis of capitalism, Marxist social science has found it difficult to explore alternatives to

---

40   Lawrence Grossberg, "On Postmodernism and Articulation: An Interview with Stuart Hall," *Journal of Communication Inquiry* 10, no. 2 (1986): 45–60; Bourdieu, *Distinction*.

41   Wright, *Envisioning Real Utopias*, 138.

capitalism, given that working class movements in the West are in decline and socialism is in retreat. The ideology of TINA prevails.

In this context the work of Erik Wright is especially important, showing that there are desirable, viable, and achievable alternatives to current capitalism. Marxist theories of the twentieth century did not show us a path to socialism, except for a ruptural transformation led by the working class, which seems to be no longer viable. Wright attempted to reformulate the concept of socialism and to find agents of transformation—not the working class, but civil society activists.

Considering Wright's many projects across his life, we can find continuity in his theoretical concern for emancipating human beings from injustice and oppression. From the outset, Wright attempted to rebuild class analysis as the core of Marxism, analyzing class inequality and class struggle in contemporary capitalism. He frequently argued that class analysis comprised three areas: class structure, class formation, and class struggle. *Class Counts* presents Wright's theory of class structure in contemporary capitalism. But rather than completing a theoretical reformulation of class formation and class struggle, he wrote *Envisioning Real Utopias*, providing a theory of social transformation dealing with the formation of collectivities and transformative activities for building non-capitalist institutions. In *Envisioning Real Utopias*, Wright did not exclusively focus on social transformation based on the working class. Instead, he tried to provide a theoretical understanding of social transformation in general and a practical road map for those searching for alternatives to capitalism.

Wright's reformulation of his thought on socialism and emancipatory social sciences was based on a synthesis of various theories developed in the late twentieth century. His zeal for socialism and emancipation was persistent throughout his life. He did not believe that the transformation of any social system would realize socialist ideals immediately, arguing instead that it would only enhance that possibility. In the final analysis, the realization of socialist ideals based on democratic and egalitarian values will depend on human agency. Social structure and social institutions will never realize those values by themselves. Furthermore, Wright warned that, due to the social system's complexity and its propensity for producing unintended outcomes, a sustainable institutional design would be difficult to achieve—a phenomenon that is discernible in the failure of institutions of capitalism and state socialism to accomplish

their goals. Nevertheless, *Envisioning Real Utopias* combines the optimism of a cool-headed Marxist sociologist with the sophisticated theory
of social transformation. It might be Wright's magnum opus, offering a
new theory of socialism and social transformation in the twenty-first
century.

Wright's last book, *How to Be an Anticapitalist in the Twenty-First
Century*, provides a simple and precise discussion of the importance of
values in shaping collective agency and movements when labor unions
are not major actors (as in many industrial capitalist countries). He
expected the core values of democracy and egalitarianism to provide a
platform for connection across different identities and interests. Wright's
emancipatory social science provides rich theoretical and practical
resources for activists as well as critical social scientists.

PART II

From Real Utopias to Class Analysis

5

If You're a Socialist You Need the Real Utopias Project, Whether You Like It or Not
Harry Brighouse

I picked up *Class, Crisis and the State* in the East Oxford Alternative Bookshop on the Cowley Road when I was sixteen. It was too expensive for me, so I read it in full sitting on the floor, under the indulgent eye of the owner, Jon Carpenter. Much later, in graduate school, Analytical Marxism drew me away from philosophy of language and into political philosophy. I read all Erik's books (except *The Politics of Punishment*), eventually even purchasing *Class, Crisis and the State*. We finally met in January 1992, when I interviewed for a job in the University of Wisconsin–Madison philosophy department. He kindly supported my staying an extra two days in Madison to attend a proto–Real Utopias Project conference. As soon as I moved here, Erik went out of his way to welcome me, deliberately offering professional and intellectual opportunities that he knew would challenge me but through which I would grow and teaching me how to interact seriously with social scientists. He thought more highly of my abilities than I did; in response, I became more able. He was, for most of our shared time in Madison, the person on campus I talked to, and collaborated with, more than any other. He

I'm grateful to many of the participants at a memorial conference for Erik held at UW–Madison in November 2019, and especially to the late Leo Panitch, whose work I *also* read on the floor of the East Oxford Alternative Bookshop and whose contribution to that conference inspired this paper. I'm also grateful to the editors, the other contributors, to the other members of the September Group, and, as ever these days, to David O'Brien and Gina Schouten for insightful comments on drafts.

conceived the Real Utopias Project during my first couple of years here. Erik's earlier work had been instrumental in changing my trajectory in graduate school; his mentorship, comradeship, and friendship were central to my trajectory thereafter.

Despite the fact that my three children were born on two continents, he and Marcia were the only adults who met them *all* before they were a week old.

What Is the Real Utopias Project?

Under Erik Olin Wright's guidance, the Real Utopias Project (RUP) has been a massive, collaborative project, involving numerous sociologists, economists, political scientists, and philosophers and investigating specific institutional designs that were either directly intended or might be adapted to play a role in implementing a more just society. The institutional designs that form the core of the project (so far) were elaborated in the lead essays to the several volumes in the RUP series,[1] in contributions to *Politics and Society*,[2] and in Wright's own book

---

1   John Roemer, *Equal Shares: Making Market Socialism Work* (London: Verso, 1996); Janet Gornick and Marcia Meyers, *Gender Equality: Transforming Family Divisions of Labor* (London: Verso, 2009); John Gastil and Erik Olin Wright, *Legislature by Lot: Transformative Designs for Deliberative Governance* (London: Verso, 2019); Bruce Ackerman, Anne Alstott, and Philippe Van Parijs, *Redesigning Distribution: Basic Income and Stakeholder Grants as Alternative Cornerstones for a More Egalitarian Capitalism* (London: Verso, 2006); Sam Bowles and Herbert Gintis, *Recasting Egalitarianism: New Rules for Communities, States and Markets* (London: Verso, 1999); Joshua Cohen and Joel Rogers, *Associations and Democracy: The Real Utopias Project, Vol. 1* (London: Verso, 1995); Archon Fung and Erik Olin Wright, *Deepening Democracy: Institutional Innovations in Empowered Participatory Governance* (London: Verso, 2003).

2   Bruce Ackerman, "Reviving Democratic Citizenship?" *Politics and Society* 41, no. 2 (2013): 309–17; Gerald F. Davis, "After the Corporation," *Politics and Society* 41, no. 2 (2013): 283–308; Archon Fung, "Infotopia: Unleashing the Democratic Power of Transparency," *Politics and Society* 41, no. 2 (2013): 183–212; John Gastil and Robert Richards, "Making Direct Democracy Deliberative through Random Assemblies," *Politics and Society* 41, no. 2 (2013): 253–81; Phillipe Van Parijs, "The Universal Basic Income: Why Utopian Thinking Matters, and How Sociologists Can Contribute to It," *Politics and Society* 41, no. 2 (2013): 171–82; Yochai Benkler, "Practical Anarchism: Peer Mutualism, Market Power, and the Fallible State," *Politics and Society* 41, no. 2 (2013): 213–51.

Envisioning Real Utopias.[3] Some designs *actually exist* in some form: for example, the Porto Alegre participatory budgeting process, the Quebec social economy movement, and, most peculiarly for many commentators (including this one), Wikipedia. Others, like universal basic income (UBI) and John Roemer's version of market socialism, have never been implemented.[4]

The sense in which all these designs aspire to be *real* is that they can, if implemented in the right conditions, be self-sustaining over time, while reproducing themselves without adverse unintended consequences. To qualify for consideration, a design must also be *utopian*: that is, some variant of it is, or could be made, consistent with some set of balanced, radically egalitarian normative principles. In *Envisioning Real Utopias*, as we'll see, Wright proposes a set of moral principles that constitute a variant of radical egalitarianism. But other versions of radical egalitarianism than his can be appealing, and different designs in the real utopias family are underpinned by subtly different variants of egalitarianism. A candidate design need not be *transitional*—that is, it need not be something the implementation of which would be necessary for, or even would contribute to, the transition to a more just society. And even if it *is* transitional, it cannot be *merely* that. In conversation Wright suggested the following test: a design is real utopian, as opposed to merely reformist, if it, or something very like it, would be a feature of a society that fully realized egalitarian ideals.[5]

To give a simple illustration: affirmative action would not count as a real utopian design, even though it may be an urgently necessary mechanism for mitigating or eliminating racial inequality, because it would not be a feature of a fully just society; a fully just society would, by definition, lack racism. By contrast, assuming it survives the scrutiny I'll discuss in the next paragraph, UBI would be real utopian, because it could be *an actual element* of an egalitarian society.

What does the scrutiny consist of? We use two tests. First, would the design, if implemented in the right conditions, live up to the defensible

---

3   Erik Olin Wright, *Envisioning Real Utopias* (London: Verso 2010).

4   Phillipe Van Parijs and Robert J. Van der Veen, "The Capitalist Road to Communism," *Theory and Society* 15, no. 5 (1986): 635–55; Roemer, *Equal Shares*.

5   If, like me, you suspect that justice might be multiply realizable, you should substitute "could" for "would." To illustrate: it doesn't seem implausible to me that a UBI *could*, but *needn't*, be part of an ideally just society. Perhaps some version of John Roemer's coupon socialism without the UBI would be just as good.

principles that animate it, or animate us? Second, is it viable? That is, could it, or some variant of it, when implemented as part of an overall package of designs in the right conditions, be stable over time without having its benefits outweighed by adverse consequences elsewhere in the institutional ecosystem within which it is nested?

The scrutiny stage of the project draws on theoretical and empirical evidence to make provisional conclusions about whether the design could work as intended. For the untried designs, such as coupon socialism and UBI, we draw on empirical evidence from other, actually existing, designs, which might not themselves qualify as real utopian. In the case of coupon socialism, for example, we learn from actual capital markets under capitalism, and in the case of UBI we learn from means-tested cash transfers. *Existing* utopian designs (such as the social economy in Quebec and participatory budgeting) yield empirical information that we can use to assess, tentatively, whether some version could be stably implemented in the right environment. Only if it passes both tests can we place it on the menu of recommendations that socialists should consider.

The RUP invites criticism and impatience from some left-wing theorists. Some complain that Wright's treatment of the *existing* utopian designs is insufficiently critical; Leo Panitch, for example, argues that the Quebec social economy and the participatory budgeting process in Porto Alegre were highly flawed.[6] Dylan Riley is impatient with the normative theorizing that is an essential element of the project and perplexed by Wright's understanding of socialism, especially given his willingness to apply the term to actually existing designs that are stably present in a *capitalist* society.[7] Several critics argue that Wright wrongly neglects class and its role in transformation.[8]

Some criticisms are posed as objections to the RUP itself, others as objections to the argument of *Envisioning Real Utopias*. The two are not

---

6   Leo Panitch, "Erik Olin Wright's Optimism of the Intellect," *New Political Science* 42, no. 1 (2020): 42–51.

7   Dylan Riley, "Real Utopia or Abstract Empiricism? Comment on Burawoy and Wright," *New Left Review* 121 (January–February 2020), 99–107; Dylan Riley, "Neo-Tocquevillian Marxism: Erik Olin Wright's Real Utopias," *Socio-Economic Review* 10 (2012): 375–81.

8   Riley, "Real Utopia or Abstract Empiricism?"; David F. Ruccio, "Review of *Envisioning Real Utopias*," *Historical Materialism* 19, no. 4 (2011): 219–27.

identical. Although *Envisioning* contains the most comprehensive argument for the RUP, most of the RUP is conducted in the RUP volumes
and other papers, by theorists other than Wright. And some of what
Wright does in *Envisioning* might sensibly be thought to be outside the
scope of the RUP. Wright sets himself three tasks: developing a critique
of capitalism that explains what is wrong with it; articulating desirable,
viable, and achievable alternatives to capitalism; and advancing a theory
of transformation from capitalism to an alternative. The third of these
was almost completely absent from the RUP before the publication of
Envisioning Real Utopias and has been almost completely absent since
its publication.[9]

Here's the plan for the current chapter: I'll respond to the objections
that do indeed apply to the RUP understood in the restricted sense,
which excludes a theory of transformation. But first I'll explain what the
RUP is and show why it, or something like it, is essential for the socialist
project. It is, in fact, *the most fundamental* intellectual task for socialists.
This is because without the RUP, or something like it, we lack even a
critique of capitalism, let alone grounds for recommending socialism as
a replacement. Perhaps, and I think this is a live possibility, *even with it*
we lack a critique of capitalism and grounds for recommending socialism. Because if no proposed design survives the scrutiny of the RUP,
then we cannot, in good faith, recommend any alternative to capitalism.
And without alternatives, we lack a critique. If so, that's too bad for
socialism.

Without a Moral Theory, You Can't Evaluate Capitalism

Wright notes the falsehood of the most deterministic version of historical materialism, which postulates that capitalism will collapse as a result
of its own contradictions, giving way first to socialism and then to
communism in which the state withers away and resources are

---

9   "The idea of the project was to focus on specific proposals for the fundamental
redesign of different arenas of social institutions rather than on either general, abstract
formulations of grand designs or on small immediately attainable reforms of existing
practices . . . [We] wanted to achieve . . . a clear elaboration of workable institutional
principles that could inform emancipatory alternatives to the existing world." Wright,
Envisioning Real Utopias, 5.

distributed "from each according to his ability, to each according to his need." This proceeds as if by the laws of nature.[10]

You might think that this view is so implausible that it would be uncharitable to attribute it to Marx, and you might be right. You might also think it is so implausible that *nobody has ever* held it. You'd probably be wrong about that, but it doesn't matter: for Wright, it is a stalking horse. According to this theory, any institutional changes we think we are driving are, in fact, determined. Because there is no agency, there's no need to look for values or normative principles to guide us or to evaluate our options. We have no options, and no choices to make!

Suppose, with Wright, that this deterministic view of history is false.[11] Instead, assume that the forms of social organization that we end up with are *in some part* the upshot of our agency. Then, in order to know what to choose—how to use our agency—we need standards by which to evaluate different institutional options. We need, in other words, what philosophers call an "ideal moral theory."[12]

Marxists have, historically, been uneasy with ideal moral theorizing. Sociologists, too, think that as scientists they are concerned simply with empirical matters. As *scientists*, they're right. But the scientists' task is only to interpret society. As *agents*, the point is to decide whether to change it and, if so, how.

And science cannot tell us what we should value. The chapters of *Envisioning* that engage in ideal moral theorizing have attracted less attention than the rest of the book.[13] But they are at the *center* of the RUP because, unless Wright is at least roughly right about the moral theory he adopts, he lacks (and we all lack) a normatively compelling critique of capitalism and, therefore, reasons even to seek, let alone to recommend, an alternative.

Disagreement about what really matters—about what is the correct ideal moral theory—is pervasive. So how could we know what is right? We have to engage in something like what the philosopher John Rawls calls "reflective equilibrium." The background assumption is that people

---

10   Wright, *Envisioning Real Utopias*; Gerald Allan Cohen, *Karl Marx's Theory of History: A Defence* (Princeton, NJ: Princeton University Press, 1978).

11   Wright, *Envisioning Real Utopias*.

12   Few Marxists persist in believing the deterministic theory of history. But some who have abandoned it do not appreciate just how significant that abandonment is.

13   Most of the direct moral theorizing is contained in chapters 2 and 3.

with different backgrounds, cultures, and experiences have different insights into, and different blind spots concerning, the truth about matters of value. We use our common human reason, in dialogue with one another, to identify contradictions and to critique and refine one another's claims and commitments. Principles and judgments that serve our interests or those of people we are close to, for example, or that reflect received opinion in our society, or are unstable, or that we have reason to suspect reflect cultural biases, are particular targets for scrutiny. They might survive the process, of course, but, like other survivors, only if the reasons offered in the process seem to support them better than conflicting alternatives. This may seem an uncertain and unsatisfactory process for addressing questions of value. It certainly does not guarantee the truth of the results, but neither does the scientific method guarantee the truth of its results. Reflective equilibrium is the best method we have—and it is what, in practice, people who are concerned with correctly judging matters of value do.[14]

It is worth noting that by any plausible outcome of that process, the prima facie case that capitalism *at its best* is better than anything else human beings have experienced so far seems quite strong. Denizens of the northern European social democracies generally have long, healthy lives; enjoy historically remarkable levels of material comfort; and experience far less material inequality, inequality of life prospects, and inequality of political power than in any other large-scale human societies in history. Capitalism appears to have brought us remarkable material wealth; high levels of leisure, art, and entertainment; enhanced communication; and, of course, the widespread availability of cleanliness and antibiotics, so that injuries (including almost all everyday injuries) and even the prospect of childbirth rarely prompt fear of mortality as they almost always did in the past.[15] The Soviet Union, its satellite countries in the Eastern Bloc, as well as the experience of China so far do not compare favorably with capitalism *on average*, let alone capitalism in its most benign forms. Ira Katznelson quotes Ralph Miliband writing about the Soviet bloc countries on the eve of their collapse:

---

14   See Norman Daniels, "Wide Reflective Equilibrium and Theory Acceptance in Ethics," *Journal of Philosophy* 76, no. 5 (1979): 256–82.

15   You can argue that government intervention was needed to ensure the timely manufacture of penicillin at scale during World War II. You'd be right. Capitalism at its best involves a good deal of government intervention.

The system entailed an extreme inflation of state power, and, corre-
spondingly, a stifling of all social forces not controlled by, and subser-
vient to, the leadership of the party/state ... The simple fact of the
matter [is] that capitalist democracy, for all its crippling limitations,
has been immeasurably less oppressive, and a lot more democratic,
than any communist regime.[16]

Given that, why should we seek, recommend, or demand something
other than capitalism?

Wright's critique begins with the claim that, despite capitalism's
remarkable productive capacity and, despite its superiority to other
alternatives that we have tried, it is nevertheless bad in eleven ways.[17]
Specifically, he argues:

- Capitalist class relations perpetuate eliminable forms of human
  suffering.
- Capitalism blocks the universalization of conditions for expansive
  human flourishing.
- Capitalism perpetuates eliminable deficits in individual freedom
  and autonomy.
- Capitalism violates liberal egalitarian principles of social justice.
- Capitalism is inefficient in certain crucial respects.
- Capitalism has a systematic bias towards consumerism.
- Capitalism is environmentally destructive.
- Capitalist commodification threatens important broadly [and,
  presumably, rightly] held values.
- Capitalism, in a world of nation-states, fuels militarism and
  imperialism.
- Capitalism corrodes community.
- Capitalism limits democracy.[18]

Wright calls these observations about capitalism "criticisms," but for reasons
that I'll explain later, I won't use that term for now. These observations are

16   Ira Katznelson, "Is Liberal Socialism Possible? Reflections on Real Utopias,"
Politics and Society 48, no. 4 (2020).
17   He could have articulated the very same ideas in more, or fewer, than eleven bullet
points. I assume eleven was a sophisticated pun, referencing Karl Marx rather than Spinal Tap.
18   Wright, *Envisioning Real Utopias*, 37.

specific ways in which capitalism is *bad*, so let's call them "bad-making features." The idea that these are bad-making features is connected to Wright's conception of justice,[19] which articulates standards according to which we can evaluate any social order:

> In a socially just society, all people would have broadly equal access to the necessary material and social means to live flourishing lives.
> … In a politically just society, all people would have broadly equal access to the necessary means to participate meaningfully in decisions about things which affect their lives. This includes both the freedom of individuals to make choices that affect their own lives as separate persons, and their capacity to participate in collective decisions which affect their lives as members of the broader community.[20]

Wright drew on a vast philosophical literature that engages with, defends, and elaborates the several elements of these standards.[21] Wright, like Marx, accepted a broadly Aristotelian theory in which human flourishing is constituted by active development and exercise of a diverse array of human capabilities, which can be multiply realized. Philosophers debate whether flourishing (understood as Wright did or otherwise) rather than, for example, material resources, should be what we measure when we think about distributive justice; personally, I think Wright is roughly right about this. They also debate whether equality, or equality of opportunity, or equal access, or some rule other than equality, should guide distribution for the purposes of justice. The phrase

---

19   Wright never makes the exact connection clear. In *How to Be an Anticapitalist in the Twenty-First Century*, he frames criticisms of capitalism just in terms of equality/ fairness, democracy/freedom, and community/solidarity, not mentioning either the eleven criticisms or the conception of justice. Erik Olin Wright, *How to Be an Anticapitalist in the Twenty-First Century* (London: Verso, 2019).

20   Wright, *Envisioning Real Utopias*, 12.

21   John Rawls, *A Theory of Justice*, 2nd ed. (Cambridge, MA: Belknap Press, 1999); Ronald Dworkin, "What Is Equality? Part 1: Equality of Welfare," *Philosophy and Public Affairs* 10, no. 3 (1981): 185–246; Ronald Dworkin, "What Is Equality? Part 2: Equality of Resources," *Philosophy and Public Affairs*, 10, no. 4 (1981): 283–345; Ingrid Robeyns, *Wellbeing, Freedom and Social Justice: The Capability Approach Re-examined* (Cambridge: Open Book Publishers, 2017); James Griffin, *Well-Being: Its Meaning, Measurement and Moral Importance* (Oxford: Oxford University Press, 1988); Richard J. Arneson, "Equality and Equal Opportunity for Welfare," *Philosophical Studies* 56, no. 1 (1989): 77–93.

"broadly equal access" glosses over these distinctions because Wright knew there was room for reasonable disagreement even among socialists, and thought that different reasonable answers might support different real utopian designs, all of which could belong in the socialist family.

Without *Viable* Real Utopias, You Can't Even *Critique* Capitalism

We need ideal moral standards if we want to make a moral evaluation of capitalism. Wright's claims about capitalism constitute a moral evaluation, as opposed to some empirical observations fancied up into pseudo-evaluative language, only because he has an ideal theory on which autonomy, freedom, democracy, and equality are good, and environmental destruction, militarism, and war are bad.[22] But, as David Estlund points out, much (though not all) of Wright's evaluation of capitalism "proceeds independently of complex questions about whether there are superior viable alternatives. Suppose there were no such alternatives. That would not change the facts about whether capitalism is environmentally destructive, fuels militarism, or limits democracy."[23]

Now I can explain my reluctance, earlier, to use the term "criticism" of Wright's claims about the bad-making features of capitalism. Having a moral theory allows us to *evaluate* something—that is, to make an estimate of how far and in what ways it falls short of some set of standards. But socialists want to do more than that. They think that the bad-making features of capitalism give us *sufficient reasons* to act against capitalism (at the right moment, in the right way) and replace it with socialism (whatever that is). A critique goes beyond evaluation and provides *reasons for action*. But recognizing capitalism's failure to fully realize justice is not enough on its own. In order for it to be a reason to act, there must be available to us superior alternatives that are viable in the sense that "if implemented, they would actually generate—in a sustainable, robust manner—the emancipatory consequences that motivated the proposal."[24] The superior alternatives would, Wright thought,

---

22   It's a more or less *true* ideal theory.
23   David Estlund, "A Little Bit Utopian?," *Crooked Timber* (blog), February 13, 2013.
24   Wright, *Envisioning Real Utopias*, 21.

fully instantiate the values he articulates. Given that he thinks those values *can* be fully realized and that we should act to realize them, he implicitly endorses the following principles of action:

- Social and economic institutions should be arranged so that all people would have broadly equal access to the necessary material and social means to live flourishing lives.

- Political institutions should be arranged so that all people would have broadly equal access to the necessary means to participate meaningfully in decisions about things which affect their lives, including freedom to make choices that affect their own lives as separate persons, and their capacity to participate in collective decisions which affect their lives as members of the broader community.

Why say that the *evaluation* of capitalism does not constitute a *critique* unless there's a superior viable alternative? Suppose that capitalism is the best we could do with respect to Wright's moral standards.[25] Then it might be reasonable to say that capitalism coexists with human suffering that we regret or would wish away if we could. But this would merely be a complaint about the human condition, not a distinctive criticism of capitalism, and certainly would give us no reason to seek to replace it. I might wish that I could run a three-minute mile in my bare feet. Suppose (very plausibly) that I routinely fail to run a three-minute mile in my bare feet. In that case we might put that down as a bad-making feature of life, but, given that doing so is impossible for any human being, let alone for me, nobody would think me *blameworthy*, or properly subject to criticism, for not doing it. Similarly, it is no criticism of capitalism that it does the eleven things cited in Wright's theses if no alternative system could do or could have done better. If there were no viable real utopias that could, unlike capitalism, instantiate the principles that Wright implicitly endorses, that would invalidate the principles themselves.

---

25 A couple of Wright's statements regarding bad-making features *presuppose* the replaceability of capitalism with something that would be better with respect to that bad-making feature. For example, if capitalism were the best we can do with respect to human suffering then, by definition, it would be false to say that it perpetuates eliminable forms of human suffering.

Why? Ideal standards can be valid without being fully implementable. Perhaps nobody could ever write the perfect novel, but having a set of standards of what a perfect novel would be like helps us evaluate actual novels and, perhaps, aids thought about how to write a very good, or even a great, novel, which some people *are* capable of doing.

But *principles* are different from *standards*. In order for a principle to be a good principle, one which actually gives us reason to act, it must be the case that we *could*, at least in some conditions, act on it. Think about how "ought" claims work at the individual level. I cannot run a mile in three minutes. I *cannot* do it; therefore, it is not the case that I *ought* to do it. Philosophers capture this idea with the slogan "ought implies can," which applies not only to individuals, but also to collectivities. Imagine five friends exploring a series of caves. A massive boulder suddenly falls to block the opening of one cave, trapping one friend inside. The boulder is so massive that it would take the strength of forty people to shift it. No four people, however strong, could do it. They are certainly obliged to try to help their friend—perhaps by searching for another thirty-six people, by looking for explosives, or by pushing food supplies through a tiny crack. But they are not obliged to shift the rock with their bare hands because that is something that they simply could not do. The principle "friends should move outsized rocks in circumstances like these" is invalid.

So if no viable real utopia can realize the values that Wright's two principles embody (that is, if nothing passes scrutiny in the RUP), then those principles are not even valid. They do not describe our obligations because they are calling on us to do something that we just could not (even collectively) do. If "ought implies can," then it is also true that '*cannot* implies *not* ought'. In order even to know whether his principles are valid, we need to know whether institutional forms are available that could realize them.

Without *Achievable* Real Utopias, You Can't *Oppose* Capitalism

Now suppose that we have reason for confidence in our principles. Then we have a critique. But the moral and prudential force of that critique is very weak indeed unless a superior alternative is actually achievable from where we stand. Suppose, for example, that the historical moment in which a viable alternative could have been implemented has passed because the existence of a very large industrial and urban proletariat was essential for their achievability. The critique of capitalism supplies *no reason at all to supersede it* in that case, because, despite the alternative's viability, it is not, in fact, achievable.

Wright says:

> Achievability is not really a simple dichotomy between the achievable and the unachievable; different projects of institutional transformation have different prospects of ever being implemented. The probability that any given alternative to existing social structures and institutions could be implemented sometime in the future depends upon two kinds of processes. First it depends upon the *consciously pursued strategies* and the *relative power* of social actors who support and oppose the alternative in question . . . Second . . . it depends upon the trajectory over time of a wide range of *social structural conditions* that affect the possibilities of success of these strategies.[26]

So achievability is probabilistic. And the normative force of a recommendation is sensitive to how achievable it is when it would be carried out, and what the costs of achieving it would be. Let me illustrate.

Consider the case in which the prospects for achieving socialism are poor though not negligible. The critique does supply reasons to enact it, but those reasons are weak, and the reasons we have to pursue improvements in capitalism instead might easily outweigh them. Consider the runner who *might* be able to shave seventy-five seconds off his time if he took the recommended steps. But suppose those steps would elevate the risk of an injury that would worsen his time. Then he has a reason not to take them, and depending on the probabilities, that reason might outweigh his reason to follow the recommendations. Or, maybe, he'd be better advised to take different steps that might shave forty seconds off his time at an only slightly elevated risk of injury.

Now consider the fortuitous case, which we hope in fact pertains, in which the prospects are good, and the costs are low. Then the normative force of the reasons to enact it are strong and more easily outweigh whatever reasons there are to refrain. The increased risk of injury is tiny,

---

26 Wright, *Envisioning Real Utopias*, 24–5.

the increased effort is small, and the likelihood of the seventy-five-second gain is very high.

So the strength of the reasons to enact socialism vary with the prospects for, and the costs of, achieving it. They also depend on *whether we know how* to enact it. Consider a coach saying, "Shave seventy-five seconds off your time." If she tells the runner how he could have trained better, specifies which exercises would have improved performance, explains the ways in which he deviated from the prescribed diet and training regime, and points out certain readily achievable technical adjustments to his form, the critique has considerable force because he knows how to enact the advice. If she says, "Well, you just *could*," she does not provide any reason at all for action because the agent does not know what steps to take. Think of a doctor in 1850 whose patient has cancer. Not only does the doctor not know how to cure cancer, he doesn't even know how to *try* to cure cancer. So even if it were true, at that time, that he *ought* to cure cancer, that would not provide any reasons for action on his part nor would it ground any serious kind of critique of him or the prevailing health care arrangements.[27]

It is very striking that the values Wright invokes when articulating the bad-making features of capitalism are not very controversial.[28] Most non-socialists value community, efficiency, human flourishing, freedom, autonomy, and democracy. The task of socialists is not, in general, to convince people that they should change what they value but to convince people that these widely shared values support principles of action and that those principles support replacing capitalism with socialism. What the RUP gives us, if some designs survive its scrutiny, are reasons to believe that the principles are valid, reasons to believe that socialism is viable and achievable, and steps that we can take, practically, to enact it. Without the RUP or something like it, we are in much the same situation as our ignorant runner and our 1850s doctor. We don't know how to do what we think would be desirable if it were achievable, or even whether it is achievable, and therefore whether we should even be socialists. If *no* designs survive the RUP's scrutiny, we have reasons to be pessimistic about the prospects for socialism that are, in turn, reasons to act in other ways.

---

27 Other considerations or principles might ground a critique. But not this one.
28 Thanks to Gay Seidman for helping me see why this matters.

Actually Existing Real Utopian Designs

Leo Panitch accuses Wright of subjecting some of his preferred, actually implemented designs to insufficient scrutiny. Of the Porto Alegre participatory budgeting process, Panitch observes that

> the consensual community identity, which had initially concentrated these basic demands around street paving and sanitation, had already by 1992 begun to fray in the face of challenges by the proprietors of unused private land where poor people had "illegally" established favelas, which made it impossible to invest in street paving and sanitation under existing law.[29]

And, of the Quebec social economy, he says:

> This so-called social economy pertained only to a very small part of the Quebec economy, even insofar as this was conceived to include the capital investment pension Solidarity Fund of the Quebec Federation of Labour, which Envisioning Real Utopias also championed. Moreover, established as it was in the wake of a series of severe defeats imposed through coercive legislation on the very public sector trade unions who were the mean social base of the social democratic Parti Quebecois, the Chantier exercise from the beginning was directly associated with the implementation of fiscal austerity and social service cuts.[30]

I don't know enough about the particular cases to adjudicate if Panitch's negative judgments of them are fair. Wright possessed, as Panitch indicates in the title of his paper, optimism of both the intellect and the will.[31] He saw the best in *people*, and his disposition in observing *institutions* was to reflect on the mechanisms that gave cause for optimism. But we should be clear-eyed, rather than unduly optimistic, in our analyses of actually existing designs: indeed, one might argue that, given the history of Marxism in power, we should

---

29 Panitch, "Erik Olin Wright's Optimism of the Intellect," 46.
30 Ibid., 48.
31 I shared neither affliction with him.

exercise an abundance of caution. Panitch's bleaker take is an important corrective.

Having said that, even if Panitch's more pessimistic judgments are
correct, the fracturing and/or failure of some design *in a hostile environment* does not always mean that it is not viable in the relevant
sense. It doesn't even mean that it, or something like it, should not be
recommended. Consider the running example again. Perhaps there is
some reason that I ought to run a mile in ten minutes (just about
realistic for me). If the course is entirely uphill, uneven, and muddy,
and I'd be running against the wind, my failure to run a ten-minute
mile *in those conditions* is not evidence that I could not do it on a flat,
dry, even course on a still day. Depending on how well or badly I do,
and the ways in which I do well or badly, you might judge that I could
run a ten-minute mile on a muddy and uneven course as long as the
wind was not against me. Or at least on a flat, dry course on a calm
day. My failure is not even evidence that you should not recommend
me to someone who needs a ten-minute-mile runner.[32] If the specific
problems that Panitch notes emanate from interaction with a hostile
environment, then they do not require us to take those designs off the
menu. Although it must always be alert to the dangers of wishful
thinking and over-optimism, the RUP is fundamentally interested in
how a design would operate within a reasonably favorable institutional ecosystem.

What Is Socialism?

A century ago, socialists thought that they understood what socialism
was. The state would own and control the means of production. The
experiences of the Soviet bloc in the east of Europe, those of national-
ized industries in the West, and the ideas of the New Left in the postwar
period shook belief that state ownership and control is either necessary
or sufficient for socialism.[33] So what does socialism mean? And what
makes something anticapitalist?

---

32 Entirely compelling evidence that you should *not* recommend me is available
on request.

33 Wright, *Envisioning Real Utopias*, 131–4.

Dylan Riley criticizes Wright: "What is the purpose of re-describing the socialist project in terms that confusingly equate it with a variety of patently non-socialist institutions and outcomes, just because these seem to be in some way tangible? . . . Re-describing present-day institutions as if they were 'partly socialist' has only a soporific function."[34] Elsewhere he says:

> In extracting the "principles" of Wikipedia, participatory budgeting, Mondragon or the university, they are in fact proceeding in a highly abstract way. For "actually existing" institutions "actually exist" in capitalist society, and *their capitalist or anticapitalist character is determined by their relationship to the whole of which they are a part. It can only be determined by putting them in the context of capitalist society, and asking whether they serve to reproduce that society or not.* The attempt to define a "real utopia," however specified, in abstraction from a notion of society as a whole, faces intractable methodological difficulties.[35]

And:

> An analogy may clarify the problem. Calling an organization "anticapitalist" just because it isn't oriented toward profitability or doesn't run on market principles is a bit like calling orange peel "anti-orangist" because it is oily and bitter, as opposed to juicy and sweet. The mistake is to isolate the parts whose relationship constitutes the thing one refers to as "an orange," whose bitter peel protects the juicy flesh . . . The Basque Country's Mondragon cooperative network, though imbued with social-Catholic values, became a capitalist firm (with a somewhat peculiar structure) through the compulsion of the market. Participatory budgeting in Porto Alegre soon became a matter of achieving democratic popular consent for limited municipal budgets. Wikipedia, conceived by the Ayn Randian Jimmy Wales, successfully mobilizes unpaid labour to provide a public good, but can hardly be said to pose a threat to capitalist property relations.[36]

---

34 Riley, "Real Utopia or Abstract Empiricism?," 107.
35 Ibid., 101,.
36 Ibid., 101–2.

Here's a possible explanation why Wright might (perhaps confusingly) have applied the terms "socialist" and "anticapitalist" to certain actually existing institutions. One core value Wright identifies concerns the organization of power relations: in a just society, power over how we live our personal lives (individual freedom) and over how we live together (social power) would be roughly equally distributed. We'd have a very robust and egalitarian liberal democracy.[37] Wright's proposal is that we understand socialism as a "way of organizing the power relations through which economic resources are allocated, controlled, and used," in contrast with the ways that statism and capitalism organize social power.[38] The proposal fits nicely with the practice of many movements that have identified as socialist, and with the rhetoric (if not the practice) of many more such movements. And it represents an empirical judgment that the organization of social power relations (in contrast with, say, personal transformation) is the key to achieving justice. When selecting designs to scrutinize, we seek designs with more, rather than fewer, egalitarian power relations. The Roman Catholic Church and NFL look unpromising; Mondragon seems a better bet. Wikipedia, though not a threat to capitalist property relations, might also be worth serious scrutiny. We are not looking for threats; we are looking for whatever has promise.[39]

Riley is right that this way of going about things isolates designs from their contexts. But if we're in the business of working out what

---

37   In a very puzzling passage Riley says that his own rational redistribution "specification . . . gives a much clearer foundation to the connection between socialism and democracy than that offered by Wright. It is not that there are two demands: democracy and socialism. The point would be, instead, that socialism as a system of rational redistribution can only exist in a highly democratic context." (Riley, "Neo-Tocquevillian Marxism," 377–8). This comment, to me, seems to get things almost exactly the wrong way round. Riley, in fact, is the one making two separate demands. Democracy is one demand, and socialism is another, and the first is merely *instrumental for* the second. Wright, by contrast, thinks that democracy is valuable in itself, and is a central *constituent of* (so not merely instrumental for) socialism, because it is *part of* justice that "all people would have broadly equal access to the necessary means to participate meaningfully in decisions about things which affect their lives. This includes . . . their capacity to participate in collective decisions which affect their lives as members of the broader community." Democracy, for Wright, is not the precondition for, or the best way to ensure, a certain desired redistributive outcome, but is, itself, part of what we should be aiming for.

38   Wright, *Envisioning Real Utopias*, 111.

39   Thanks to David O'Brien for this observation.

to recommend and whether to recommend it, I don't see any other way to proceed. A natural way of reading the italicized comments in the above quote seems to be that we can only judge a design socialist if it is already a working component of an ecosystem of existing institutions that, together, meet socialist goals. If so, we can never judge a design as socialist until we already have socialism; indeed, if we take Riley's orangist analogy seriously enough, we couldn't judge a design socialist until we had *worldwide* socialism. To not know whether a design is worth recommending until socialism has been enacted might be entirely satisfactory if we are just sociologists.[40] It is much less so if we are activists, trying to win the hearts and minds of the people whose commitment and sacrifice is essential for the transformation.

The RUP might not work if the institutions of contemporary capitalism were relevantly like the components of an orange. All the things you find in an orange, Riley seems to assume, are both essential constituents of the orange and essentially orangist.[41] But Wright believed—and I think rightly—that not all the things you find in capitalism are essential to capitalism, or are essentially capitalist. Capitalism has room for irritant institutions, some of them hard won through political struggle, others simply testaments to human creativity and generosity, individual and collective. Its ecology combines different elements, some of which are at odds with others. It hampers, but does not eliminate, alternatives. If capitalism were monolithic, then we could hope (in vain, unfortunately) that the crudely determinist theory of history discussed earlier is true. In that case, though, we would have no agency, so recommending socialism would be pointless, and not only because we could have no way of knowing what we were recommending.

Riley's preferred definition of socialism is "a system of rational redistribution in which the allocation of the social surplus is allocated through substantive rationality," and he interprets "substantive rationality" to involve a process that operates "not behind the backs of social actors, but according to agreements based on public discussions governed by rules of rational critical discourse."[42] Suppose this is a good definition of

---

40 I'm not *even* a sociologist.
41 I don't know enough about oranges to have an opinion, myself.
42 Riley, "Neo-Tocquevillian Marxism," 377.

socialism.[43] Recommending it is analogous to saying, "Eat better and train harder." It's *something*. But the correspondent would be foolish not to ask, "Just *what* should I be adding to and cutting from my diet, and *what* exercises should I be adding to and dropping from my exercise regime; and what reasons can you give me for thinking that these changes will lead to improvement?" Analogously: "Just what exactly are the rules of rational critical discourse, how will they be enforced, and how will a more just society be sustained?" If you answer with the level of detail that respectful rational discourse requires, you're explaining what socialism is. You're engaging in the RUP, whether you realize it or not.

The Unmysterious Absence of Class Analysis

In his wonderful article commemorating Wright and celebrating his work, Michael Burawoy recognizes the two major projects of Wright's career and describes him as shifting "t."[44] David Ruccio asks, "What happened to class analysis? After introducing it in chapter 3 it seems to drop out of the book, until his return to the issue of working-class politics toward the end."[45] Riley thinks that the neglect of class in *Envisioning* is a "major and highly paradoxical (given its author) flaw," leading, among other things, to a "radically incomplete conceptualization of socialism."[46]

Class analysis is not relevant to the task at hand. I've asked you to see the RUP as principally about establishing what values we should use for evaluation, what principles should guide us in scrutinizing designs that contribute to realizing those values. Establishing values and principles are fundamentally philosophical tasks. The scrutiny component requires empirical engagement, but given Wright's answers to those philosophical questions, which require the elimination of class distinctions, any successful design will not contain or allow for class distinctions. So we do not need to consider class analysis when assessing a design's viability.

---

43   It isn't.
44   Michael Burawoy, chapter 1 of this volume, "A Tale of Two Marxisms," p. 17.
45   Ruccio, "Review of *Envisioning Real Utopias*," 255.
46   Riley, "Neo-Tocquevillian Marxism," 376.

Class analysis *is* pertinent to understanding capitalism, and understanding *our* capitalism *here and now*, in turn, is essential for establishing which, among the (perhaps small) number of viable designs, are sufficiently attainable to be worth recommending. This is why class analysis does recur in the parts of *Envisioning* that are about strategies for transforming society, the part of the book that I have invited you to consider not part of the RUP, strictly speaking. Wright knew what tools were appropriate to which tasks.

Conclusion: A Defense of Blueprints

Like many Marxists, Wright resisted the language of blueprints. He says: "Particularly in the Marxist tradition, radical intellectuals have insisted that wholesale redesign of social institutions is within the grasp of human beings. This does not mean, as Marx emphasized, that detailed institutional blueprints can be devised in advance of the opportunity to create an alternative."[47]

In deference to Wright I have avoided the term "blueprint." But I think the RUP is a process of . . . well, scrutinizing blueprints. Socialists who think they have no obligation to offer real, practicable designs thereby evince disdain for those whom they are inviting to make commitments and sacrifices and to take the risk that everything goes wrong. As Wright says, "Vague utopian fantasies may lead us astray, encouraging us to embark on trips that have no real destinations at all, or, worse still, which lead us towards some unforeseen abyss."[48] If they are not offered a blueprint, how can anyone judge whether those commitments, sacrifices, and risks are worth taking? You wouldn't ask to redesign someone's house, still less ask them to pay for it, and still less to risk their lives for it, without offering a blueprint. "Trust me, we'll work it out together," or, worse, "Trust me, *you'll* work it out," or "Trust me, *I'll* work it out," sound like empty promises at best and attempts to disguise a hidden agenda at worst. Basic respect requires one to offer up for consideration, scrutiny, revision, or rejection a proposal that they have already diligently scrutinized themselves. If any designs pass

---

47   Wright, *Envisioning Real Utopias*, 7.
48   Ibid., 6.

muster in something like the RUP, the approach socialists should take is to say: "We've drafted a blueprint. We've worked hard on it, using the expertise available to us, and we think there's a good chance it will work to realize the values we share. You can reject the blueprint. Maybe you have a better one. Let's compare them! And of course, if you accept ours, it's not written in stone, any more than yours if that's the one we settle on. They're *blueprints*, not commandments. We'll work, together, on revisions, so that we can make the house we share the best it can be, as we build it together."

The riskier and costlier the transition, and the less detailed and well-scrutinized the blueprint, the more disdainful the offer. Coincidentally (and fortunately), the less likely it is to win support. Who knows if there will be second chances if we get it wrong next time? Especially if—as experience has shown is possible—we get it catastrophically wrong.

If you're a socialist you need the Real Utopias Project, whether you like it or not.

6

Class Counts for Real Utopias: The Implementation of Free Mass Transit in Seven Brazilian Cities
João Alexandre Peschanski

My doctoral research was partially inspired by a single sentence from *American Society: How It Really Works*, a book Erik Olin Wright coauthored with Joel Rogers. The book was mandatory reading for undergraduates enrolled in SOC 125: Contemporary American Society, for which I was a teaching assistant in 2010 under Erik's supervision. In chapter 6, Erik and Rogers write, "[Mass transit] rides could be free because even with free tickets, the sum of all the positive externalities is likely to exceed the financial costs of building and running a comprehensive public transportation system."[1] This sentence is, as far as I know, the first scholarly mention Erik had ever made regarding free mass transit, and it fascinated me.

Mobility was not explicitly within the scope of the original *Envisioning Real Utopias* research agenda, even though the topic became increasingly relevant as Erik moved this agenda forward. For instance, in *How to Be an Anticapitalist in the Twenty-First Century*, he expanded on his

An initial version of this work was presented at the IV ISA Forum of Sociology, February 2021. Parts of this work rely directly on my unpublished PhD dissertation: "Free Fare, a Real Utopia," University of Wisconsin–Madison, Department of Sociology, 2019. My research was supported by a University of Wisconsin–Madison Graduate Fellowship, the Faculdade Cásper Líbero Interdisciplinary Research Center Fellowship (2020), and the São Paulo Research Foundation Grant 2013/07699-0.

1 Erik Olin Wright and Joel Rogers, *American Society: How It Really Works* (New York: W. W. Norton, 2010), 101.

argument from 2010, mentioning free mass transit as an example of a nonmarket economic organization (chapter 4). Mobility was not part of my research agenda either, as my early work as a graduate student with Erik at the University of Wisconsin–Madison focused on the developmental state and class dynamics during the Brazilian military dictatorship. Yet, the idea that we could envision a fee-free transportation model strongly resonated with me and would come up as a discussion topic in several informal meetings with my adviser over the years.

In 2011, I wrote an op-ed called "Economic Reasons for Free Public Transportation" for the Brazilian weekly *Brasil de Fato*, building upon the argument from that excerpt in *American Society*.[2] Erik included a presentation on free mass transit at the 2012 American Sociological Association's Annual Meeting, whose theme was "Real Utopias: Emancipatory Projects, Institutional Designs, Possible Futures."[3] The session—called "Post-fossil Conversation and Free Public Transport"— was led by Mario Candeias from the Rosa Luxemburg Foundation.

Then, something that would have been hard to predict happened: in 2013, a national mass movement erupted in Brazil with a specific call for "free mass transit." In the context of simultaneous transport fare increases in several municipalities, especially São Paulo, the Free-Fare Movement (Movimento Passe Livre, or MPL) called for and organized the first demonstrations of this increasingly contentious period, not only reacting to fare increases, but also putting the possibility of a free public transportation system on the political agenda. The op-ed that I wrote in 2011, sparked by Erik's sociology, was massively circulated on the internet and included as background reading on the Free-Fare Movement's website. A revised version was included later that year in the book *Rebel Cities: Free Fare and the Protests That Took Over the Streets of Brazil*, which sold over fifty thousand copies, and I published two scholarly pieces on the topic.[4] At this point, Erik convinced me I

2 João Alexandre Peschanski, "Motivos econômicos pelo transporte público gratuito," *Brasil de Fato*, July 15, 2011.

3 "Real Utopias: Emancipatory Projects, Institutional Designs, Possible Futures," 107th Annual Meeting of the American Sociological Association, Denver, Colorado, August 17–20, 2012, asanet.org/sites/default/files/2012_am_final_program_c_optimized.pdf.

4 João Alexandre Peschanski and Renato Moraes, "Os protestos de junho e a agenda propositiva: Um argumento teórico," *Lutas Sociais* 17, no. 31 (2013): 111–24; and Peschanski, "El pase libre en Brasil y la Sociología de las Posibilidades," in *Demodiversidad:*

should change the topic of my dissertation and investigate free mass transit instead, which I eventually did.

I defended my dissertation, "Free Fare, a Real Utopia," in September 2019, with Gay Seidman as my official adviser and Erik in my heart. Erik had passed away eight months earlier and had only read the theoretical framework and one of the cases I investigated. Erik and I had planned to work on a volume on free public transportation for the Real Utopias Project; we saw it as part of a socialist agenda and as a contrast to the devastating Uberization model.

At the time I finished my dissertation, there was widespread hopelessness on the Brazilian left. The country had shifted from experiencing growing prosperity and social security in the 2000s and early 2010s to facing hastily declining socioeconomic security and emerging anti-democratic discourses and practices. The election of right-wing extremist Jair Bolsonaro as Brazil's president in 2018 accentuated the emergence of dystopian processes in Brazil and made me feel that the genuine goal of my work—to explore a real utopia!—was, to say the least, misplaced.

On January 8, 2019, I spoke to Erik for the last time. My dear friend Tatiana Alfonso Sierra paid him a visit and connected us. At some point, Erik asked me what I thought about writing my thesis in the current Brazilian context. He listened to my answer and replied, "Finish the thing!" It is when hope is scarcest that we need real utopias the most.

Free Mass Transit *Is* a Real Utopia

Free fare, or free mass transit, is a relatively simple policy: the provision of public transportation services in a given community without collecting fares. Obviously, no transportation system is cost-free—some mechanism of social payment must in the end cover at least the operational costs—but what is free is access to transport. The prevailing definition in the literature encompasses transportation systems that adopt free access to public transportation at all times or at specific times (i.e., off-peak or

Imaginar nuevas posibilidades democráticas, ed. Boaventura de Sousa Santos and José Manuel Mendes (Madrid: Ediciones AKAL, 2017).

weekends). Systems that provide free access to specific demographic groups—the elderly, students, public employees—are not considered free-fare systems, since these are exceptions in a system in which user fees are collected and where in many cases these benefits are cross-subsidized by overpricing fares for other riders. "Full free fare" refers to a system where there is no user-fee collection—in a public transport vehicle or any other space, such as a station or a platform before or after boarding.[5] My research only focused on full free fare.

The viability of a free-fare proposal must take into consideration an understanding of costs and benefits, unintended consequences, and medium- and long-term dynamics of institutional implementation. Skeptics have claimed that free fare is a fantasy. For instance, Fernando Haddad, a social scientist, Workers' Party intellectual, and São Paulo's mayor during the 2013 Free-Fare Movement protests, told the press that it would be easier to ensure free trips to Disney World for all citizens. However, by 2018, a free-fare system had been implemented in more than a hundred cities in the world.

From a theoretical perspective, the total price of the free-fare proposal might be justified if the positive social impacts serve as the rationale for funding the mass transportation system. The social impacts are especially salient if the free-fare model is implemented alongside policies that strongly limit the use of individual cars, with positive impacts including the drastic reduction of pollution and traffic and related social costs. This approach is especially relevant for large cities, where social problems associated with dependance on individual car use exist on a larger scale. Air pollution and excessive noise are public health problems and thus generate medical costs for citizens and the state.[6] Other expenses related to the private transport mode include maintaining a network of traffic inspectors to organize cities with heavy traffic; the hospital costs associated with traffic accidents, a major cause of public hospitalization in Brazil, as well as respiratory diseases, which are partially caused by pollution from high individual car use; and the loss

5 Joel Volinski, *TCRP Synthesis 101: Implementation and Outcomes of Fare-Free Transit Systems* (Washington, DC: Transportation Research Board, 2012).

6 Qi Zhao et al., "Trends in Hospital Admission Rates and Associated Direct Healthcare Costs in Brazil: A Nationwide Retrospective Study between 2000 and 2015," *Innovation* 1, no. 1 (2020): 100013.

of productive time to traffic jams.[7] These expenses are covered by citizens and the state, especially in cases where automakers systematically externalize the social problems that their products generate. The core theoretical justification of the free-fare proposal is that mobility should be considered a political good, which in the aggregate directly and indirectly contributes to social welfare.[8]

Public transportation ought to be understood as a public good that benefits even those who do not rely on mass transit. It benefits all of society, since it lowers the negative impacts associated with transportation (pollution and traffic). From this perspective, to charge for the use of mass transit might be understood as an economic injustice: though the service benefits everyone, only the users pay for it. In a certain sense, to charge for the use of public transportation becomes a form of exploitation of the users by the nonusers. Costs associated with a system of public transportation should thus be shared by all who benefit from it— they should be divided up among all citizens.

I understand the implementation of free fare as a potential step toward socialism. This bold statement relates to at least two major research directions around alternatives to capitalism in the twenty-first century. First, there has been a renewal of sociological thinking about alternatives in the last fifteen years or so. At least two independent initiatives in this revitalization are worth mentioning. One, led by Boaventura de Sousa Santos, is currently organized as the research project ALICE. On the project's fundamental premise, Sousa Santos explains, "Alternatives are not lacking in the world . . . What is indeed missing is an alternative thinking of alternatives."[9] This project has been developing a new sociological epistemology, advancing alternative institutions influenced by traditions and practices of the global South. A second initiative, led by Erik, has been called the Real Utopias Project.[10] This is mostly a theory-driven project aimed at providing

---

7   Guilherme Szczerbacki Besserman Vianna and Carlos Eduardo Frickman Young, "Em busca do tempo perdido: Uma estimativa do produto perdido em trânsito no Brasil," *Revista de Economia Contemporânea* 19 (2015): 403–16.

8   Derek Galey, "License to Ride: Free Public Transportation for Residents of Tallinn," *Critical Planning* 21, no. 1 (2014): 19–33.

9   Boaventura de Sousa Santos, *Democratizing Democracy: Beyond the Liberal Democratic Canon* (New York: Verso, 2005).

10   Erik Olin Wright, "Preface: The Real Utopias Project," in Archon Fung and Erik Olin Wright, *Deepening Democracy: Institutional Innovations in Empowered Participatory*

a renewed understanding of social power in political and economic configurations. Both initiatives shift our attention away from the grand narrative of the alternative to the dominant system of social relationships, instead exploring possibilities of socially grounded institutional innovations.

To investigate institutional alternatives, such as the free-fare proposal, implies the development of a sociology of possibilities. The description and diagnosis of the functioning and consequences of social norms are necessary tasks for a science of social emancipation; not to envision an alternative could lead sociology to a dead end. Without a developed account of possibilities, the best one can hope for is the improvement of institutions within the constraints of the existing social order; otherwise, the capacity and opportunity to develop a better alternative can only occur once the dominant system of relationships is undone. Although the latter approach has characterized most classic emancipatory traditions in the social sciences, the idea that "after the revolution" people would be able to transform principles into concrete social and economic institutions consciously and without much difficulty seems implausible.

Second, an emergent body of literature on what Erik's student David Calnitsky has termed the "policy road to socialism" reconsiders the role of the state in non-ruptural strategies for moving beyond capitalism.[11] This literature has revived to some extent classical discussions about the role of incremental, or reformist, changes in broader transformation agendas. It has also highlighted the investigation of criteria that might be used to assess whether policies are moving toward alternative social relationships. A critical assessment of an alternative institution's emancipatory potential depends on gauging its potential compatibility with other alternative institutions and whether it is reproducible in a general alternative system of social relationships.

To assess the desirability of alternative institutions in his renewed socialist agenda, Erik introduced the idea of measuring the institutions according to moral principles, especially equality, democracy, and

---

Governance (New York: Verso, 2003); Erik Olin Wright, *Envisioning Real Utopias* (New York: Verso, 2010).

11   David Calnitsky, "The Policy Road to Socialism," *Critical Sociology* 48, no. 3 (2021): 397–422.

sustainability.[12] He broadly defines equality as a pillar of social justice: "In a socially just society, all people would have broadly equal access to the social and material conditions necessary for living a flourishing life." The principle of democracy is framed in terms of deep democracy: "In a fully democratic society, all people would have broadly equal access to the necessary means to participate meaningfully in decisions about things that affect their lives." Sustainability, from Erik's perspective, relates to the assertion that "future generations should have access to the social and material conditions to live flourishing lives at least at the same level as the present generation." With less emphasis, he also mentions other principles, such as freedom, community, and solidarity.

Mobility is the key normative element in assessing free-fare policies. It involves the circulation of people, objects, and information. A simple definition emphasizes the process of circulation as moving from one location to another and the meaning people assign to that movement.[13] On the one hand, this definition emphasizes the production of mobilities (the social process by which moving and its meanings are constituted within and by power dynamics) that structure and influence social processes. This emphasis is on the material conditions and implications of mobility. It is worth noting that *not* moving around is also an element of this definition of mobility, as the notion of community normally involves settling in a particular space for the purposes of interaction and mutual connection. On the other hand, this definition of mobility also pertains to subjective expectations and strategies where a person's identity is influenced by their understanding of space and movement. This understanding is affected by how technologies of mobility and communication evolve and by their impact on how an individual connects to other people or travels to other places unimpeded by how far away they are. The definition of mobility that I rely on is closely related to Erik's understanding of social justice, in terms of mobility's importance for providing access to the conditions for living a flourishing life.

12 Erik Olin Wright, "Transforming Capitalism through Real Utopias," *American Sociological Review* 78, no. 1 (2013): 1–25.
13 Tim Cresswell, "The Right to Mobility: The Production of Mobility in the Courtroom," *Antipode* 38, no. 4 (2006): 736–54; Vincent Kaufmann, *Les paradoxes de la mobilité: Bouger, s'enraciner* (Lausanne, Switzerland: Presses polytechniques et universitaires romandes, 2008); John Urry, *Mobilities* (Cambridge: Polity, 2007).

To think of free mass transit as a step toward socialism or, in Wright's language, as a real utopia makes sense as long as the policy being proposed or implemented is rooted in a system of moral values linked to an emancipatory social science normative agenda. However, to claim that free fare is a real utopia may be controversial—as are most, if not all, public-good-grounded real utopias—since free fare is nonetheless compatible with and functional to the reproduction of the dominant system of social relationships. I will assume—as Erik would probably have said—that free fare is at least a "way station," an intermediate step toward a real utopia, as it embodies the principles of larger institutional innovation and helps us move in that direction.

Viable Implementation

Since the 1960s, proponents of the idea of public transportation as a public good have defended free-fare proposals.[14] The proposal gained momentum because in that decade, the volume of public subsidies to sustain systems of public transportation grew. In the United States, federal subsidies increased through the 1960s; in the 1970s, the National Mass Transportation Assistance Act authorized partial free-fare experiments in two medium-sized cities, Denver, Colorado, and Trenton, New Jersey. These experiments lasted for about a year between 1978 and 1979 and were implemented only during off-peak hours. Results in the two cities were similar: there were many new passengers, no significant impact on the number of circulating cars, and increasing degradation of the quality and security of the public service.[15] An independent experiment was set up in Austin, Texas, for fifteen months between 1989 and 1990, with similar results.[16] These experiments were the object of strong methodological critiques,[17] yet free-fare detractors used the experiments'

---

14   A. H. Studenmund and David Connor, "The Free-Fare Transit Experiments," *Transportation Research Part A* 16, no. 4 (1982): 261–9.

15   James D. Orrell, David C. Hodge, and Tim R. Strauss, *Fare-Free Policy: Costs, Impacts on Transit Service, and Attainment of Transit System Goals; Final Report* (Olympia: Washington State Department of Transportation, 1994); Jennifer Perone and Joel Volinski, *Fare, Free, or Something in Between* (Tampa: Center for Urban Transportation Research, University of South Florida, 2003).

16   Volinski, *TCRP Synthesis 101*.

17   Orrell, Hodge, and Strauss, *Fare-Free Policy Costs*.

results to describe the proposal as non viable. For several decades free mass transit had little resonance, especially in developed countries.

In the twenty-first century, in the context of increasing environmental concerns about the universal dependence on individual automobiles, discussion about the free-fare model has experienced a resurgence, now with a stronger environmental focus. Contemporary defenses stress the need to simultaneously make the public transportation system free and to limit the use of cars, especially those with only one occupant. Many of the benefits of establishing a free-fare system won't be realized unless there is a decline in car usage and culture (which in turn depends on disincentives to drivers or even banning cars from city areas) and investing in anti-consumerist environmental literacy, as well as on the implementation of a high-quality public transportation system in which people can also enjoy the ride as a leisure activity. Price sensitivity for public transportation is lower in the case of "exclusive users"—that is, people who depend fully on collective transportation, such as youth, the elderly, and the disabled. Even if the fee for mass transit is low, users are unlikely to use it if they have the choice of driving their own car. This group of potential users is more sensitive to the improvement of service quality and increased costs associated with owning and driving a car, such as gas and parking.[18]

Free public transportation is already implemented in some places. In 2018, it existed in at least 112 cities, largely in the wealthiest parts of the world. What we know from programs in Europe and North America is that they are more likely to emerge in college towns, winter sports resorts, and small towns with large rural areas.[19] In larger cities, the transition from a fee-based to a free transportation system is normally influenced by the level of public subsidies for mass transit and by broader efforts to reduce car circulation in downtown areas.

In Europe, free-fare systems have been implemented in several cities since the late 1990s. Hasselt, a town of seventy thousand inhabitants in Belgium an hour away from Brussels, implemented the system in July 1997 in response to an increased urban population and large

18   Todd Litman, "Transit Price Elasticities and Cross-Elasticities," *Journal of Public Transportation* 7, no. 2 (2004): 37–58; Cynthia Chen, Don Varley, and Jason Chen, "What Affects Transit Ridership? A Dynamic Analysis Involving Multiple Factors, Lags and Asymmetric Behaviour," *Urban Studies* 48, no. 19 (2010): 1893–1908.

19   Volinski, *TCRP Synthesis 101.*

investments to improve urban life. Immediately after the implementation of free fare, the number of mass transit users grew by 900 percent;
it continued to grow, reaching a total increase of 1,300 percent by 2013.
The operational costs of such a large mass transit system increased four
times in less than twenty years and led to a temporary interruption of
free fare in 2013.[20] In 1997, Templin, a small health resort of fourteen
thousand residents in western Germany, about a hundred kilometers
from Berlin, adopted a free public transportation model with the initial
goal of reducing automobile use. Ridership increased 750 percent in the
first year and even more in the second year, but only 10–20 percent of
these new riders were car users. The largest contingent was composed of
pedestrians and cyclists, which brought a secondary benefit: by reducing the size of these vulnerable groups—at least in a car-dominated society—the number of traffic accidents dropped.[21] In 2009, Aubagne, a
French city of one hundred thousand residents seventeen kilometers
outside Marseille, also implemented a free-fare system. Ridership
increased 142 percent between 2009 and 2012, and there was a 10
percent reduction in the number of cars.[22]

The most studied free-fare case is Tallinn, the capital of Estonia,
which implemented a free-fare model in January 2013. The implementation of the system did not lead to a significant increase of bus riders.[23]
However, in Lasnamäe, the poorest region of the city predominantly
inhabited by Russian immigrants and marked by high levels of unemployment, ridership increased 10 percent. Before implementation, the
public transit service was already highly subsidized, and fares covered
only 33 percent of operational costs. A preliminary questionnaire

20   Nils Fearnley, "Free Fares Policies: Impact on Public Transport Mode Share and
Other Transport Policy Goals," *International Journal of Transportation* 1, no. 1 (2013):
75–90; Raf Canters, "Hasselt Cancels Free Public Transport After 16 years (Belgium),"
Eltis, August 1, 2014.

21   Karl Storchmann, "Externalities by Automobiles and Fare-Free Transit in
Germany: A Paradigm Shift?," *Journal of Public Transportation* 6, no. 4 (2003): 89–105.

22   Maxime Huré, "Gratuité des transports collectifs: De l'expérience sociale à l'alternative politique?," *Métropolitiques*, November 16, 2012.

23   Taavi Aas, "Free Public Transport in Tallinn: Financial, Environmental and
Social Aspects," Union of the Baltic Cities Joint Seminar on Sustainable Transport
Solutions, Tallin, Estonia, April 11–12, 2013 ; Oded Cats, Triin Reimal, and Yusak Susilo,
"Public Transport Pricing Policy: Empirical Evidence from a Fare-Free Scheme in
Tallinn, Estonia," *Transportation Research Record*, no. 2415 (2014): 89–96; Galey,
"License to Ride."

indicated that 49 percent of the population felt unhappy with the fare price. After voters approved a referendum to adopt a free-fare system, with 75 percent in support, a model was created with the official goal of reducing traffic jams and pollution as well as improving mobility. The impact of the model was measured by comparing the months before and after implementation. Among other findings, the assessment observed that the city attracted around ten thousand new residents, whose taxes have helped fund the project.

In developing countries, the social dimension of free-fare systems has wider resonance. In many of these cases, a key question is how expenses should be paid for: with progressivity, the free-fare system might improve conditions for the most vulnerable populations and help reduce social inequalities. Moreover, even though individual automobile ownership has increased in many developing countries, median incomes have generally remained low for most of the population and thus public transportation is the only alternative.[24] This social dimension is generally at odds with the reasoning behind the defense of the free-fare proposal in richer countries, where objections commonly cite the poor administration of the system or the poor quality of transportation.[25] Systematic case studies on the implementation of free mass transit models in developing countries are still lacking. The next section will describe examples in Brazil, relying on primary research.

Free Fare in Brazil

Public transportation is almost exclusively used by the poor in medium and large Brazilian cities. This is especially true in São Paulo, Rio de Janeiro, and other state capitals, where bus roads have accompanied urban sprawl, in a process that has expelled the urban poor to the outskirts. In São Paulo, for example, low-skill workers—who live far away from their work—spend on average several hours a day using public transportation.

---

24 Daniel Santini, *Passe livre: As possibilidades da tarifa zero contra a distopia da uberização* (São Paulo: Autonomia Literária, 2019).

25 Lúcio Kowarick, *A espoliação urbana* (Rio de Janeiro: Paz e Terra, 1979); Eduardo de Alcântara Vasconcellos, *Transporte urbano nos países em desenvolvimento* (São Paulo: Annablume, 2000).

Since the late 1980s, public transportation has remained under the scope of the municipal administration. At the end of the military dictatorship, responsibility was transferred from the federal government to cities. Local governments now had to choose how to set the mass transit system and, under strict federal regulation, had to cover expenses, including an obligation to provide fee-free transportation for the elderly and half-price transportation for students. During this process of transferring responsibility, hundreds of cities were unable to cope with the new regulations; as a result, many small and mid-size cities, especially in the rural areas, still have no public transportation system at all. In communities that have implemented a system, it has often been organized as a sort of partnership with a private consortium, in what we call a "concession." In this model, companies sign a contract with the city government and expect to run the service on a for-profit basis.

In general, Brazil's urban public transportation systems have been described as precarious and inefficient, and fees have remained surprisingly expensive, accounting on average for one-third of the median salary in Brazil. The combination of a public service that is both bad and expensive has contributed to pervasive social unrest regarding transportation. The unrest peaked with the 2013 cycle of protests, mainly led by the Free-Fare Movement but building on several years of smaller contentious events, especially in the cities of Salvador and Florianópolis.

In this context, free-fare proposals were launched in Brazil. In the late 1980s, Workers' Party mayor Luiza Erundina proposed a fee-free policy for São Paulo, but her attempt was blocked by the city council. Almost at the same time, Paulínia, a city in a wealthy rural region, adopted free mass transit, which lasted until the late 1990s. In 2016, a number of Brazilian cities ran free mass transit systems, seven of which are the focus of this section. They are as follows, organized by the state in which they are located:

- Minas Gerais: Monte Carmelo and Muzambinho;
- Paraná: Ivaiporã, Pitanga, and Tijucas do Sul;
- Rio de Janeiro: Maricá; and
- São Paulo: Agudos.[26]

---

26 Márica was not included in my dissertation.

The cases vary in several important dimensions (Table 6.1). The cities had significantly different population sizes. Assessments of social well-being were also strikingly different: some cities had high social well-being, while others had recently experienced social decay, associated with increasing impoverishment and outmigration. Some cities had a mostly urban population and an economy that mostly relied on industry, while others were mainly rural. In some cases, municipal territory was wide; other cities were among the smallest in their states. Politically speaking, mayors were both from the left and the right, progressive and conservative. Some cities had large university campuses, but most of them did not. Some of these cities had a functioning free mass transit system before 2013; some implemented these programs only after the Free-Fare Movement protests.

Table 6.1. Data on Seven Cities in Brazil with Free Fare in 2016

City	Population (estimated)*	Human Development Index*	Year of free-fare implementation
Agudos	37,023	Medium	2002
Ivaiporã	32,035	Medium	2001
Maricá	157,789	High	2015
Monte Carmelo	47,682	Low	1993
Muzambinho	21,026	High	2011
Pitanga	32,015	High	2011
Tijucas do Sul	14,537	Medium	2015

* All data are from the year that free fare was implemented.

The implementation of free fare happened in the context of municipal experimentation with providing mass transit in Brazilian cities, particularly in the 1990s and 2000s, and that form of experimentation occurred in the larger context of systematic precarization of public transportation and the creation of a political framework in which city governments took up the role of supervising and managing social services, including transportation. Experiments have been conducted across several aspects of public transportation provision—funding, management, operation, planning. The particular kind of transportation-system experimentation city governments have attempted is context-dependent; and the reason why some experiments were successful is related to the particular path the policy went through between its inception and its implementation. In my dissertation and a previous publication, I focused on the political processes that led to the inception of, and reforms within, the free public transportation systems in Brazilian cities.[27] Free-fare implementation was usually associated with local leaders proposing the policy on a populist ticket or as part of a local developmental agenda where they faced no or little opposition from the city council. In the next section, I will explore how class dynamics might have affected the implementation of free fare, looking particularly at class formation among capitalists in these cities.

Class and State Dynamics

How do class interests affect preferences for the creation of free fare? The question is not significantly different from what Erik investigated in his analysis of a different real utopia through the parable of the Shmoos in a well-known piece of scholarly literature in which he connects material interests to universal basic income.[28] What we learn from this parable is that, with regard to universal basic income, social classes have diverging preferences, shaped by their position in the system of social relationships.

However, there are major differences between a theoretical exercise, such as a discussion of the parable of the Shmoos, and an empirical account of the implementation of free-fare policies in Brazil. One such difference is the role of the state. In Brazil the free-fare proposal did not magically appear in the seven cities but was conceived and implemented by city governments, sometimes having emerged first as a major agenda topic during a particular leader's campaign. The implementation of the policies could be called "free fare by decree" since the initiation of the policy required little, if any, social mobilization. Only in Maricá did free mass transit emerge as part of a radical agenda, influenced by the 2013 protests. Another difference is that I look exclusively at capitalists' interests, particularly with regard to the political process of class formation.

---

27 João Alexandre Peschanski, "The Free Fare in Brazil and the Sociology of Possibilities," in *Demodiversity: Toward Post-abyssal Democracies*, ed. Boaventura de Sousa Santos and José Manuel Mendes (London: Routledge, 2020): 165–88.

28 Erik Olin Wright, *Class Counts: Student Edition* (Cambridge: Cambridge University Press, 2000).

I assumed that there were two types of capitalists in the cases I have investigated: the owners of the private company that was running the transportation system before free fare was implemented, and the general group of capitalists who were not part of the transportation business.

In Agudos, Monte Carmelo, and Muzambinho, no conflict existed between the city government that implemented free fare and bus company owners; thus, implementation was fast. No official provision of collective transportation had existed in Monte Carmelo and Muzambinho before implementation. In Agudos, there was a privately run service, but it was bankrupt and indebted to the city.

In Tijucas do Sul and Ivaiporã, the decision to implement free fare followed a longer administrative procedure and class-based negotiation. In these two cases, bus companies lobbied against the government proposal and tried to block the implementation of the free transportation system, especially through legal pressure and media campaigning. The decision to implement free fare often was made after a long, tense period in which companies pushed to increase user fees to reap even larger profits. However, conflict between the government and the bus companies did not escalate because

- the policy's implementation happened at an opportune moment of a company's contract expiring, leaving the city the option not to renew it and implement free fare instead;
- companies received some compensation, including through the sale of their used vehicles to the city; and
- although companies lost control over intra-municipal lines, they remained in control of inter-municipal lines, which still operated under a user-fee model.

In Pitanga and Maricá, an enduring conflict arose. Conflict led to high levels of uncertainty over the service provider, as cases trying to block the development led to contradictory rulings and rose through the appeals courts. In both cities, at one point both the user-fee system and free-fare system ran simultaneously on some routes. In Brazil, this is arguably against the law, as a route is supposed to have an exclusive provider. This led to the matter being heard in the courts. At some point, each form of transportation system ran intermittently, as decisions from local and state judges ordered one system or the other to halt its service for a certain period. In the case of Pitanga, an agreement was reached after two years of conflict: the company-run and the free-fare service would coexist, each on a specific line; in fact, the free-fare bus occasionally ran advertisements for the paid-for service.

The situation in Maricá has evolved differently. The proposal for free fare was part of a broader agenda by the leftist mayor Washington Quaquá of the Workers' Party. He wanted to transform Maricá into "the city of utopias." Reaction from conservative sectors and corporate lobbies was fierce. The company that ran mass transit in Maricá was one of the largest transportation corporations in Brazil, and it sought to block the free-fare policy through court appeals and political mobilization. "Permanent tension" and "class warfare" were words used to describe the reaction to Quaquá's agenda. In this scenario, social mobilization played a major role, and activists aligned with the city government to push the transformative agenda forward.

Free fare is an impactful policy, in the sense that it modifies the social system's dynamics, and can lead to changes in class-based political behavior and interests. Nevertheless, these actions and interests are not necessarily easy to identify empirically. In the seven cases, I have investigated how bus companies and their lobbies were able to rally other capitalists to support their agenda, reflecting a loose identification of class interests.

One scenario involved the creation of a class coalition, which was what happened in Agudos and Maricá. In Agudos, the bus company owners attempted to rally influential members of the local economic elite to oppose the free-fare proposal. Yet capitalists strongly supported the implementation of free mass transit as it was associated with a local developmental strategy that attracted factories—who saw not having to cover transportation costs as an incentive—and that could boost local commerce as routes went through the shopping areas. In Maricá, a class coalition emerged against Quaquá's socialist agenda, which included the creation of a local currency (mumbuca), the provision of a universal basic income, and the implementation of free fare. Right-wing politicians and companies from several sectors established a coalition to oppose Quaquá's policies. As court disputes between the bus company and the city government escalated and received more press attention, the unified capitalist conservative opposition called for and organized protests.

In Monte Carmelo and Muzambinho, there was no evidence of any conflict or coalition-building among local capitalists with respect to free fare. In Tijucas do Sul and Ivaiporã, conflict arose between groups of small producers: as free fare increased people's mobility, small producers that had settled in areas with limited transportation access were unhappy that their potential customers could now shop in other areas of the city, especially downtown. The city government had to modify the bus schedule in order to create incentives for people to buy what they needed in their local communities. In Pitanga, the bus company was active in mobilizing other relevant economic players against a fare-free transportation system. Yet as the city government and the company reached an agreement, other companies demobilized.

State-capitalist relationships and capitalist class formation appear to be major factors in determining the implementation process of free-fare policies across the seven Brazilian cities that I have investigated. Table 6.2 identifies how conflict between bus companies and the city government and the presence of a capitalist-wide coalition have affected the implementation paths for Maricá, Agudos, Pitanga, Tijucas do Sul, Ivaiporã, Monte Carmelo, and Muzambinho.

The investigation of these cases and the impact class interests have on the implementation of free fare leaves us with at least two major questions. First, under what conditions will a free-fare system become sustainable? The circumstances in which the system was implemented appear to be relatively extraordinary: a strong local leader, an ambitious developmental agenda, and a specific class equilibrium. These circumstances are often only transitory and cannot be the basis for enduring policymaking. Part of the answer to this first question may lie with an element that begs further investigation: the people. To the extent that a policy improves living conditions, it is not unlikely that people will feel entitled to the benefits that this policy generates and, when necessary, will mobilize to act against the dismantling of public transport. In the Brazilian case, this hypothesis may have even more resonance as the 2013 protests around mobility have spread the notion that free fare may be framed in terms of political contention. To investigate this hypothesis, it would be necessary to look at whether the evolution of the free mass transit model has been accompanied by local organizing and movement building.

Table 6.2. Class Dynamics during the Implementation of Free Fare in Seven Brazilian Cities

		Type of relationship between bus companies and the city government	
		Conflict	No conflict
	Coalition	Maricá	Agudos
Capitalist class formation	No coalition	Pitanga Tijucas do Sul Ivaiporã	Monte Carmelo Muzambinho

A second question is, what are the conditions for the replication of free fare, and what are the forces of opposition to this policy? Despite its predominance, neoliberal logic was not strong enough to prevent the emergence of the free public transport policy. It is ironic that in the cases I have investigated, the agents of change were usually right-wing politicians, sometimes in alliance with capitalist coalitions. There are famous studies of the conditions in which capitalists have acted against the interests of the market, but what is striking in the Brazilian cases discussed here is that free fare is a firmly local policy, and, except in the case of Maricá, it was dissociated from a broader transformative agenda. On the one hand, to understand the conditions for replication of free fare could depend on studying the political economy of mobility, in particular the hegemony of bus companies. On the other hand, it could depend on investigating the fiscal and legal constraints faced by municipal governments, which eventually create non-trivial obstacles to political experimentation.

Erik concluded *How to Be an Anticapitalist in the Twenty-First Century* (2019) with a discussion of what he called "real politics," regarding the creation of alternative institutional arrangements and the political capacity to erode capitalism. Following this logic, I think these cases offer strong evidence that free public transportation is viable and should be considered part of the real-utopia agenda—and that class analysis offers a useful lens through which it is possible to clarify the way forward.

7

The Cooperative Market Economy: The Promise and Challenge of Mondragon
Marta Soler-Gallart

In his book *Envisioning Real Utopias*, Erik Olin Wright describes the Mondragon Corporation as a real utopia. He writes, "What we can do is look at what is generally regarded as the world's most successful group of worker-owned cooperatives: Mondragon in the Basque region of Spain." Erik started engaging with scholars working on successful "cooperativism" in order to build an analytical framework for understanding the conditions of viability for the extension of what he called "real utopias." He changed his view about cooperativism after talking to researchers studying cooperatives of the Mondragon group, especially after visiting them in the Basque Country.[1] The visible social and economic effects of their democratic structure led him to include cooperatives as a real utopia, an institutional example of a potential pathway to social empowerment. An internal cooperative strategy led Mondragon to become one of the largest industrial groups in Spain, competing in international, capitalist markets and contributing to the region with one of the lowest Gini indexes in the world, as well as its surprising success in maintaining jobs throughout the 2007–8 economic crisis. During his trip to the Basque Country, Erik and the Spanish scholars spoke with Mondragon workers and their relatives as well as with managers and

---

1   Gisela Redondo, Ignacio Santa Cruz, and Josep Maria Rotger, "Why Mondragon? Analyzing What Works in Overcoming Inequalities," *Qualitative Inquiry* 17, no. 3 (2011): 277–83.

trade unionists, initiating a large international network for the study of cooperatives as a viable alternative on a global scale.

The study of the Mondragon experience can actually provide new insights into class analysis, not dissimilar from Erik's earlier work. During the second half of the twentieth century, the dominant social relations of production, and even the very existence of the idea of social classes, started to be questioned. Erik, however, made an effort to maintain the concept of social class by renewing and adapting it to new times, and a new society.

Mondragon is an example of how a "modern" working class, different from that of the nineteenth century, has been able to build a new and alternative economy. The designers and founders of the Mondragon project were people who belonged to the working class. It was these worker-owners, not investors, who built the project's successful co-ops; they overcame the traditional capitalist class by establishing limits on executive salaries and improving working conditions for all workers, thus eliminating forms of exploitation. In this case, workers were the real agents of transformation. Consequently, and echoing Marx's insight, the worker-owners of Mondragon Corporation demonstrated that capitalists are not necessary to have a productive and competitive economy.

By including Mondragon in his real utopias analysis, Erik presented an alternative to capitalism in the twenty-first century, where the people—members of the cooperative—are themselves agents of transformation. He showed that rather than being pessimistic about the reproduction of inequalities emerging from capitalism, we can be optimistic about the possibility of recreating positive models and successful actions across the entire planet.

First Visit to Mondragon: Erik Discovers a New Alternative

In 2007, like many other countries, Spain was submerged in a serious economic crisis, which led to a dramatic loss of jobs and social benefits. Facing this reality, CREA (Community of Research on Excellence for All), of which I served as director, decided to create a group focused on the study of real alternatives to the capitalist economy, following the research that some members of CREA had been conducting for over twenty years, with a strong emphasis on the Mondragon experience. At that time, Erik was still skeptical about cooperatives; however, he changed his view after talking to researchers, including Ramón Flecha, founder of CREA, especially after he visited us in the Basque Country for a guided tour of Mondragon.

Let me set the context for Erik's change of mind. In May 2008, Erik was invited to Barcelona to share his research on Envisioning Real Utopias at the Catalan Sociological Association and to conduct a seminar at the University of Barcelona. At a meal with some CREA colleagues, Flecha shared with him our research on Mondragon as a successful cooperative group and proposed the possibility of creating an international network focused on the study of these real alternatives to a capitalist economy.[2] The ostensible social and economic effects of cooperatives' democratic structure made Erik decide to include the cooperative market economy as a "real utopia"—one of the pathways to social empowerment.

Until that time, Erik had not viewed cooperatives as viable alternatives. Within the capitalist context, he had argued, they either marginally subsisted in sectors that received little interest from capital investment, surviving on state subsidies or the self-exploitation of workers, or were officially called cooperatives but in practice were capitalist enterprises. However, through strong arguments, Flecha showed him that was not the case at Mondragon, which was a strong cooperative group capable of competing in global contexts through the creation of new business forms designed to overcome capitalist domination without the organization losing its humanist principles.

Erik's discussions with Flecha and other CREA members would lead to a collaboration on a study of cooperatives as real utopias. Still, it was necessary for Erik to get to know Mondragon firsthand by talking to the people directly involved. Erik was excited about the idea of being able to verify what he had been told and carry out his own in-depth research. Thus, four months later, in September 2008, Erik, Flecha, Teresa Sordé (a researcher from CREA), and I went to Mondragon, in a trip full of curiosity, discovery, and passionate discussion.

---

2   Redondo, Santa Cruz, and Rotger, "Why Mondragon?"

During that first trip, Erik spoke with the workers, their families, managers, and researchers from the LANKI Institute of Cooperative Studies at Mondragon. He also engaged in dialogues with people who were less sympathetic to cooperatives, including members of trade unions. He got to know the characteristics of Mondragon directly and its difficulties and the arguments of its detractors. In many of these interviews he implemented what he called the "red button" theory. While speaking to or interviewing people who offered strong arguments against the corporation, he would ask them, "Imagine you have a red button here, and if you press it, the Mondragon cooperatives disappear. Would you press the button?" Regardless of how critical some people were of Mondragon, whenever Erik posed this question, everyone's response was always the same: they would not press the button. This thought experiment was important because it showed the impact of Mondragon and, at the same time, pointed out that the existing criticisms were not so powerful as to justify giving up on the project. The inquiry of the "red button" theory confirmed to Erik that Mondragon was a viable non-capitalist alternative that should be included in his list for what would become *Envisioning Real Utopias*.

On that visit, Erik took a picture of himself at an assembly line of Fagor, one of Mondragon's cooperatives, and sent it to his friend Michael Burawoy, to signal his faith in cooperatives. Burawoy quickly responded, saying, "Not bad for a beginner." They had argued a lot about worker-owned cooperatives, and Michael had failed to convince him. He used to ask us, "What have you done to Erik that now he is into cooperatives?" For many years, in our meetings of the international network for the study of cooperatives, Erik used to say that somewhere in the world there is a car with an engine piece made by a sociologist.

Through these diverse conversations with us and with people involved in Mondragon, Erik learned the entire history of the cooperative group, as well as the internal strategy that led Mondragon to become one of the most important industrial groups in Spain (as I will explain in more detail in the following sections). Mondragon broke the perception that cooperatives are not a viable alternative because they can compete within a capitalist context; since its founding, Mondragon has offered an alternative to the capitalist enterprise. In 1943, the young priest José María Arizmendiarrieta, who "called for human action to change the course of history," founded a professional school in Mondragon, viewing education as key to social and economic transformation.[3] Indeed, education has remained an essential factor of success in Mondragon since its very foundation. In 1956, along with five of his students from the professional school, Arizmendiarrieta created the first industrial cooperative, Ulgor (which later became Fagor). However, his vision was broader than just one cooperative operating an appliance workshop, so their initiative did not end there. Step by step, they expanded, until they managed to create a group of more than 150 cooperatives, including a banking company, a social security system, and a university. His vision and initiative to promote new lines and maintain core values has enabled Mondragon to continue until today, with great success worldwide.

That first visit of Erik's to Mondragon, which involved close contact with the members of the corporation and exposure to the intense work they carried out, as well as to the enthusiasm of all the people involved and the stories Flecha shared as the delegation walked across the city of Bilbao, marked the beginning of Erik's study of cooperatives as a viable alternative on a global scale.

What Is Different about Mondragon?

In his book *Envisioning Real Utopias*, Erik writes: "What we can do is look at what is generally regarded as the world's most successful group of worker-owned cooperatives, Mondragon in the Basque region of Spain. Examining the factors that have contributed to its success and some of the dilemmas it faces may help clarify the real utopian potentials of cooperatives as a pathway to social empowerment."[4]

According to the World Cooperative Monitor, Mondragon is the first cooperative group in the world.[5] It is also one of the first business groups in the Basque Country, as well as one of the largest such enterprises in Spain, with 79,931 employees distributed in four main areas of activity: 2,220 in financial, 37,809 in industrial, 38,523 in retail, and 1,379 in its

3   Ramon Flecha and Ignacio Santa Cruz, "Cooperation for Economic Success: The Mondragon Case," *Analyse and Kritik* 33, no. 1 (2011): 157–70.
4   Erik Olin Wright, *Envisioning Real Utopias* (London: Verso, 2010), 240.
5   World Cooperative Monitor, *Exploring the Cooperative Economy*, 2019.

research area. Internationally, it has more than 138 production plants and, outside of Spain, has more than 14,100 workers.[6] Sixty-five years of history endorse this corporation as one of the world's most outstanding examples of worker-owned cooperatives.

During the financial crisis of the 1970s, values of cooperation and solidarity moved Mondragon to adopt measures to support the cooperatives that were most negatively affected. These and other measures resulted in an annual 3.3 percent increase in employment between 1976 and 1986 in Mondragon, during a period in which unemployment was rising across Spain. Similarly, in 2012, when many companies had to close down and more than 5 million people became unemployed in Spain, the members of Mondragon made tough decisions, such as reducing their wages to avoid firing other members and to help prevent the cooperatives that were struggling from having to shut their doors. These are just some of the actions inspired by Mondragon's focus on maintaining its corporate values of participation, social responsibility, cooperation, and innovation. Scientific research has observed the enormous transformative and emancipating potential of this approach.[7]

As part of CREA's endeavor to study real alternatives to the capitalist economy, Flecha and his colleague Iñaki Santa Cruz carried out research on successful cooperative actions for many years.[8] They are both from the Basque Country and had been interested in Mondragon since the 1960s, when they were students at Deusto Business School. Flecha and Santa Cruz have summarized Mondragon's success by identifying six key unique characteristics of the corporation.[9]

First: *democracy and transparency*. Mondragon's democratic organization gives all members access to all information concerning the cooperatives and allows them to participate in decision-making under the rule of "one person, one vote." Information channels are well established

6   Mondragon Corporation, *Annual Report 2020*.

7   Teresa Morlà-Folch et al., "The Mondragon Case: Companies Addressing Social Impact and Dialogic Methodologies," *International Journal of Qualitative Methods* 20 (2021): 1–9.

8   Ramón Flecha, "European Research, Social Innovation and Successful Cooperativist Actions," *International Journal of Quality and Service Sciences* 4, no. 4 (2012): 332–44.

9   Flecha and Santa Cruz, "Cooperation for Economic Success."

for the purposes of transparency. The organizational structure, which is based on cooperative members' assemblies, guarantees collective decision-making. From the level of the meetings of the *consejillos* (small councils) between worker-members of the same shop floor, to the general assembly, there are a number of different structures allowing the voices of all workers to be heard. In other words, a space is created where decisions are made and actions are taken that affect the entire company.

Second: *solidarity in profit for economic growth*. A system of reinvestment and redistribution of the profit from each cooperative allows Mondragon to grow and innovate while maintaining its communitarian values.

Third: *solidarity among workers across the corporation*. In times of recession, two solidarity mechanisms in Mondragon are fundamental: mutual economic support between cooperatives and the reallocation of workers. These mechanisms reflect values that Erik identified as the pursuit of community/solidarity.[10] At the level of the individual cooperative, there have been measures such as the adjustment of temporary staff, reduction of salary levels, capitalization of special payments, and waiving of charges. At the inter-cooperative level, the relocation of members and compensation for losses have been facilitated through the Inter-cooperation Solidarity Fund.

Fourth: a *more egalitarian pay scale*. Mondragon executives tend to earn less than managers in capitalist companies, while mid-level technicians tend to earn more in Mondragon than their counterparts in capitalist companies. When Mondragon was created, a wage ratio of 1 to 3 was established in the cooperative between the worker with the lowest salary and the highest manager. Today, the wage ratio within most cooperatives is 1 to 4, and in some of them 1 to 6, but if we analyze the overall wage differential, it is significantly much smaller than in other companies. From this ratio, we can deduce that most Mondragon managers receive around 70 percent of the salary earned in similar positions in the competitive market. These policies aim to bring managers' salaries closer to those of similar positions in the market so that cooperative managers do not leave for other companies. While Mondragon's middle and senior management employees earn less than they might earn in

---

10   Erik Olin Wright, *How to Be an Anticapitalist in the Twenty-First Century* (London: Verso, 2019).

similar positions in other companies, they prefer to stay in Mondragon because it is a project deeply rooted in their community. They have many benefits and advantages and, most importantly, job security. In short, they are owners of the cooperative.

Fifth: *maximum job security and strong limitations on temporary employment*. No more than 20 percent of workers in a company can have temporary employment status, and usually they are offered the option of becoming members.

Sixth: *specific advantages for members*. Members have several advantages, such as being able to choose between taking early retirement, leaving the cooperative and receiving compensation, or continuing to work in another cooperative when their own jobs are threatened by external market forces.

These six features are present across the corporation and help form its democratic culture and shared values and beliefs. While we cannot establish causation between these cooperative features and the low levels of income inequality found in the Mondragon region, we can identify a clear correlation.

Cooperativism: A Working-Class Culture

Since Mondragon was founded, education has been a key dimension of the project, embedded in the corporation's DNA. Mondragon's cooperative values and its democratic culture are transmitted to workers through ongoing training, and all workers are involved in the development of skills directly linked to their work as well as management skills. Furthermore, the cooperative culture is transmitted through university education (Mondragon University, created in 1997, is itself a cooperative within the Mondragon Corporation group). Erik in fact points out that education and training helps to guarantee "equal access," tearing down any barriers so that all agents can participate.[11] For this reason, a large number of Mondragon's managers have been trained within the corporation itself, and their link to the corporation is deeply rooted in cooperative culture and its values. In other words, the corporation itself generates talent that is committed to this organization of labor. In

---

11   Ibid.

general, the cooperative culture is deeply rooted among its workers: their life trajectories are closely linked to this corporation that also guarantees them job security. Consequently, turnover is lower in Mondragon than in other companies.

In addition, Mondragon is constantly seeking formulas to expand the cooperativist culture beyond the corporation. The Centro de Formación Ikasbide Otalora (Ikasbide Otalora Cooperative and Management Educational Center), created in 1984, has contributed to the corporation's success and expansion. The availability of postgraduate training and courses for promoting cooperative education and dissemination stands in marked contrast to the lack of education about the management of cooperative companies in most business schools. Indeed, to manage a company in which workers are at the same time owners and participants in decision-making processes requires a professional education that differs from the training needed for managing capitalist companies. Hence, Ikasbide Otalora attracts people from all over the world who want to learn about cooperative management, and its impact is outstanding: whereas in 1988, more than half of Mondragon's executives came from outside the corporation, today, most executives in Mondragon have been trained internally and risen from junior positions.[12] This contributes to Mondragon's expansion of its cooperativist culture around the world, creating a pool of good, effective, and honest professionals for the management and direction of cooperative companies everywhere.

The Challenge of the Global Market

Although most cooperatives tend to be locally based, Mondragon, whose motto is "Humanity at Work," has been competitive both in national and international markets. The Mondragon Corporation has 103 cooperatives, 122 subsidiary firms (some of them mixed cooperatives), one mutual assistance organization, eight foundations, ten support

---

12   Imanol Basterretxea and Eneka Albizu, "Management Training as a Source of Perceived Competitive Advantage: The Mondragon Cooperative Group Case," *Economic and Industrial Democracy* 32, no. 2 (2010): 199–222.

entities, and thirteen international services.[13] While most of MC's coop-eratives, including its headquarters, are located in the Basque Country, subsidiaries are based in other parts of Spain and in countries such as Germany, France, the United Kingdom, Brazil, India, China, and the United States.[14] In fact, Mondragon's internationalization is one of the most hotly debated issues about the corporation today.

Mondragon has proved that being committed to egalitarian and democratic values and being successful in the capitalist market are not opposed and can actually go hand in hand. In fact, by maintaining both its democracy and solidarity and its competitiveness, the Mondragon model has been both more efficient and more equitable than its main-stream counterparts. However, the corporation has also encountered numerous challenges during these years, including detractors who question the group's cooperativist nature. The most prominent chal-lenge Mondragon has encountered, as highlighted by Flecha and Ngai, has been figuring out how to maintain cooperative values while pursu-ing expansion and internationalization. Like other worker cooperatives that want to be competitive in a globalizing market, Mondragon faces the dilemma of expanding domestically and internationally without losing those values, and without negatively affecting employees' conditions.[15]

Mondragon increased its internationalization in the 1990s as the corporation had long discussed the strategy as a necessary measure for remaining economically competitive. The process of internationaliza-tion mainly consisted of the creation and acquisition of capitalist compa-nies, which some scholars have described as contradicting Mondragon's cooperative values.[16] Mondragon has developed two main strategies to address this challenge: first, creating mixed cooperatives, and second, extending what they call the Corporate Management Model. "Mixed cooperatives" are subsidiary companies that have been transformed from the capitalist model but are only partly worker-owned. The rest of

---

13   Mondragon Corporation, *Annual Report 2014*.

14   Marta Soler-Gallart, *Achieving Social Impact: Sociology in the Public Sphere* (New York: Springer, 2017).

15   Ramon Flecha and Pun Ngai, "The Challenge for Mondragon: Searching for the Cooperative Values in Times of Internationalization," *Organization* 21, no. 39 (2014): 666–82.

16   Flecha and Ngai, "The Challenge for Mondragon."

the cooperative is usually owned by the parent cooperative, or even by third parties such as Mondragon Inversiones. This option allows workers who are unable to own the company, or unwilling to take the risk, to share their cooperative with other capital holders. The aim with a mixed cooperative system is to promote significant transformation, to not simply convert the company directly into a cooperative but bring about a cooperative culture. Moreover, this model, whether it is temporary or permanent, enables further cooperativization. In their analysis of internationalization strategies, Flecha and Ngai show that mixed cooperative organizations can overcome barriers to expanding the cooperative culture through the combination of three spheres of participation: capital, profit, and management.[17]

A second strategy is the implementation of the Corporate Management Model (CMM), a general tool created to unify the management of all cooperatives of the group and its subsidiaries, bringing the management and participation of workers in the subsidiaries closer to the structure of the parent cooperative. The CMM is characterized by corporate development, self-management, and communication; the parent cooperative is responsible for developing and implementing these three principles in the subsidiaries. *Corporate development* entails promoting assemblies (such as the social council or the governing board) as a meeting point for discussing the collective project. In other words, it is a way to promote the participation of everyone in the management of the company, encouraging new forms of worker involvement in Mondragon's subsidiaries. *Self-management* emphasizes the importance of horizontal structures as opposed to hierarchical ones, and encourages responsibility, as well as teamwork, at all levels. *Communication* ensures transparent channels of information. CMM provides some general guidelines, which each company adapts to its specific context and peculiarities, whether they are or are not cooperatives. These strategies—mixed cooperatives and the implementation of the CMM—do not necessarily guarantee that subsidiaries are transformed into cooperatives. They are intermediate steps toward making subsidiaries more democratic than conventional capitalist companies.

The commitment to internationalization makes Mondragon competitive in international markets, with subsidiaries setting up near the

17   Ibid.

companies they work for to guarantee supplies. However, notably, this situation does not involve the relocation of the cooperative to another country, as such a move could threaten to reduce workforces or production levels of the parent cooperative in the Basque Country. While it has widened market options, the parent cooperative remains the owner of the subsidiaries. Accordingly, the cooperative's parent firm and the subsidiaries follow the same form of management, while still recognizing that each subsidiary must follow the labor laws of the country in which it is based.

Mondragon is a different model from that of a conventional capitalist company. Its parent company is a cooperative. It participates in the capitalist market because it knows that it cannot isolate itself from the capitalist world and still be competitive. However, at the same time, it follows its values, hoping to generate a fairer society. In line with Erik's analysis of real utopias, Mondragon, by acting on its values, encourages the erosion of the capitalist system from within, showing that other ways of managing a company are possible. Through these and other strategies to overcome such dilemmas, Mondragon challenges the widespread assumption that cooperatives cannot simultaneously maintain their core values and be large, growing, self-sustainable, and stable.

Mondragon as a Real Utopia

The business model of Mondragon was included in Erik's examples of real utopias because while most cooperatives are embedded in the local or regional economy, Mondragon had become an economic actor on a global scale.[18] Erik writes that even though worker-owned cooperatives represent viable alternatives to capitalist firms, they rarely figure significantly in theories of alternatives to capitalism. Indeed, prior to learning more about Mondragon, he had accepted the criticism often directed toward worker cooperatives: that they could only survive in small niches, unless they chose to leave cooperative values behind in order to expand and engage in more effective business practices. However, defying this logic, the global expansion of Mondragon has actually helped the cooperative stay geographically rooted and preserve local jobs. The

---

18   Ibid.

dynamics embedded within Mondragon, along with the way the cooperative confronted the challenges of the market, fascinated Erik. He reflected on this different model of creating and organizing labor, hoping to understand its strategies concerning replication and the transferability of that cooperative experience. Coming to view cooperativism as a possible element in the emancipatory transformation of capitalism, he points out:

> Perhaps the oldest vision for an emancipatory alternative to capitalism is the worker-owned firm. Capitalism began by dispossessing workers of their means of production and then employing them as wage-laborers in capitalist firms. The most straightforward undoing of that dispossession is its reversal through worker-owned firms. In most times and places, however, worker cooperatives are quite marginal within market economies, occupying small niches rather than the core of an economic system. One striking exception is the Mondragon Cooperative Corporation in the Basque region of Spain.[19]

Erik determined that, since their economic activity is based on democracy and equality, worker cooperatives could prefigure an emancipatory systemic alternative.

I have already mentioned that one of the challenges Mondragon faces in being competitive in today's globalized market is maintaining solidaristic processes that prevent its individual cooperatives from going bankrupt. In his book *Envisioning Real Utopias*, Erik discusses this and a range of other tensions attributed to the Mondragon group's complex governance structure: between solidarity across cooperatives and the economic interests of individual cooperatives, between democratic structure and managerial autonomy, and between decentralized decision-making and a more centralized coordination across cooperatives. Despite these challenges, tensions, and dilemmas, Erik acknowledges that senior management is still elected by workers, and major company decisions are made by the board of directors or general meetings that represent members. Mondragon remains, as Erik describes

---

19 Erik Olin Wright, "Transforming Capitalism through Real Utopias," 2011 Presidential Address, *American Sociological Review* (2012): 10.

worker-owned cooperatives, "one of the central expressions of a demo-cratic egalitarian vision of an alternative way of organizing economic activity."[20] Hence, Mondragon shows not only that it is possible for a worker cooperative to be as efficient as capitalist firms, but also that its cooperative values—such as the collaborative work process, worker-owners' commitment to the cooperative's success, and a closer align-ment between workers' and managers' interests—can actually make it more efficient and productive than capitalist firms. Its cooperative and solidaristic values make Mondragon, in Erik's words, "an emergent form of a *cooperative market economy* rather than simply a cooperative firm within a capitalist market economy."[21]

What does the inclusion of Mondragon in Erik's *Envisioning Real Utopias* mean? It relates to a key element of Erik's understanding of real utopias—the idea of reproduction by replication: "an experi-mental process in which we continually test and retest the limits of possibility and try, as best as we can, to create new institutions which expand the limits themselves. In doing so we not only envision real utopias but contribute to making utopias real."[22] In other words, Erik presents Mondragon as an inspiring model for other cooperatives, which in turn contributes to helping other entrepreneurial busi-nesses become emancipatory cooperatives. Of course, Erik could see that Mondragon was an exception, a unique case: "The Mondragon Cooperative Corporation is an example. Such firms remain a hybrid economic form, combining capitalist and socialist elements, but the socialist component has considerable weight."[23] But rather than simply studying the cooperative's uniqueness and its key features for its own sake, as Flecha and Santa Cruz did, we can also explore how a cooperative like Mondragon can become successful and in turn create a real utopia.[24] Rigorous analysis of real utopias can contribute to identifying successful practices for possible replication around the world.

As I noted earlier in the chapter, and as Erik pointed out in *Envisioning Real Utopias*, Mondragon is not exempt from tensions and

20   Wright, *Envisioning Real Utopias*, 236.
21   Ibid., 241.
22   Ibid., 373.
23   Wright, "Transforming Capitalism," 18.
24   Flecha and Santa Cruz, "Cooperation for Economic Success."

contradictions, and today it still faces important challenges and dilemmas as it seeks to remain rooted in its cooperative values while succeeding in the global capitalist market. However, such challenges do not diminish the opportunities that Mondragon offers, allowing us to learn from the strategies and actions that have led to its success in order to help other enterprises find a pathway toward utopia. In other words, to quote Erik, "rather than attempting to specify the design for the final destination, the strategy is to examine specific mechanisms which move in the right direction."[25]

A "Modern" Working Class Builds a New Alternative

In some of the debates Erik and our team held in the Basque Country with university professors and trade unionists during that visit, it became clear once again that many Marxists are opposed to cooperatives and that they believe Marx opposed them as well. That mistake is not unusual; similar criticisms have been raised in many different forums, including international conferences and sessions with experts in critical economy. If Althusser wrote *Reading Capital* without having read it, we should not be surprised that many of those who say they are experts in critical economy speak and write about Marx without having seriously read his works. These kinds of mistakes are easily identified by those who have read and debated *Capital* and other key works.

Marx not only was in favor of worker cooperatives, but he knew them and praised them. In fact, in the 1864 "Inaugural Address of the Working Men's International Association," he states:

[There] was in store a still greater victory of the political economy of labor over the political economy of property. We speak of the co-operative movement . . . The value of these great social experiments cannot be overrated. By deed instead of by argument, they have shown that production on a large scale, and in accord with the behests of modern science, may be carried on without the existence of a class of masters employing a class of hands; that to bear fruit, the means of labor need

---

25 Wright, *Envisioning Real Utopias*, 246.

not be monopolized as a means of dominion over, and of extortion against, the laboring man himself.[26]

Like many other thinkers, Marx thought that alternatives to the capitalist system would be created by a pre-communist socialist system, which would be reached through a revolution promoted and led by the dispossessed working class. Consequently, what was important was the analysis of existing social classes and the struggle for that socialist revolution. Marx believed that taking time to analyze cooperative movements— which, according to him, were not going to play a relevant role in such a revolution—would have been an unnecessary distraction from that larger effort; from his perspective, analyzing social groups that did not easily fit into categories such as the working class or the bourgeoisie was irrelevant, because the most important topic was the struggle between those classes. In that same inaugural address, he argued that while cooperatives demonstrated that production on a large scale is possible without exploitation, the dominant classes—who, knowing cooperatives' potential, try to discredit them as "utopias of the dreamers"—will prevent the expansion of cooperatives through various political means and economic monopolies. Therefore, he says, class struggle becomes a necessary precondition:

However excellent in principle and however useful in practice, co-operative labor, if kept within the narrow circle of the casual efforts of private workmen, will never be able to arrest the growth in geometrical progression of monopoly, to free the masses, nor even to perceptibly lighten the burden of their miseries . . . It is perhaps for this very reason that plausible noblemen, philanthropic middle-class spouters, and even keen political economists have all at once turned nauseously complimentary to the very co-operative labor system they had vainly tried to nip in the bud by deriding it as the utopia of the dreamer, or stigmatizing it as the sacrilege of the socialist. To save the industrious masses, co-operative labor ought to be developed to national dimensions, and, consequently, to be fostered by national means. Yet the lords of the land and the lords of capital will always use their political

26   Karl Marx, *Inaugural Address and Provisional Rules of the International Working Men's Association*, 1864, 11.

privileges for the defense and perpetuation of their economic monopolies. So far from promoting, they will continue to lay every possible
impediment in the way of the emancipation of labor . . . To conquer
political power has, therefore, become the great duty of the working
classes.[27]

At the end of the twentieth century, cooperative movements were very
diverse. Many of them included companies with excellent values, but
they were reduced to business activities that were not competitive in the
market economy. These cooperatives did not offer an alternative to the
capitalist companies and were frequently known to have exploitative
labor conditions. Many did not even join trade-union struggles for the
improvement of workers' lives. It is therefore understandable that many
critical scholars, like Erik in his earlier years, have shown little interest
in cooperatives, perceiving them as marginal experiments.

At that time, Marx's class analysis was not developed enough for
understanding the evolution of capitalist societies, and many thinkers
began to insist that class analysis was not useful for our times. Some
even argued that social classes no longer exist. Taking a different and
much more rigorous perspective, Erik undertook the difficult and
important task of enriching the analysis of social classes within contemporary capitalist societies, introducing new concepts that were crucial
and clarifying. But his class analysis expanded when he discovered
Mondragon, which he realized included a successful construction of the
working class through companies managed and self-organized by workers, who achieve better labor conditions than workers in capitalist
companies. The Mondragon cooperatives were not insignificant nor
were they marginalized by economic or political monopolies. Instead,
they proved successful in the competitive market. Mondragon was a
clear example of how a non-capitalist real utopia could expand, growing
in numbers and outreach, and thus contribute to the erosion of
capitalism.

In Erik's discussion of real utopias, class struggle disappears as a
precondition (which is clear in his discussion of the ruptural strategies
of social transformation). Diverging from Marx, the Real Utopias
Project proposes that, rather than class struggle, it will be the

---

27   Ibid, 11.

expansion of successful non-capitalist initiatives, self-organized by workers, citizens, and civil society, that will provide the possibility of democratic transformation. Obviously, this possibility does not come without obstacles and difficulties, which Erik started to address in *Envisioning Real Utopias* and his analysis of real utopias' viability. Others have also studied these issues; many of the researchers mentioned in this chapter, with whom Erik also collaborated, are studying the challenges that Mondragon has faced in its global expansion, as well as the continual search on the part of the cooperative members (a "modern" working-class contingent) for ways to maintain the values of democracy, solidarity, and humanity in the organization of labor within their companies.[28]

Final Words

Through his analysis of real utopias that are already making steps toward possible alternative horizons, Erik was able to see possibilities for the transformation of our world. That is why he included Mondragon as one of those utopias, co-organizing and actively participating in seminars and debates held by the international network for the study of cooperatives, where he promoted the exchange of analyses of cooperative experiences as well as the dissemination of the Mondragon success story. The first meeting took place in the summer of 2009 in Barcelona, followed by a series of workshops exploring an array empirical examples of pathways to a cooperative market economy in places as different as Madison, Barcelona (again), Buenos Aires, Johannesburg, and Padua, Italy. In these meetings, in addition to deeply probing the Mondragon experience, we were able to debate other cooperative experiences, such as Argentina's *recuperadas*, the United States' union co-op model, and the municipal incubation of cooperatives. In addition, this international network helped promote the research and careers of several young researchers who carried out doctoral dissertations on cooperativism.

---

28   George Cheney et al., "Worker Cooperatives as an Organizational Alternative: Challenges, Achievements and Promise in Business Governance and Ownership," *Organization* 21, no. 5 (2014): 591–603.

Erik initiated this work, which will continue, as other scholars have committed to using sociological knowledge to envision alternative futures. Erik's work on real utopias has undoubtedly left a legacy for all of us. Research on real-life contemporary successful actions around the world that are making lives better, and providing the conditions for human flourishing, is, as he used to say, more necessary than ever. Real utopias, such as the cooperative market economy, are true alternatives to capitalism; by working on them, we contribute to a pathway toward a more democratic, egalitarian, and just society.

8

Who Will Help Decommodify Housing? Race, Property, Class, and the Struggle for Social Housing in the United States
H. Jacob Carlson and Gianpaolo Baiocchi

There is a poster in the Havens Wright Center for Social Justice that says, "Class consciousness is knowing which side of the fence you're on. Class analysis is figuring out who is there with you." Though we graduated nineteen years apart (Gianpaolo in 2001, Jake in 2020), each of us spent our formative years in the orbit of the Havens Center at University of Wisconsin–Madison's sociology department. Like so many other students of Erik's, we were taken by his way of thinking and have modeled our careers around the way he connected his political commitments to meticulous scholarly work. We both found our way to Erik after some time doing political work before graduate school, and the Erik we met was one deeply committed to real utopias, which also shaped our own thinking. It was fitting that while the two of us met for the first time at the annual meeting of the American Sociological Association, our collaboration started with a forward-looking report for the Right to the City Alliance on models of decommodified housing.

Our collaboration became more intense with the onset of the COVID-19 pandemic. We lent our efforts to the #CancelRent movement in the United States, and our conversations took an explicit real utopian turn when we were asked by staffers for a member of Congress to develop a "transformative proposal." It took us several months of dialogue with movement activists, nonprofit housing practitioners, congressional staff, and others to develop what we would call the Social Housing Development Authority and, later, the broader real utopian proposal we are calling "Social Housing 2.0." As we continue to discuss the possibilities for a viable future in which access to housing is not exclusively determined by the market, the question on nearly everyone's mind is how to get there. Who, exactly, might stand to win or lose in such a transition, and who might be in the coalition to push for it? The task of figuring out exactly who might be on our side of the fence if not there already, as the Havens Center poster urges us to do, is as important as it is complicated in the racialized "homeowner's society" that is the United States.

This essay is an effort to address those questions by drawing on the variety of analytical tools that Erik created (or at least our interpretation of them). Every roadblock we hit, we have tried to imagine what Erik would advise; once you got to know his ways of looking at things, you can trick yourself into guessing what he might say. It's a trick, since his actual opinion was often quite different from your expectations, but always thoughtful and insightful. We regularly feel a pang of sadness knowing that we'll never get a chance to hear his thoughts on these issues but hope that he would be happy knowing so many people are working on them.

In response to the ongoing harms caused by the United States's highly commodified housing system, there is a growing call for "social housing" institutions that could "decommodify" housing. Examples of such institutions include community land trusts, tenant cooperatives, mission-driven nonprofits, well-functioning public housing, and others. In contrast to most affordable housing policies in the United States, social housing projects do not simply involve housing subsidies for the less fortunate or for for-profit developers. While the institutional designs may vary, what today's social housing proposals have in common is that they impose structural restrictions on speculation and profit-making and that they include some degree of democratic resident control. Still, despite this growing demand for social housing, there is little agreement on what the term even means in the US context, let alone the institutions and policies necessary for a transition to a full system of robust social housing. All of these require particular agents of change who can bring such a housing system into existence and, more importantly, keep it going.

Erik Olin Wright spent the better part of three decades re-founding Marxist class analysis. Among his contributions, Erik showed with characteristic clarity that (1) a class analysis was based on a class structure that delineated objective material interests, (2) for certain locations in that class structure, some of those interests might be in contradiction with each other, and (3) exploitation was central to class analysis. The core purpose of class analysis is fundamentally about identifying actors and forces in anticapitalist struggles and their potential for building and exercising political power. Indeed, a core motivation for Erik's insistence that exploitation formed the foundation of class analysis was ultimately a strategic one: the exploited have power. Those who reside in a contradictory location have indeterminate interests, because they are simultaneously exploiters and exploited, and as a result they can be *either* allies or enemies.

In his later years, Erik shifted his focus to the Real Utopias Project, exploring institutional designs that are either feasible or actually existing in the world today. Real utopias prefigured a more emancipatory world of tomorrow. A core motivation for this framework was Erik's skepticism of the possibility of a socialist rupture to create a sustainable and democratic society that would not slip back into capitalism, or worse. The goal was to discover institutions that could *erode* capitalism to the point where eventually we find ourselves in "something like socialism." In this project, the core questions were around the desirability, achievability, and viability of particular institutions: Do we want it? Could we get it? And if we got it, could we keep it?[1]

In this essay we explore the real utopia of social housing, borrowing from Erik's insights about class analysis to develop an account of the agents who might bring it into existence. We first describe the broad contours of what we call "Social Housing 2.0," which draws from a variety of previous instances of decommodified housing. After briefly discussing the desirability and viability of social housing, we then focus the rest of the paper on questions of achievability. We elaborate the basis of an emerging coalition of supporters for social housing, and finally, we explore the institutional strategy and politics of a transition to a more robust system of social housing.

---

1   Erik Olin Wright, *Envisioning Real Utopias* (London: Verso, 2010).

Social Housing 2.0: A Real Utopia

In the last few years, the discussion among housing activists has moved from a critique of gentrification, displacement, and other manifestations of the housing crisis to a search for an alternative vision. "Social housing" has emerged as a slogan and a goal of housing justice and tenant organizers in the United States. Despite this interest, there is little agreement on what exactly social housing might be, other than something different from the current form of market housing and something which would be both accessible and affordable. Frequent examples include contemporary community land trusts, Vienna's social housing, midcentury US limited-equity cooperatives, and less commonly, US public housing. There is even less clarity on how to achieve this goal, given the deeply entrenched legacy of private market housing.

We have come to treat social housing, and our specific proposal of Social Housing 2.0, as a real utopia. It implies more than a vague call for the decommodification of housing. Taking a cue from Erik's argument for putting the "social" in "socialism," adding "social" to housing foregrounds "social empowerment dimensions" and civic participation. Social housing requires imagining a kind of housing whose production, distribution, and management is guided by deeply democratic principles, a logic of intentional inclusion, and an ethos of care and environmental stewardship. It is important to build institutional designs that insulate housing from the market, but social housing must also work to rebuild our connection to communities and address inequality. Social housing implies a bottom-up element that renders it incompatible with exclusively top-down statist directives, even if its scalability and durability requires it to be in some way publicly backed.

What we are calling Social Housing 2.0 is a kind of housing provision that is (1) non-speculative, (2) democratically controlled by residents, and (3) publicly backed. "Non-speculative" housing means that the price of housing and access to it are not solely determined by the private market. This type of insulation from the free market usually involves price controls on rents and resale values established by the state or the institution that provides the housing. "Democratic control" refers to real, accountable decision-making over the management of the housing itself. "Public backing" stipulates that the state has a responsibility to financially and institutionally support housing. This does not necessarily mean that the government is the direct provider and manager of all housing, but it should ensure that housing is treated as too important to fail. This would additionally include financial tools, technical support, and accountability to ensure that democratic control does not reproduce the same exclusionary dynamics that have taken hold particularly in white homeowner communities.

We call our proposal "social housing" because it recognizes the social value of housing to a society. But we dub it "2.0" because it builds on, and responds to, the lineage of other social housing projects of the past and present. Social Housing 1.0 includes the midcentury welfare state programs and experiments like Britain's council housing, Austria's limited-profit housing associations, or indeed public housing projects of the United States. Those forms of housing were provided partially or fully outside of the free market, and they were publicly backed, typically directly constructed by the national government. These large-scale, non-market housing schemes provided what is today mostly an under-appreciated success: in some European countries they housed nearly a third of their population, helping to underwrite upward social mobility and a reduction in inequality for two generations of Europeans. While US public housing was inspired by European social housing through the writing and advocacy of Catherine Bauer, it was sabotaged in its early days by real estate interests and instead became a symbol of government ineptitude.[2] Still, at its peak it provided affordable homes to over 1.4 million families.[3] Public housing in the United States was structurally inhibited from benefiting broad sections of the population, including the middle classes, leading to its progressive marginalization. As neoliberalism grew over the latter part of the twentieth century, European social housing also was increasingly residualized as housing for the poor, and it lost some of its political support.

The political difficulty in creating new, government-constructed and -managed housing has led many in the United States and the global South to pursue non-statist forms of decommodified housing. These include urban housing cooperatives formed by former squatters, community land trusts (CLTs), and cooperative offshoots of social

2   Alex F. Schwartz, *Housing Policy in the United States* (New York: Routledge, 2015).

3   Ibid., 164.

movements or labor unions, among many others—what we might call "Social Housing 1.5." Many of these projects have been, in Erik's words, "interstitial," because of their small scale. Some, like CLTs, have been replicated and adapted via nonprofit advocacy networks. Others, like tenement syndicates in Germany, have developed autonomous funding models to build new housing. Social Housing 1.5 models create organizational mechanisms to insulate the housing from the private market without relying on state regulations. A CLT owns the land via a nonprofit while allowing restricted purchases or rentals on top of it. A limited-equity cooperative sets price caps on the resale of an owned unit, while rental cooperatives collectively set shared rent levels. Relatedly, these housing models also foreground mechanisms of democratic control that Social Housing 1.0 models typically did not. The limitation of these models is most notably their lack of public backing, which limits their ability to grow in scale, as well as the possibility to hold them accountable if they abandon social justice goals and become exclusionary.

The real utopia of Social Housing 2.0 thus draws from both midcentury examples, marked by strong public backing that made possible large-scale interventions into the housing market, and contemporary cases, marked by bottom-up democratic decision-making that has shaped countless smaller experiments in community housing provision outside the market. The result is a set of institutions and structures that decommodify housing. In this context, "decommodify" means reducing the extent to which housing is treated as an asset and governed by market logics. "Reducing" the influence of markets suggests that decommodification can lie on a spectrum, with *stronger* constraints creating housing that is *more* decommodified—without necessarily requiring a wholesale removal of all market mechanisms. Social housing 2.0 is not a particular *type* of housing but rather a *system* of housing that sets out design principles and institutional supports to ensure that housing is a right and that can operate at a scale necessary to solve the problem. It can—and should—take diverse forms, since copying and pasting housing models may not work in certain communities, and institutional monocropping can make housing vulnerable to economic instability.

To make Social Housing 2.0 a reality, though, will require both avoiding the mistakes of the previous generations of social housing, and facing the particular challenges of introducing social housing at scale today, which is unavoidably a question about politics and social actors.

Today's Agents of Change

There is no major city in the United States today without a multitude of tenants' rights groups. "Gentrification" has in the span of a decade crossed from left-wing academic journals into everyday language. From coast to coast, a loosely organized, intersectional, and bottom-up movement is coalescing around housing "justice." This movement is driven by the idea that housing is inextricable from a range of other issues such as racial justice, poverty, the environment, immigration, and the rights of the formerly incarcerated. But if the 2008 financial crisis hardly moved the needle for most policy makers, for a generation of housing activists, it did precisely that. Now, their questions are beginning to break into national policy debates—questions of collective ownership, decommodified land, and housing under democratic control. What might such housing look like? Fighting evictions and foreclosures and capping rents are critical for defending renters and low-income homeowners from predatory real estate developers, and for transferring resources and power from the speculative market back into the hands of residents.

Scholars have increasingly noted the dynamic, multifaceted, and militant nature of today's tenants' movements in the United States, particularly in some urban centers. Indeed, movements appear to have entered a new phase that has only intensified since the pandemic.[4] Vollmer describes New York's current movement as "post-autonomous and post-identitarian."[5] Weaver, while describing a socially heterogeneous movement, talks of a move from a defensive posture to one demanding rent cancellation and beyond.[6] Up until recently, the movement was led mainly by Black and brown women, who, owing to the dynamics of racial capitalism, were most likely to be long-term renters. However,

---

4   Justin Kadi, Lisa Vollmer, and Samuel Stein, "Post-neoliberal Housing Policy? Disentangling Recent Reforms in New York, Berlin and Vienna," *European Urban and Regional Studies* 28, no. 4 (2021): 353–74; John Baranski, *Housing the City by the Bay: Tenant Activism, Civil Rights, and Class Politics in San Francisco* (Redwood City, CA: Stanford University Press, 2019).

5   Lisa Vollmer, "Changing Political Collectivities in Times of Crisis: Tenant Protest in Berlin and New York," in *Urban Change and Citizenship in Times of Crisis*, ed. Bryan S. Turner et al. (London: Routledge, 2020), 97–117, quote on 97.

6   Celia Weaver, "From Universal Rent Control to Cancel Rent: Tenant Organizing in New York State," *New Labor Forum* 30, no. 1 (January 2021): 93–8.

changes in the housing market since 2008 have seen an influx of hetero-geneous younger renters locked out of homeownership, creating a broadened, more radical, base. The movement in New York State, for example, is "diverse and multi-generational, with thousands of young people following the lead of the women of color who have led the move-ment for years." Weaver sees in the current context the possibility of more radical demands to decommodify housing, "using state action to acquire properties and leverage disinvestment to convert thousands of homes into publicly and democratically controlled land/housing."[7] Globally, scholars have begun to describe a convergence in this new phase of urban social movement organizing centered on the pillars of the right to housing and community control.[8]

Yet we know that despite the sympathetic analyses of observers, urban social movements and tenant movements in particular have not always wound up particularly unified or defending radical plat-forms. Describing Britain's tenant movement of the 1970s and 1980s, Cairncross, Clapham, and Goodlad note that as a political identity, tenancy fell to second place behind class as the movement was "divided on the basis of social class, status and consumption position . . . and rarely [displayed] a strong orientation towards collective, militant, protest action."[9] A variety of examples from Europe, South Africa, and Brazil, show that tenants' movements are not always united or radical in their demands.

Class has long been used as a framework to organize forces for social justice. But does it make sense to speak of tenancy in terms of class rela-tions? Housing has long been a site of mobilization and struggle of the marginalized against the powerful, a core focus for Marxists. Some identify housing organizing as a conflict over collective consumption and social reproduction in capitalism.[10] Others point to indeterminacy

---

7   Weaver, "From Universal Rent Control to Cancel Rent," 98.

8   Anna Domaradzka, "Urban Social Movements and the Right to the City: An Introduction to the Special Issue on Urban Mobilization," *VOLUNTAS: International Journal of Voluntary and Nonprofit Organizations* 29, no. 4 (2018): 607–20; Philipp Reick, "Toward a History of Urban Social Movements," *Moving the Social* 63 (2020): 147–62.

9   Liz Cairncross, David Clapham, and Robina Goodlad, "The Social Bases of Tenant Organisation," *Housing Studies* 8, no. 3 (1993): 179–93.

10   Manuel Castells, *The Urban Question: A Marxist Approach* (London: Edward Arnold, 1977).

on the class question as "urban conflicts in developed capitalist societies . . . clearly [cannot] be reduced to the contradiction between capital
and wage labour because they [involve] the state as well as other popular
classes."[11] Today's activists do speak of class, though not in the traditional Marxist sense. It is not uncommon for activists to refer to "the
tenant class" or to the "Renter Nation"—describing a collective group of
people who share interests as unpropertied renters and who would, in
principle, stand to gain in the socialization of housing.[12] Movement
analyses vary in how precise or expansively they define this group. Some
analyses, such as the perspective put forward by Right to the City,
include lower-income or highly indebted owners ("bank tenants");
high-income renters, however, are often not included.[13] Other analyses
note that while working-class people are at the core of the tenant class,
middle-class and white-collar tenants have certainly appeared as vocal
participants in today's movements.

Contradictory Class Locations within Housing Relations

The need to figure out who is on which side of what fence in order to
make social housing possible calls for an analysis of political forces and
identities. So, is class analysis relevant for housing? Some have attempted
to generate such an analysis, positing that one's "means of residence"
constituted the basis for "housing classes," and that in turn shaped class
interests and class consciousness, which additionally shaped racist attitudes.[14] Yet most Marxists argue that classes are only defined with respect
to the means of production and that other types of economic or consumer
assets, while important, do not form the basis of class location per se.[15]

---

11   Paul Hendler, "The Tyranny of Concepts: Assessing the Housing and Urban
Political Theories of Manuel Castells," South African Sociological Review (1989): 23–36.

12   Weaver, "From Universal Rent Control to Cancel Rent"; Right to the City
Alliance, Rise of the Renter Nation: Solutions to the Housing Affordability Crisis, Homes
for All, June 2014.

13   Right to the City, Rise of the Renter Nation.

14   John Rex and Robert Moore, Race, Community and Conflict: A Study of
Sparkbrook (London: Oxford University Press, 1967).

15   Peter Saunders, "Beyond Housing Classes: The Sociological Significance of
Private Property Rights in Means of Consumption," International Journal of Urban and
Regional Research 8, no. 2 (1984): 202–27.

Even if one does not believe that housing can constitute a basis for class relations (though we believe it does), a number of insights from Marxist class analysis, particularly the work of Erik, are useful for understanding the housing question. Erik describes the three "fundamental theses of class analysis: (1) What you *have* determines what you *get*, (2) What you *have* determines what you *have to do to get what you get*, and (3) *What you have to do to get what you get* determines *whose interests are opposed to your interests*."[16] Housing shapes the answers to all of these questions.

As we argue below, the configurations of *property rights* and *market power* determine how someone secures the use value of housing, whether they can use that housing to also generate exchange value, and who in the sphere of housing has opposing interests to them. As with traditional class analysis, a housing class analysis can demonstrate (1) the ways that property ownership shape objective interests, (2) how ownership of property can create antagonisms between actors or sets of actors, (3) that while the system of property rights can generate interests, some of those relations may also generate contradictions, and (4) that rearranging property rights can be a core element of emancipation.

There are two dimensions of our housing class analysis: the *property rights* a resident or household has with regard to their residence (as owners or renters) and whether they have high or low *market power* to acquire that residence. The first dimension concerns the property rights for the resident. Owners and renters have fundamentally distinct relationships to housing. Owners have freehold rights, including the right to use the property and sell the property. These rights may be partially encumbered, such as when a bank provides a loan to purchase the property that entitles it to sell the property through foreclosure in the event of the owner's default. In the end, these property rights entitle the owner

---

16 This exact phrasing came from Fall 2013 lecture notes of his "Class, State, and Ideology" course. Wright talks about "the fundamental metathesis of class analysis"— the idea that class, from a Marxist perspective, had important implications for individuals and institutions (Erik Olin Wright, *Approaches to Class Analysis* [Cambridge: Cambridge University Press, 2005], 21). However, to our knowledge he did not write in his published work that these three criteria were the "fundamental theses." The first two were described as two propositions on the effects of class on individuals (ibid, 22). Erik Olin Wright, "What Is Class?" (lecture, "Class, State, and Ideology," University of Wisconsin–Madison, 2013).

to the proceeds of the sale, conditional on also paying back the lender, if necessary. As a result, these rights can be incredibly lucrative, particularly in hot market conditions. By contrast, renters have leasehold property rights, which confer to them usage of the property for a specified duration but do not give them the right to sell the property. Their specific rights are stipulated in a contract with the owner of the property, the landlord. Ownership rights are established by real estate law, while tenants' legal rights are codified in landlord-tenant law. Ownership and tenancy operate in largely separate markets: home sellers set prices based on comparable homes for sale, while landlords set rents based on comparable homes for rent. Given these distinctions, we should analyze owners and renters separately, and largely not in *direct* relationship to one another.[17]

The second dimension is the amount of market power a potential resident has to acquire a given property. Currently, markets are used to allocate nearly all housing in the United States. Access to a home, whether owned or rented, relies on the purchase or leasing of a dwelling, and the price is set via a competitive market. In a competitive market, high-market-power actors can outbid those with less market power, or at least drive up the price. The aggregation of such competitive bids across a similar class of commodity can lead to market-wide price increases for those commodities. With enough inequality in wealth and income, those with low market power can be excluded from the markets, leading to the consolidation of property ownership at the top of the income distribution. Sellers and landlords set asking prices based on prevailing market conditions, while buyers and renters bid against other prospective residents for the use rights of the property in question.[18]

---

17   There are some linkages in the owner and renter markets. The value of land may, for example, lead increases in aggregate home prices to also push up rent prices. While by and large, a home searcher looks *either* for a rental *or* for a home to purchase, dynamics in one market can affect the other, such as when high home prices lead prospective buyers to stay in the rental market longer.

18   "Bidding" among prospective home buyers is common, especially in hot housing markets. This puts buyers in sometimes aggressive competition with each other, as bidding wars can quickly drive up the purchase price of a home. In contrast, it is less common that a rental unit is put up for a direct bidding war, though that *does happen* in tight rental markets. More common is that a landlord will receive multiple applications for a unit and will select a tenant based on things like credit history, available income and assets, rental history, and other traits.

Unlike some other commodity markets—which can respond to price increases by increasing the production of identical items—each housing unit is unique because it sits on a specific coordinate on the globe. Land is a finite resource; as Mark Twain said, "They're not making it anymore." Housing supply can be increased to bring down aggregate prices, but at the end of the day, one occupant will get the housing unit and everyone else will not. Thus, in the bidding for a particular housing unit, those with greater market power can outbid those will less power. The analysis of these two dimensions produces a matrix of housing class locations, depicted in Table 8.1.

Table 8.1: Housing Class Analysis: Property Rights and Market Power

	Rents	Owns
High Market Power	**High-Market-Power** Renter	**High-Market-Power** Owner
Low Market Power	Low-Market-Power Renter	Low-Market-Power Owner

There are some complexities in this analytical structure. The first is an issue of temporality. The price of housing is determined *before* the moment of acquisition. A prospective occupant will go through a process of negotiation before they ever have any direct property rights to the home. The result of that negotiation will nonetheless shape the ongoing costs of living there, either through monthly rental payments or, in the case of typical owners, through mortgage payments. This cost of living mostly stays constant for the duration of the property right, which for owners is indefinite and for renters is the length of the lease.[19] Thus, it is important to understand the conditions when those prices are set, which is before the actual acquisition of the property. While housing tenure constitutes an ongoing use value for the resident, it does not generate new commodities or exchange values during the period of that tenure, since exchange value for a property is only

---

19 There are a few qualifications to this. The first is that for owners, they are usually responsible for property taxes, which may increase over time as land values go up. Second, the costs of homeownership also include upkeep of the property, which may fluctuate over time. Lastly, while the lease contract stipulates the rent payments for the duration of the *lease*, it does not determine the price of the full *occupancy*, as renters may renew a lease, though under potentially a higher rent.

realized at the point of resale. The exception to this is of course the landlord-tenant relationship, where landlords regularly collect rents from their tenants.

This leads to another complexity. While prospective residents may bid for a housing unit, there is ultimately another agent who determines the agreed-upon price prior to the moment of acquisition. This is the *current* property rights holder, that is, the seller in the ownership market and the landlord in the rental market. As the seller or landlord, their interest is to get the highest price, given the conditions of the market. This places potential occupants of that residence in competition with each other, as they bid for the right of occupancy or ownership. With few exceptions, the competitor with the most market power is likely to win out.

Given the way that market competition creates antagonism between low- and high-market-power renters and owners, there is an important issue of temporality in the emergence of contradictions in the system. Especially for owners, there is a contradiction between their interest *prior* to acquisition and their interests *after* acquisition. Prospective owners want to be able to buy low, but then they hope the property value will continue to increase, so that they can eventually sell high. But both of these prices are set by broader market conditions. Prior to acquisition, a low-market-power future owner is competing with higher-market-power future owners and would prefer that they stay away from the desired property. Yet, after acquisition and at the moment of a subsequent resale, that same owner has an interest in high-market-power buyers bidding up that property, as well as other properties in the area. This speculative rationale is part of what drives "gentrification," where people may buy housing at a low cost and, as conditions change in the neighborhood, reap large returns on resale.

Meanwhile, renters do not have the ability to gain any returns from a resale. Still, there are contradictions in this process. Higher-market-power renters can use their resources to crowd out poorer renters, thus gaining access to housing units that would have otherwise been occupied by those low-market-power renters. Yet high-market-power tenants risk being subsequently in competition with even-higher-market-power renters. Again, the process of gentrification is illuminating. Gentrification often starts with slightly more affluent households moving into poor neighborhoods, but as time progresses, those initial in-movers risk future displacement, as market conditions draw in higher-market-power in-movers, who further push up rents in an area.[20]

Thus, while high-market-power renters benefit from housing commodification at an initial time, low-market-power owners benefit from it at a later time. The identification of this temporal contradiction means that *high-market-power renters and low-market-power owners occupy contradictory locations within housing relations.* The indeterminacy of their interests means that they could side with low-market-power renters against the commodification of housing or with the high-market-power owners in support of expanded commodification (seen in the middle-shaded cells in Table 8.1).

Affordable housing policy in the United States has only focused on one quadrant: low-market-power renters. By altering property rights and the structures of market power, Social Housing 2.0 can help resolve the contradictions between those low-market-power owners and high-market-power renters. These groups will be important for the emerging political coalition to transition away from free market housing.

Race into Profit: Racial Capitalism and Residential Property

It is impossible to consider housing and residential property in the United States without discussing racism. The literature on racial capitalism provides effective tools to understand the connections between structures of economic and racial oppression. Scholars who have studied racism and capitalism argue that while the former predates the latter, they interact with one another to produce new forms of domination.[21] Instead of increased commodification that would "free people from domination based on personal status," capitalism has produced differences and new forms of domination.[22] As Bonilla-Silva has argued, these

---

20   Phillip Clay, "The Process of Black Suburbanization," *Urban Affairs Review* 14, no. 4 (1979): 405–24.

21   Cedric J. Robinson, *Black Marxism* (Chapel Hill: University of North Carolina Press, 1983); Eduardo Bonilla-Silva, "Rethinking Racism: Toward a Structural Interpretation," *American Sociological Review* 62, no. 3 (1997): 465–80; Michael Omi and Howard Winant, *Racial Formation in the United States* (London: Routledge, 1994).

22   William H. Sewell, "The Capitalist Epoch," *Social Science History* 38, no. 1–2 (Spring/Summer 2014): 1.

are distinct forms of advantage and disadvantage.[23] Capitalist housing is a clear example of this, and recent scholarship has begun to discuss it in racial capitalist terms.[24] Free market housing both excludes people from its benefits and leverages racism to maximize profits. As Virdee puts it, "In symbolically and materially revaluing some parts of the subaltern population while simultaneously devaluing others, elite deployment of racism aims at engineering a chasm in identification such that those who have been revalued become indifferent to, even complicit in, the suffering and degradation of those subalterns marked as 'racially inferior,' including within the same geographical space."[25]

Racial projects have long been inextricably tied with government and private sector efforts to expand markets and profits. New Deal institutions like the Federal Housing Administration turned the United States into a nation of homeowners while explicitly excluding Black families from those opportunities. The private real estate market, in conjunction with government policy, withheld housing opportunities and financing from neighborhoods of color, commonly known as "redlining." Even institutions like the Home Owners' Loan Corporation, which gave substantial volumes of refinanced loans to Black homeowners struggling in the wake of the Great Depression, did so mostly to bail out the white lending institutions that issued the mortgages.[26] All of these policies were part of an explicit effort to encourage private homeownership in contrast to renting.[27]

These policies shaped how people understood their own economic opportunities with respect to racial others. As Faber summarized the thesis of Kenneth Jackson's *Crabgrass Frontier*, "By giving federal backing to the idea that proximity to people of color necessarily leads to property value decline, these policies created a powerful financial

---

23   Bonilla-Silva, "Rethinking Racism."

24   Jennifer L. Fluri et al., "Accessing Racial Privilege through Property: Geographies of Racial Capitalism," *Geoforum* 132 (2022): 238–46; Scott N. Markley et al., "The Limits of Homeownership: Racial Capitalism, Black Wealth, and the Appreciation Gap in Atlanta," *International Journal of Urban and Regional Research* 44, no. 2 (2020): 310–28.

25   Satnam Virdee, "Racialized Capitalism," *Sociological Review* 67, no. 1 (2019): 35.

26   Todd M. Michney and LaDale Winling, "New Perspectives on New Deal Housing Policy: Explicating and Mapping HOLC Loans to African Americans," *Journal of Urban History* 46, no. 1 (2020): 150–80.

27   Gail Radford, *Modern Housing for America: Policy Struggles in the New Deal Era* (Chicago: University of Chicago Press, 1996).

incentive for white communities to segregate themselves."[28] Even as fair housing laws sought to outlaw discrimination, the housing market continued to profit from, and reinforce, racism and inequality. As Keeanga-Yamahtta Taylor puts it, "The real estate industry wielded the magical ability to transform race into profit with the racially bifurcated housing market."[29] The result is a *ten-to-twenty-fold difference in household wealth* between white and Black households. There is a large gap between Black and white homeownership rates, and African Americans are more likely to be recent homeowners, own homes in segregated neighborhoods, have risky mortgages, and face more volatile neighborhood markets. The influence of racism in housing cannot be understated. Markley et al. demonstrate the importance of the racial appreciation gap in the housing market in Atlanta: a "neighborhood's racial composition has a more salient impact on home price change than its income."[30]

The market financially rewards racism in housing, *irrespective of the biases any individual might have.* Social housing removes those rewards and redistributes housing opportunity. Today, the preexisting homeowners in a gentrifying neighborhood, regardless of their own personal feelings about it, have an economic interest in the ensuing rise in property values, whatever the causes or consequences may be. Low-market-power white homeowners may consider their interests to be more aligned with those of well-off homeowners than with renters or with a coalition behind social housing. A robust social housing system would do away with this racial bonus for homeowners in white neighborhoods. This is why there is a long line of anti-racist thinking that proposes social forms of housing, including the Black Panthers' Ten-Point Program, which called for private housing and land to be converted into cooperatives to build "decent housing" backed by the government.

While social housing undermines the structural incentives for racism, on its own it likely will not alleviate otherwise persistent racial biases. To think about this transition seriously means facing the very real

---

28   Jacob W. Faber, "We Built This: Consequences of New Deal Era Intervention in America's Racial Geography," *American Sociological Review* 85, no. 5 (2020): 740.

29   Keeanga-Yamahtta Taylor, *Race for Profit: How Banks and the Real Estate Industry Undermined Black Homeownership* (Chapel Hill: University of North Carolina Press, 2019), 11.

30   Markley et al., "The Limits of Homeownership."

possibility of racial backlash. There is certainly precedent for this, particularly when thinking about white homeowners, from the famous homeowners' revolts in California in the 1970s to the resistance to scattered-site public housing in Yonkers in the 1980s made famous by the HBO mini-series *Show Me a Hero*. The history of labor organizing in the United States is marked by instances of a lack of solidarity between white workers and non-white workers—the results of which provide temporary rewards for white workers while hurting all workers in the longer term. No institutional fix obviates the need to shift consciousness. Scholars and strategists emphasize the importance of "transformative organizing" when reaching those sectors, a way of organizing that seeks to transform subjects and their horizons away from narrow demands.[31] Thus, the struggle for housing would gain positive synergy from parallel movements for gender, environmental, political, and—most notably—racial justice.

The Strategy and Politics of Transition

How do we actually create social housing in a capitalist society? We do not have the ability to instantly remove speculation from the housing market. Real estate plays an outsized role in the United States, touching almost every sphere, from politics to pensions. People are materially and ideologically bought into the current system. Two-thirds of US households own their home, and many of the remaining renters aspire to become homeowners. The vast majority of rental housing also is held by private landlords. Whatever the long-term vision of social housing might be, a transition strategy that includes intermediary policies, institutions, and social movements will be needed.

Erik described a strategy of "eroding" capitalism in which the introduction of viable alternatives can both protect people from the ongoing harms of the system as well as incrementally blaze a path toward a new kind of society.[32] The idea is that you do not ever directly attempt to

---

31   Bill Fletcher Jr., "How Race Enters Class in the United States," in *What's Class Got to Do With It? American Society in the Twenty-First Century*, ed. Michael Zweig (Ithaca, NY: Cornell University Press, 2004), 35–44.

32   Erik Olin Wright, *How to Be an Anticapitalist in the Twenty-First Century* (London: Verso, 2019).

"smash" the system, but, using the metaphor of an ecosystem, you rather introduce an "invasive species" that eventually crowds out the old capitalist institutions. But in order for this to be successful, there needs to be both conditions that allow the institution to "take hold" and provisions to ensure that negative side effects are minimized. To the first point, we will next discuss types of coalitions of actors who can help support the emergence of social housing. Then, in response to the second point, we will describe types of transitionary institutions that can help smooth the process of transformation away from our current housing system.

Table 8.1 shows us which groups are most likely to support social housing. Low-market-power renters have no material interest in preserving market housing and would receive the greatest benefit by transitioning toward social housing. In contrast, high-market-power owners have benefited from the current housing system and would have little incentive to change. The other diagonal cells—low-market-power owners and high-market-power renters—are where people's relationships to market housing could be called contradictory: in certain ways they both benefit from, and are harmed by, the current arrangement. Thus, while low-market-power renters might theoretically form the core of a pro-social housing coalition, these other two groups could be brought on board if the conditions were right for them.

How do we bring people in those contradictory locations along in support of social housing, given that they are partially invested in the current system? Erik noted the importance of "symbiotic" strategies, which solve concrete problems for those invested in an existing system.[33] The main "problems" for low-market-power owners include the high cost of purchase, financing, and maintenance, which in the context of broader economic volatility can place these households one step away from foreclosure. High-market-power renters are similarly affected by high rents but also by the lack of housing in desirable locations. Erik was also fascinated by institutions and policy models that essentially "down-titrate" people's exposure to capitalism, most notably the Meidner plan. With social housing, there will need to be programs that both expand the supply and share of housing built outside of the traditional market, as well as address the ongoing problems of commodified

---

33 Wright, *Envisioning Real Utopias*.

housing. Next, we describe a series of potential programs to address these issues.

The first is to use government funding to build lots of new social housing. This has been the demand in the US of the Homes Guarantee platform, which calls for the creation of millions of new units of quality, green public housing. The expansion of housing supply is a core need for tenants living in substandard conditions and paying exorbitant rents. Expanding supply would also theoretically help reduce prices in the broader rental market. The impacts of creating new social housing would be substantial, yet the policy does not address the possibility of converting rental and ownership units currently held in the private market.

One proposal for a real utopian transitionary institution is what we are calling the Social Housing Development Authority (SHDA).[34] The SHDA seeks to transfer housing out of the free market and into the social housing sector. It does this by first focusing on the acquisition of distressed real estate assets. Currently, when a property goes into financial distress, it eventually works its way through various foreclosure or short sale proceedings, which ultimately land it back in the private market, usually going to a real estate speculator looking to buy property cheaply. The SHDA uses the power of the state to intercede, acquiring the property before the private market can. Next, the SHDA rehabilitates the property to livability standards as well as upgrading it with green building materials to help address the climate crisis. Last, the SHDA transfers it to the social housing sector—either to a nonprofit organization, a tenants' cooperative, a community land trust, or a public housing authority. To facilitate this transfer, and to provide a renewable and independent flow of resources to the housing entity to do its work, the SHDA provides low-cost financing to the acquiring institutions.

An institution like the SHDA could create a number of positive outcomes. Residents who live in substandard housing would have access to the means to improve the livability of their home. Current and future residents of the social housing would benefit from low-cost places to live. By crowding out real estate speculators, the SHDA would undermine the forces that drive up the cost of housing. Even for properties

34 Gianpaolo Baiocchi and H. Jacob Carlson, *The Case for a Social Housing Development Authority*, Urban Democracy Lab, November 2020.

that were not acquired by the SHDA, the throwing of water on parts of the overheated housing market could bring down the overall temperature. We have also suggested that the SHDA would not be limited to acquiring residential property; it could also convert hotels or commercial space into residences for the homeless (as is currently being done in New York City and Seattle) or expand the overall supply of social housing through new construction. By focusing on a more feasible section of the housing market (distressed assets), the SHDA can start to incubate a more robust institution that would be capable of implementing a broader social housing program.

Many policy tools are even more effective at the federal level, which has more expansive powers, especially for financing. Yet, as we have seen, new federal programs can be difficult to get off the ground, particularly in the face of a gridlocked federal government. In contrast, while financial resources may be smaller at the local level, political opportunities may be more fluid. Already, new "tenant opportunity to purchase," or TOPA, laws have been passed in multiple cities and states over the past few years. Many places have established new affordable housing trust funds with the explicit goal of encouraging the growth of tenant cooperatives and community land trusts.

Even with a large-scale public investment, the reality is that social housing would likely be created or converted incrementally. If social housing has the kind of ripple effects in a community that we believe it could, each new social housing project would in turn have effects on the surrounding market-rate rental and ownership properties. When an institution like the SHDA acquires and converts a distressed property, it would help stabilize surrounding property values. Some evidence exists, for example, that properties around community land trusts acquire higher property values. While arguably better than if it were acquired by an investor, this nonetheless can in some cases increase the market forces affecting nearby housing, potentially spurring gentrification. These all will interact with the racial dynamics of the housing market, and it is also not unreasonable to expect that in some communities the development of social housing projects will trigger hostilities (like those that currently exist in some places toward public housing). The local externalities of social housing will be highly contingent, but additional policies like rent control could ensure that social housing does not provoke unintended dynamics with market housing.

Conclusion

One of the less specified elements of Erik's real utopian writing has been the question of who exactly would be the agents of the proposed transformations. In *How to Be an Anticapitalist in the Twenty-First Century*, Erik writes a concluding chapter offering ideas on who these agents might be. Making explicit his break with more determinist Marxisms, Erik writes that "actual" class has become too fragmented to be an agent; instead, it is the interplay of identities, interests, and values that would unite a political subject up to the task. In this account, contingent political struggles rather than unfolding economic conditions take center stage—an argument that could run the risk of becoming detached from an analysis of capitalism. In his homage to Erik, Burawoy links these struggles to the pendulum of commodification and decommodification of Polanyi. For Burawoy, contemporary agents of social transformation have grievances that center on capitalism, yet they are also pushing toward new visions of a more emancipatory future. "Only a powerful 'counter-hegemonic' ideology," he writes, "can make the market an object of socialist struggle, given its capacity to naturalize its own working."[35]

Part of Erik's rationale for a strategy of *eroding* capitalism was that all societies contain elements of capitalism and socialism, and the goal was to push things *toward* the latter, without pre determining what a complete system of socialism might look like. Doing so helps incrementally shift people's consciousness about what is possible and helps minimize transition costs that could disrupt the path forward. It thus acknowledges the strategic benefit of hybrid institutions that may contain elements of the prior system. Even if they have restrictions on profit-making, many actually existing instances of social housing are quasi-ownership models. In the interregnum, such models will be useful as transitionary platforms in countries with high homeownership rates. Decommodifying housing need not—and we argue should not—rely on only one type of housing, whether that be government-managed public housing, land trusts, cooperatives, or any others. Whenever one of these

---

35 Michael Burawoy, "A Tale of Two Marxisms: Remembering Erik Olin Wright (1947–2019)," *New Left Review* 121 (January–February 2020): 91–95. It appears as chapter 1 of this volume.

instances takes hold, it can demonstrate to others that an alternative is possible. But for social housing to be viable and achievable as a system, it will require social movements and popular opinion to force the state to use its resources to both jumpstart and maintain the conditions to ensure housing as a right and a social good.

9

The Emancipation Network: Discovering Anticapitalist Institutions within Brazilian Capitalism
Ruy Braga

"Capitalism breeds anticapitalists."

> Erik Olin Wright, *How to Be an Anticapitalist in the Twenty-First Century.*

Although the struggle to democratize access to the Brazilian public university education system is old, it was only after a Brazilian delegation participated in the Third World Conference against Racism, Racial Discrimination, Xenophobia and Related Forms of Intolerance, promoted by the United Nations in 2001, that the issue of racial quotas moved to the forefront of the federal government's agenda. After Lula's election in 2002, affirmative policies were approved in 2003 and implemented in Brazil's public university system from 2004 onward and were finally confirmed as constitutional in 2012 by Brazil's Supreme Court.

However, as is often the case in Brazil, the approval of a new law only created an arena of struggle defined by the tension between legality and reality, requiring an intensification, rather than relaxation, of popular mobilization from collective actors who supported the new policy. Between the approval of the quota system and the recognition of its constitutionality, Brazilian public universities went through a period of intense disputes, with an alliance between the student movement and the Black movement positioned in the front line of defense.[1]

---

1   Sidney de Paula Oliveira, *Cotas raciais istemaema universal: Um estudo sobre o acesso de estudantes negros(as) na Universidade Federal de São Paulo* (São Paulo: Dialética, 2021).

By the mid-2000s, undergraduate students at the University of São Paulo (USP) were increasingly involved in the debate over quotas, especially because of the failure on the part of their university—the largest public university in Brazil—to implement the policy. While many federal universities began to emphasize inclusion of Black and Indigenous students, USP began slowly to discuss a new evaluation system for public school students, with no mention of ethno-racial criteria. The university's student and Black movements were moved to act on two major fronts: on the one hand, they pressured the university council through alliances with pro-quota sectors of the academic bureaucracy; on the other, they mobilized students through direct action.

One of these initiatives involved an effort to create new popular preparatory schools for the admission exam that selects students for USP. These preparatory courses help public school students who otherwise would struggle to compete on equal terms with students who have attended better-resourced private schools.[2] With the reconstruction of the Cursinho da Poli (located at USP's Engineering School) and the creation of the Butantã popular prep school in 2005, named after the neighborhood where the university's main campus is located, the alliance between the Black and student movements established what would become the Emancipation Network, today the largest national movement for the democratization of access to university education.

In this chapter, I will argue that in different ways, the history and structure of this social movement not only illustrate the purpose of the Real Utopias Project (RUP) which Erik Olin Wright launched in the early 1990s, but also illuminate central aspects of the relationship between Marxist sociology and emancipatory social movements—especially those related to the transmission of critical knowledge from academia to civil society. This shift of ideas and energy from academia to civil society helps us to clarify not only Erik's project, but also the basic relationship between science and utopia in his sociology. In Brazil, the Emancipation Network has tried to address the challenge represented by the relationship between Marxism and social movements,

---

2   After resisting for a decade and a half to adopt a racial quota system, in 2018 USP finally gave in and introduced affirmative policies for that year's admission exam.

illustrating how projects constructed within a contemporary context might begin to create a real utopia.

In its most general formulation, I interpret Erik's RUP as being first a theory capable of identifying anticapitalist institutions within capitalism that can form part of a socialist order. In the case of the racial quota system, for example, it is necessary to consider the notion of "transition" underlying radical transformations: since the different structural dominations of capitalism will not automatically disappear during the transition to socialism, the shift will require institutions capable of strengthening systemic emancipatory arrangements. In this sense, determining what extent a public policy driven by a social movement transforms capitalism and to what extent it simply reproduces it is a complex challenge that cannot be solved abstractly. The socialist potential of an institution as a "party-movement," for example, depends on many factors, including the radicalism of its political program and the strength of its collective action.

Here I will argue that, contrary to what some of its critics claim,[3] Erik's RUP has a prominent role in the new party-movements that have emerged in the past two decades in both the global North and South.[4] Naturally, considering the different constitutive dimensions of this theory, it is important to locate the space that these new political experiences occupy in the general framework of the project. For the purposes of this case study, we will focus on just one of the three modalities ("ruptural," "symbiotic," and "interstitial") of social transformation that Erik identified: the interstitial transformation, which most accurately expresses the political experience represented by the Emancipation Network and which, in the framework that Erik laid out, is the kind of social transformation that results "from the cumulative effect of moves within existing rules of the game."[5]

If it is not possible to speak of "dismantling capitalism" when we refer to the democratizing that arises from new party-movements acting

---

3   Dylan Riley, "Real Utopia or Abstract Empiricism? Comment on Burawoy and Wright," *New Left Review* 121 (January–February 2020): 99–107.

4   For example, the recent merger between the Movement of Homeless Workers, the Emancipation Network, and the Socialism and Freedom Party led to Guilherme Boulos becoming a major leader of the Brazilian left wing and runner-up for mayor of São Paulo in the 2020 election.

5   Erik Olin Wright, *How to Be an Anticapitalist in the Twenty-First Century* (New York: Verso, 2019).

under neoliberal hegemony, can the interstitial transformations brought about by these actors create opportunities for "dismantling capitalism," through the intersection of struggles for public housing, the democratization of access to public education, and movements against racism as well as those in favor of gender equality? In our understanding, Erik's RUP not only helps us to theorize the social practice of these party-movements, but also to politicize the social science that underlies his utopian project. However, this back-and-forth between theory and politics demands a closer look, which I will do through an overview of Erik's intellectual trajectory.

From Science to Utopia: Proposing the Challenge

Jorge Luis Borges once said that each writer "creates his own peers," changing our conceptions of both the past and the future of an author. In this sense, Michael Burawoy's statement that "Erik moved from a class analysis without utopia to utopia without class analysis" could definitively shape perceptions about Erik's intellectual trajectory, altering our interpretation of both the past and the future of his work.[6]

The argument is quite clear: Erik changed the meaning of his Marxism that made him world famous, from the meticulous work of observing the social structure to a no less meticulous work of mining "real utopias"—that is, projects, institutions, and processes capable of challenging capitalism. Michael suggests that a kind of "epistemological break" occurred; instead of moving from critical humanism to the science of history, as in Althusser's well-known interpretation of the young Marx, Erik navigated a path in the reverse direction, from scientific Marxism to a critical and humanistic Marxism. Here I propose an argument that complements Michael's perspective, but which requires a repositioning of the observer's perspective. It is like a parallax: the object does not actually move, but the eye captures a slightly different angle on the observed object.[7]

---

6   Michael Burawoy, "A Tale of Two Marxisms: Remembering Erik Olin Wright (1947–2019)," *New Left Review* 121 (January–February 2020): 67–98. Reprinted as chapter 1 in this volume.

7   This slight adjustment will be useful so that I can start from Erik's Real Utopias Project in order to interpret the empirical object of this chapter.

First, I would say that the idea of an "epistemological break" is, of course, quite suggestive. However, it misses an essential issue both in the trajectory of Erik's thought and in his political transformation. After all, contrary to what Althusser thought about the young Marx, there was never really a break between the critical-humanist Marx and the scientific Marx. Marx's trajectory beginning with his "Theses on Feuerbach" was, above all, political and revolutionary, driven by this young Hegelian's discovery of the recently formed French labor movement.[8] The same can be said of Erik: I do not really see a "break" in the dynamics of his thinking, but a dialectical overcoming of the limits of his scientific Marxism, driven by a political shift in focus, from the academy to civil society.

We know that in the name of scientific Marxism, Erik challenged sociology in the academic field. The proof of his remarkable success lies in the fact that throughout the world, his works have risen to canonical status in the sociology of social stratification. We must then ask, what happened to the combative drive of his early work on social classes, which aimed to defeat positivist sociology? Michael has noted that from the 1980s the relationship between Erik's Marxism and his sociology, at least with regard to the theme of social classes, gradually became more accommodating, more ecumenical and pluralist.[9] In other words, after becoming his generation's outspoken Marxist critic of sociology, Erik seems to have reconciled himself to sociology.

In dialectical terms, this accommodation happens when the subject retracts and realizes that there has never really been a serious conflict pushing them forward—that is, when it turns out that opponents have always been more or less on the same side. Thus, reconciliation preserves previous moments, simultaneously denying and conserving the core issues by elevating them to a new synthesis. Or, in dialectical language: when something becomes its opposite and therefore contradicts itself, it expresses its essence. This seems to be the case for the relationship between science and utopia in Erik, as his focus shifted from an emphasis on analyzing structures to the recognition that capitalist reification prevents the realization of our potential as a society and as a species.

8   Michael Löwy, *The Theory of Revolution in the Young Marx* (Chicago: Haymarket Books, 1972).
9   Burawoy, "A Tale of Two Marxisms."

Why isn't the transformation of something into its opposite—from a sophisticated and world-renowned scientific Marxism into a no less attractive utopian Marxism—astonishing? First, because utopia had always been there: Erik was a radical in his youth, attracted by the combination of the struggle for civil rights, the mobilization against the Vietnam War, and the rise of the counterculture.[10] In other words, knowing the political context helps us to appreciate the continuing presence of this "negative state," which attempts to realize latent potentialities by combating reified structures. At first, this battle emerged in Erik's eyes as an attack on the positivist professional sociology carried out in the sociological field itself, but then it turned to attacking society itself.[11]

This is not just my opinion: the fact that his research program on social class has become part of the canon of social stratification demonstrates his victory in this arena. Some will say that his challenge has been absorbed in some way by mainstream sociology. I disagree; it is more a capitulation by the discipline of sociology than an absorption of class analysis. However, even this victory could not represent a revolution in the relationships of forces in the field, as this can only be achieved through what Gramsci called "great politics," that is, through struggles capable of "reproducing or transforming social structures, founding or preserving states, etc."[12] And it was to the domain of "great politics" that Erik moved in the early 1990s, armed with his RUP.

Here it is worth remembering that, according to a certain theoretical tradition of dialectical Marxism, it is not that intellectuals by themselves arbitrarily "create" concepts; their formation is rather a subjective development under the direction of organic intellectuals. This is the problem that Gramsci described as "unity between theory and practice": how can organic intellectuals elaborate and make coherent the problems posed by the masses?[13] In other words, with his RUP, Erik imbued existing collective experiences with a flagrant anticapitalist potential. Whether

---

10   Erik Olin Wright, "Falling into Marxism; Choosing to Stay," in *The Disobedient Generation: Social Theorists in the Sixties*, ed. Alan Sica and Stephen P. Turner (Chicago: University of Chicago Press, 2005).

11   Erik Olin Wright, *Class, Crisis and the State* (London: New Left Books, 1981).

12   Antonio Gramsci, *Cadernos do cárcere (v. 3)* (São Paulo: Civilização Brasileira, 1999), 21.

13   Antonio Gramsci, *Selections from the Prison Notebooks*, ed. and trans. Quintin Hoare and Geoffrey Nowell Smith (New York: International Publishers, 1992), 333.

or not this potential will develop satisfactorily, revealing its disalienating essence, does not depend on the individual will of the organic intellectual, but on the political activity of the masses. Ultimately, it is a question that only class struggle can answer.

In other words, it is possible to perceive in the passage from class analysis to the RUP a dialectical victory, which preserved the radicalism of Erik's work and raised it to a higher political level: after all, the struggles would no longer take place within the academic field, but in society itself. And, in fact, Erik never set out to arbitrarily "create" real utopias but rather to "universalize" their existence; that is, to understand their emancipatory "essence" by articulating them in a coherent "totality."

But what "totality" are we talking about? In addition to the scope and limits of the real utopias analyzed in *Envisioning Real Utopias*—that is, Mondragon's cooperatives, Porto Alegre's participatory budget, the universal basic income program, and Wikipedia—Erik bequeathed to us something even more precious: his new program offered an outline of the political subject in the twenty-first century, capable of totalizing the emancipatory potentials of these different experiences. It is not a question of the working class in an orthodox Marxist sense.[14]

But how could a new political subject arise when at the same time internationally established Fordism in the post–Second World War era was collapsing and neoliberalism was rising on a world scale? The Fordist working class seemed completely undone, leaving today an unarticulated set of subordinate groups struggling to redefine and trace their own class boundaries. Inspired by E. P. Thompson, I refer to this moment as "classless class struggle," when the crisis of capitalist globalization universalized popular resistance to the advances of accumulation by dispossession, without, however, giving rise to politically progressive solutions.[15] Perhaps this may suggest an interpretive key to Erik's displacement of classes in favor of real utopias. He understood that classes are being remade on a global scale and decided to embrace the work of building new class-based identities through the project of real utopias.

In summary, I argue that after the collapse of the Soviet bloc, Erik decided to move from a class analysis with weak theoretical elaboration

---

14   Erik Olin Wright, *Envisioning Real Utopias* (New York: Verso, 2010).

15   E. P. Thompson, *The Making of the English Working Class* (London: Victor Gollancz, 1963).

about utopia to a strong concern with utopia befitting a moment of global reconfiguration of social classes. Here we come to Erik's manifesto: *How to Be an Anticapitalist in the Twenty-First Century* (2019). Although it is true that utopian thought is based in the contradiction between reified states and emancipatory potentialities (and the possible overcoming of that contradiction), the anticapitalism defended by Erik does not exclude political parties, but rather makes them a likely bridge between bottom-up and top-down strategies for overcoming capitalist contradictions. In Erik's words:

> Protests and mobilizations outside of the state can be effective in blocking certain state policies; they are not by themselves effective in robustly changing the rules of the game in progressive ways. For this to happen, external protests must be linked to political parties able to pass needed legislation and implement new game rules. And this requires political parties capable of competing effectively in electoral politics.[16]

It is clear that we are not referring to the old communist parties of the past, but to the new party-movements that have multiplied around the world—Podemos in Spain, the American DSA/Our Revolution, the Portuguese Left Bloc, La France Insoumise, and so on. For Erik, the multiplication of party-movements indicated that the very reproduction of capitalism creates anticapitalist forces that combine collective interests and moral values, such as equality, solidarity, and freedom. Furthermore, capitalist alienation prevents the development of human potential. Therefore, the question is how to articulate interests and values in a movement capable of facing capitalism. Since the socialist experience of "crushing" capitalism through political revolutions proved problematic and insufficient, it is up to Marxism to elaborate and make coherent the current problems posed by the masses, in order to advance the task of emancipating humanity from capitalist alienation.

To this end, Erik considered it essential to combine two major political strategies. On the one hand, it would be necessary to domesticate and tame capitalism by combining the strengthening of mixed economy

---

16   Wright, *How to Be an Anticapitalist*, 140–1.

forms with a strong regulation of capital: social protection, public services, financial regulation, and so on. On the other, it would be essential to strengthen the resistance and the experiences of "flight" from capitalism—that is, to boost social movements marked by direct action and led by citizens, consumers, environmentalists, immigrants, young people, people of color, cooperatives, unions, rural workers, and the homeless.

On the last page of his last book, Erik ends his work with two major findings: "Popular dissatisfaction with capitalism is expanding," and "There are increasingly serious efforts to create new political formations, sometimes within the traditional leftist parties and, at other times, in the form of new parties."[17] From the combination of these two findings emerges the question of *how to create political actors who can erode capitalism*. The notion of class remains central, even if it has to be reconceptualized. After all, eroding capitalism implies reducing the power of capitalists. The most natural social base for this political actor is the working class, whose evolving lived experience, marked by exploitation and domination, creates a fluid context for constructing emancipatory collective identities.

Therefore, it is necessary to deal with the problem of "competing identities." That is, in the face of the contemporary plurality of oft-conflicting identities, such as race, ethnicity, gender, and sexuality, how can we forge shared emancipatory values capable of politically unifying these identities without stifling their plurality?

From University to Civil Society: Accepting the Challenge

Over the past fifteen years, the Emancipation Network has explored this question, seeking answers to the great challenge of updating a strategy of social transformation that results from the cumulative effect of social movements, acting under the existing rules of the game—rules that must undergo extensive reform from time to time. Formed by seventy-two university-preparatory schools located in poor communities, peripheral urban areas, and favelas in Brazil's eighteen main urban centers, the Emancipation Network spans the five regions of Brazil and

---

17   Ibid., 182.

includes around 120,000 poor, Black, and urban periphery–dwelling students.

It is by far the largest popular education project in Brazil. Classes are offered completely free of charge, as the Emancipation Network is self-managed and self-financed, relying only on grassroots funding and direct support from poor communities. The network also has agreements with city halls and universities allowing it to use public school facilities for university-preparatory classes. All teachers, as well as educational coordinators, are volunteers.

Since its creation in 2005, the Emancipation Network has been organized as a social movement rooted in resistance to the process of knowledge commodification that predominates in Brazil's university system. It is, therefore, a social movement inspired by the conception of university education as both a social right and a public good. This general orientation is evident in the defense of universal access to public, free, and quality higher education in Brazil—and in the movement's focus on democratizing access by supporting poor, Black slum dwellers as they prepare for the entrance exam.[18]

In Brazil, the public university is a historically elitist institution owing to a recruitment process based on an entrance exam, called the *vestibular*, which favors candidates from the private education system. Only after the introduction of the racial quota system in the early 2000s did democratization of university access begin. Within this context of the expansion of access, the Emancipation Network began: its purpose is to increase the chances of young Black students, poor people, and slum dwellers to overcome the exclusionary barrier of the *vestibular*. In addition, when a network student enters the public university, they often become a prep teacher, helping other Black students. This is a "virtuous circle" that helps explain the national growth of the Emancipation Network in the 2010s.

The main source of theoretical and political inspiration for the network is Paulo Freire. A guardian of Brazilian education, internationally renowned for his development of a critical pedagogy rooted in poor

---

18 Throughout this preparation, the network's educators act as political subjects debating with students on not only the curricular contents that are evaluated in the entrance exam, but also, above all, on the inequality between social classes, structural racism, the oppression of women, homophobia, and the environmental crisis.

communities, Freire called for contextualizing and centering relations of exploitation and domination to encourage students to build their own trajectories as political subjects. Popular education was the main battleground, and the Emancipation Network was formed through the efforts of young students who, after attending the public university, decided to continue this movement by remaining embedded in poor communities. These young people moved from academia, where they were trained above all in the humanities, to civil society, where they become popular educators.

It is not necessary to go into detail about the history of the formation of the network here, but it is important to highlight some aspects. After the creation of the Cursinho da Poli at (USP in 2005—a school specializing in preparing students for the *vestibular* at the Escola Politécnica's student union—the network quickly expanded to favelas and peripheral neighborhoods of the city. In 2009, it expanded further to Rio Grande do Sul with the creation of the Che Guevara school in the city of Porto Alegre. In 2010, a redoubled effort led to the opening of six more schools in the São Paulo region. The next two years saw the network expand to other cities. During this period, many "opening classes" of the network were held in public places in the city of São Paulo; in addition, on what was called "USP Day," students from the network in São Paulo and in the interior of the state were taken to visit the USP main campus.

In the first half of the 2010s, some moments were particularly memorable for the Emancipation Network's activists and students. During the protests known as "June Days" in 2013 and following the protests of 2015, the network was actively engaged, organizing street demonstrations and supporting student occupations of public schools, especially those that housed Emancipation's prep schools. Both the 2013 and 2015 protests were marked by calls for "decommodification," as students demanded the right to free public transport and more investments in public education. Considering the close links of these movements with the Emancipation Network, it is not surprising that coordinators see these moments as central to the national expansion of Emancipation Network schools. As one coordinator, Naiara do Rosário, explains,

> After June 2013, our public was much more open to debate these themes: racism, feminism, LGBT-phobia . . . In 2015 the schools were occupied and we participated, because the people who were

occupying the schools already knew us. With their support, we made a booklet on how to occupy the schools. And we started to gain a lot of visibility at that time, as students from other states asked for information about the Emancipation [Network] from our schools in São Paulo. And these mobilization processes ended up being reflected in our forums and in the creation of the network's organizational charter containing our principles and which started to guide the national network.[19]

How to Create Collective Actors

Beginning in 2003, the nationalization of the movement prompted network coordinators to organize periodic meetings, resulting eventually in the creation of the Universidade Emancipa (Emancipation University) in June 2018. This was a project designed for the training of popular educators, whose main concern was to help activists and educators engaged in the network increase their political and pedagogical skills through courses offered by different specialists linked to public universities.

The Emancipation University also organized virtual courses through USP and other partner universities, such as Rio de Janeiro State University. This feature of the project proved very useful when the coronavirus pandemic arrived in Brazil in March 2020. Above all, the new context brought new challenges, as the network sought to keep students involved with virtual activities, even in predictably precarious learning conditions. In addition, a large-scale socio-reproductive crisis spread across the country's urban peripheries and slums, hitting the incomes of working families, many of whom began to live again with the scourge of hunger.

In response to the crisis, the Emancipation Network organized several solidarity campaigns throughout 2020, distributing food baskets and school material to support students' families, including remote internet access kits. In addition to relying on collective funding campaigns, the network's activists involved communities and institutions linked to prep schools, seeking to ensure the distribution of food and educational resources so that classes would not be interrupted. Despite the

---

19   Interview with Naiara do Rosário, coordinator of the Grajaú school, São Paulo, October 15, 2020.

unevenness of the results, the network managed to remain active throughout the pandemic period without interrupting any school. Naiara do Rosário explains,

> As we joined forces with the Nós da Sul [a homeless workers' movement based in São Paulo city], we were able to quickly map the needs of the neediest families, where they were in the neighborhood's regions and so on … The solidarity campaigns were very important to strengthen the relationship with the students' families, as until that moment we didn't have a very strong relationship with the families … With the campaigns, this reality is changing, as the families realize that we are on their side, acting to strengthen and defend the community.[20]

In Brasília, the network created a partnership with the student movement and groups of young people from the periphery, highlighting the importance of Black women's leadership in sustaining the solidarity campaign. The coordinator Raquel Vieira says,

> In fact, this "politics of the care" was very important in creating our solidarity campaign. The Black women in the network talked with the students and we decided to make a first survey of how many families were in need during the pandemic. And that's kind of tricky, because it's a very intimate conversation. Nobody likes to open up about it. But it was this politics of care, because we are all Black women, that facilitated this survey. Then we went looking for resources [via] online funding, and when we managed to distribute the first food baskets in partnership with the student union at UnB [University of Brasília] and with the collectives Juntos and Juntas, it was based on the information that the Black girls brought.[21]

In fact, when interviewing network activists, it was possible to see a reconfiguration of political struggles involving Black youth: during Workers' Party (PT) governments, between 2003 and 2016, policies

---

20   Ibid.
21   Interview with Raquel Vieira, adviser to federal deputy Fernanda Melchionna (Psol), specialist in public management, and coordinator of schools in the cities of Ceilândia, Santa Maria, and Paranoá in the Federal District, December 9, 2020.

such as the racial quotas system created a new field of political disputes for Black youth. Even at USP, a university historically resistant to discussions of quotas, and also the birthplace of the Emancipation Network, the dispute over the elaboration and implementation of a more democratic system of access to the university helped to strengthen the movement. The coordinator Naiara do Rosário says,

> Before I joined the student movement, I had already seen Emancipation people working in the struggles of the student movement at the university for racial quotas. USP wanted to implement a "merit" system and Emancipation fought for social inclusion of Black students. There was a public hearing in the state parliament and I went because I was a freshman. And that was when I approached the network.[22]

Here it is important to note that since the Workers' Party government first held presidential power the democratization of access to public universities in Brazil has become a political field linked to broader demands for universal social rights, capable of helping working families to overcome poverty and social inequality. As one coordinator, Maíra Cordeiro, explains,

> In fact, the racial quota system helped our movement a lot because it brought students with this Indigenous and Black profile to the public university. Thus, we were able to make the connection between activism inside and outside the university, in the neighborhoods and in the academy . . . Unintentionally, the quota policy provided the opportunity for us to continue agitating after finishing studies at the university. With the quotas came the hope of getting out of poverty . . . This is what attracts activists to our network.[23]

However, this expectation for individual progress quickly collided with the limits of a development model that has simply not been able to

---

22   Naiara do Rosário, October 15, 2020.
23   Interview with Maíra Cordeiro, Portuguese teacher, graduated from the State University of Pará, coordinator of the Emancipation Network school at UFPA, November 1, 2020.

absorb many young people into occupations compatible with their skills, especially since the 2015–16 economic crisis.

As is well known, young people entering the labor market, especially Black youth and those living in the urban peripheries, were hit hardest by the dismantling of the Brazilian worker protection system—a crisis that was deepened both by the unemployment crisis of mid-2010 and by labor reform in 2017. It is not surprising that young Black people, especially women, constitute the main audience mobilized by the Emancipation Network. After all, for the many boys enduring long days as delivery workers, there is no time to think about going to university.

With the spread of unemployment and informal work, public education was the only thing left for Black women hoping to escape poverty. Given the political experiences of this portion of Brazilian youth, it is understandable that key dynamics have shifted from unions and political parties—traditional spaces of political socialization linked to labor regulation—to movements within poor, Black, and peripheral communities demanding housing and popular education. It is also understandable that the national coordinators of the Emancipation Network seek to create and cultivate links with corresponding movements in other countries. Naiara do Rosário says,

> In 2017, for example, people from Black Lives Matter (BLM) visited us here in Grajaú and got to know our "Carolina de Jesus Space." We realized how similar we are . . . although there is a difference . . . The Emancipation [Network] acts in a more centralized way and BLM is more dispersed than us. There, each group acts in a different way . . . In our prep schools this happens a little too, there are a lot of schools that act in a decentralized way. But we have a national coordination. And it seems that they [BLM] are not concerned about trying to centralize their politics.[24]

Convergence around the anti-racist struggle through the democratization of access to higher education is not only a way to mitigate inequality, but also to protect Black youth from police harassment and violence in poor communities. Coordinator Vanderléa Aguiar takes up the theme:

---

24   Naiara do Rosário, October 15, 2020.

In my church, there's always going to be that obstacle to political conversation. And Emancipation came up with this talk about how the public university can change the lives of these young Black people, about how access to university can help stop this extermination of Black youth by the police . . . At the prep school in São Gonçalo, almost 90 percent of women are Black . . . We saw only Black women and asked ourselves: "But where are the Black men from São Gonçalo?" Then, with the Degasi [a project of the Emancipation Network for adult education developed within the prison system in Rio de Janeiro], we found out where they were. We found out that all these youth were in jail . . . Going to university is a matter of survival for these young people.[25]

An Anticapitalist Strategy for the Twenty-First Century: Intersecting Interstitial Movements

The combination of social violence associated with structural racism and the rare opportunities for socio-occupational progress available to Black youth tends to reconfigure their expectations about the future, nurturing both a sense of social injustice and values associated with solidarity and equality. This set of political tendencies is elaborated daily by the educators of the Emancipation Network through "talking circles" and "master classes" that discuss structural racism, the oppression of women, inequalities, and, above all, forms of resistance to social injustice through intersectional movements.

In this sense, if passing the college entrance exam for young Black people is the movement's immediate objective, the process of popular education supported by Emancipation Network activists reveals a project designed to connect resistance to the commodification of social reproduction of poor communities and, at the same time, to strengthen support for policies linked to the democratization of access to public goods. In both cases, the network is aiming at an interstitial transformation that could result from the cumulative effects of movements (the

25   Interview with Vanderléa Aguiar, nursing assistant, evangelical, resident of the favela "Morro dos Macacos" in the North Zone of Rio de Janeiro, coordinator of the Vila Isabel prep school, October 28, 2020.

feminist movement, anti-racist movement, etc.) that arise within capitalism. The axis that combines resistance to commodification "from below" and the strengthening of public policies "from above" is, undoubtedly, intersectionality. As one coordinator, Nina Becker, explains,

> The Emancipa Mulher was a project initially created by Joana Burigo, Winnie Bueno, and Luciana Genro based on a course called "Laudelina de Campos Melo," given by them in honor of the first unionized domestic workers in the country. The intersectional strategy was already there: a feminist, anti-racist course in support of the unionization of domestic workers . . . So we created the books that tell the story of feminist waves, provide a synthesis of academic gender research, highlighting the importance of feminism in the history of Marxism, and bring contemporary discussions about gender and work, gender and social class, and gender and racism. There are five books that guide our educators.[26]

As an intersectional social movement organized by young Black women, concerns about the representativeness of leadership—an issue that had been relatively overlooked when the network was created in the mid-2000s—emerged as a priority after 2015, during the process of expanding the network nationwide. Raquel Vieira says, "Without underestimating other people, we really think that Black women need to be at the forefront of the movement that faces the issues that hit them most strongly. This focuses the coordination on the school and the education movement in a more committed way. Contact with students is closer."[27]

As is easily identified in the discourse of the movement's coordinators, the Emancipation Network seeks to organize itself around an effort to rebuild the political subject through an anticapitalist education supported by intersectionality. Thus, the aim of the schools is not only to help students pass the entrance exam, but also to support them in becoming agents of social transformation in the mode of Paulo Freire's pedagogy of liberation. To this end, the network is associated with other

---

26   Interview with Nina Becker, sociology teacher and coordinator of Emancipa's schools in Porto Alegre, November 12, 2020.
27   Raquel Vieira, December 9, 2020.

social movements, in particular those linked to the defense of the environment, popular housing, and the struggle against racism, encouraging the political engagement of students and educators in poor neighborhoods and communities where prep schools operate. Despite the plurality of initiatives identified in the various schools, the general orientation is to "politicize the territory," organizing poor workers in their places of residence. Coordinator Nina Becker, explains,

> Race and gender issues became more evident when we created an adult literacy project in partnership with the Movement of Homeless Workers [MTST] in late 2016. It was a project focused on the most peripheral neighborhoods of the city, especially in the Restinga neighborhood [Porto Alegre]. And our audience was made up exclusively of women, workers, and many Black women who were single and illiterate mothers. The project helped us organize these women and deepen our presence in the neighborhood. Thus, we were able to support the politicization of this community through partnership with the MTST.[28]

Politicizing the territories where the movement operates is, above all, a reflection of the current reconfiguration of the subordinate classes in Brazil. Since the 2015 economic crisis began, a sudden increase in unemployment, underemployment, and informal employment rates has devastated the most important Brazilian social movement—that is, the unions. It is a process easily understood by younger social activists. "The normal thing for us is to organize the workers through the union," says Sara Azevedo, physical education teacher and school coordinator. "But we saw that unionism here in Belo Horizonte is very weak. Unionists do not speak the language of young people; they are more concerned with the union itself. This is even more true after the labor reform that ended the union tax."[29]

It is worth adding that, in parallel to the advance of outsourcing during the 2000s and informal work in the 2010s, there has been a significant strengthening of the neo-Pentecostal evangelical movement.

---

28   Nina Becker, November 12, 2020.
29   Interview with Sara Azevedo, physical education teacher, coordinator of the school "Emancipa BH" in Belo Horizonte, November 6, 2020.

The "elective affinity" between neo-Pentecostalism and popular entrepreneurship—both in terms of moving poor workers away from the so-called grammar of rights and in bringing them closer to traditionalism centered on "family values" (patriarchy, sexism, "machismo," etc.)—tends to discipline the subaltern classes in the sense of intensifying competition for opportunities in the informal market.

In a way, popular religiosity gradually occupied the void that had been created by the dismantling of Brazil's labor protections and the weakening of the grammar of social rights. If the prospect of a better future through access to retirement has become unattainable for 40 million informal workers, the mutual support system provided by the neo-Pentecostal churches in the communities seems to be the only hope for collective protection.

During the process of establishing roots in poor neighborhoods and urban peripheries, the Emancipation Network perceived the strengthening of popular neo-Pentecostalism as a great enigma to be solved. After all, this is perhaps the most important manifestation of the current remaking of Brazil's subaltern classes, intertwining precarious work, communities, and political behavior. Recognizing the plurality of the evangelical field, Emancipation's prep schools, rather than antagonize popular religiosity, decided to approach churches that were open to dialogue.

"When I was tutoring the teenagers from the church, the Emancipation [Network] appeared," says Vanderléa Aguiar.

> We got a little suspicious . . . So I went to the inaugural class and said: "That's what we need here at the church!" Because you know: the Black youth of the favela will never think that the university is reachable . . . The Emancipation started small and now works in several rooms of the church . . . As it is a project with volunteers and free, focused on young people here in the community [in Vila Isabel] who were already attending our projects, and because the church rooms were half empty during the week, the council approved . . . Jesus talks about social justice, he talks about how society should be, and I talk about Jesus from my social conception; that's why I think the Emancipation does the work Jesus told us to do here on earth.[30]

---

30   Vanderléa Aguiar, October 28, 2020.

With respect to the recomposition of the country's subaltern classes, Vanderléa Aguiar's account reflects a decisive dimension of the current moment, notoriously marked by the advance of popular neo-Pentecostalism in communities and slums: a kind of reflexive interregnum, capable of problematizing certain aspects of religiosity by emphasizing values such as equality, solidarity, and social justice. Through the interstitial approach to social transformation based on the intersection of race, class, and gender, the Emancipation Network has been able to offer participants new perspectives on the normative conflict shaped by the dismantling of Fordist solidarity and the strengthening of popular entrepreneurship.

Final Considerations

Without theorizing this interstitial approach, at least in the beginning, the activists who created the Emancipation Network realized that struggles could no longer be confined to the field of academia, but had to advance into society itself. It is hard to imagine an example of training social agents more in line with the model posed by Erik Olin Wright at the end of his manifesto. And it is worth highlighting the way in which the network took root in the neighborhoods at a time when the dismantling of the Fordist working class set the conditions for the remaking of the collective identities of subaltern social groups, favoring the emergence of new community leaders committed to the defense of education, public health, the environment, racial equality, gender equality, and the struggle for popular housing.

Together, these individual and collective experiences turned the Emancipation Network into a force articulating multiple resistances of an interstitial nature, proposing public policies capable of democratizing public education at the university level—all aimed at promoting racial and gender equality. And the proximity of a significant part of these young leaders to the Socialism and Freedom Party meant that candidates supported by the Emancipation Network won elections, both in 2018 (in the cases of federal deputy of São Paulo, Sâmia Bomfim, and state deputy of São Paulo, Mônica Seixas) and in 2020 (in the case of the city councillor of São Paulo, Luana Alves).[31]

---

31 In fact, movement coordinators estimate that in the elections of 2018 and 2020,

As we know, Erik meticulously scrutinized Porto Alegre's participatory budget in his masterpiece, *Envisioning Real Utopias*. Today, unfortunately, the experience that mobilized the sociological imagination of so many researchers around the world no longer exists. Tragically, southern Brazil became the region to express the strongest support for Jair Bolsonaro, a far-right politician.

Yet even in the face of the obvious historical defeat of one of his favorite real utopias, I doubt Erik would be pessimistic. After all, in the city where the World Social Forum was founded, Porto Alegre, a new generation of social transformation agents is continuing the democratizing task of the participatory budget by other means: politicizing the territories through a real utopia. Erik's legacy is in good hands.

---

the Emancipation Network won three parliamentary mandates through its elected educators, and another fifteen mandates supporting allies across the country.

PART III

From Class Analysis to Real Utopias

10

The Politics of Contradictory Class Locations: A View from India
Rina Agarwala

I think of Erik as a teacher. Unfortunately, I never had the honor of formally being one of his graduate students. Rather, I was one of the thousands of students who learned from Erik from afar. As a graduate student outside Madison, I devoured his articles and books. I read and reread them hundreds of times. I used them as textbooks to understand class and, perhaps even more so, exploitation—a concept that I still find extremely powerful and clarifying. Many years later, I had the gift of getting to know Erik at a more personal level, as a friend and mentor, through my interactions with him on the *Politics and Society* editorial board. Over dinners we discussed why pessimism is intellectually lazy and how optimism takes far more analytical rigor and heft. During our meetings, I enjoyed watching him think through difficult questions and critique arguments with his vintage clarity. Even more exciting was watching him be persuaded by others' arguments and change his mind, while remaining so admirably tethered to his core commitments. I marveled at his unending curiosity, his willingness to keep learning, and his refusal to become intellectually complacent—clearly the easier path for a scholar of his stature. And I tried hard to learn from his exemplary way of handling tense group dynamics, and even personal attacks on his character, with unyielding grace. But most important to me was that I got to share many personal and touching—and to me very unexpected—conversations with him about family and parenting. In all these many ways, Erik was and remains a teacher to me.

Among the many things I learned from Erik, one of the most influential has been his early work on those sitting in contradictory class locations (or what he referred to as "CCL"). These workers operate in a range of class locations and thus do not fit neatly into the traditional class categories of "bourgeoisie" or "proletariat." I was immensely grateful to him for his willingness to study and make legible the most complex and understudied aspects of class structures with simple, accessible language, evidence, and constructs, not to mention his famous two-by-two tables.

Although Erik's interest in CCL during the 1970s and 1980s was motivated by questions concerning the growing (and relatively privileged) "middle classes" in advanced industrial societies, his work held a special, and perhaps unexpected, resonance for those of us studying the working poor in the global South at the turn of the millennium. At the time, neoliberal economic policies fostering greater privatization and decreased state control over markets were approaching the height of their popularity throughout the world. As a result of these policies, some countries could point to increased national rates of economic growth and a fraction of people whose incomes had indeed risen. But within the aggregate figures, and the minority of exceptions notwithstanding, was a picture of dismay for the world's poor masses. Neoliberal policies failed woefully to deliver on the promise to expand the middle class to include the majority. Instead, increased privatization benefited those already endowed with access to resources (including material and ascriptive). And increased global market competition led to stagnant industrial growth in so many countries, which in turn led to continuing underemployment for millions of people. Neoliberal policies also destroyed state welfare systems and (perhaps even more importantly) betrayed long-standing ideals of social support and redistribution.

In this context, it may seem ironic that Erik's work on the relatively privileged middle classes in advanced industrial countries became pertinent to those of us studying the failures of neoliberalism in the global South. But we might credit neoliberal governments for ensuring that connection. In order to retain legitimacy with their citizens, neoliberal governments throughout the global South were celebrating a new "fix" for the millions of poor workers seeking but failing to find employment: namely, "self-employment," "micro-enterprise," and "small-and medium-business ownership." Although the self-employed and small-business owners enjoyed far fewer material, political, and social resources than the middle-class managers, supervisors, and experts that Erik analyzed, they sat in the very same CCL that Erik had defined and clarified. In other words, neoliberal governments in the global South had not only made CCL into a space for the upwardly mobile, professional, and managerial elite that Erik highlighted, but they also offered CCL as the only viable option of survival for millions at the bottom of the class structure.

From my perspective, it seemed obvious that those of us interested in the emancipatory future of the working classes must study those in CCL in greater depth. The number of workers in CCL—as self-employed or micro- and small-business owners—was rapidly growing, and their attempts to become "entrepreneurs" were increasingly idealized by national governments (in the North and South). Baffled by how little guidance I found in the sociological scholarship on labor and development, I found Erik's work provided an unusually clear road map on *how* to conceive and define, as well as empirically map and count, the complex CCL of the contemporary era. In addition, his early work hinted at *why* we should care about conducting such analyses. In his 1980 *Theory and Society* article, for example, he wrote that his preoccupation with class structure "enters theory primarily as part of the explanation of the constraints on social change and the foundations of class formations."[1] In other words, Erik argued that by understanding the structure of CCL, we will be better able to understand the politics of those in CCL. His work never depicted the transition from structure to politics as automatic or determined; indeed, most scholars (including Erik) had conceded by then that such transitions are always contingent on a myriad of social, political, and historical forces. But from Erik I learned that a more precise understanding of class structure promised more precision for our analyses and understanding of class politics.

The reasons for the dearth in scholarship on either the structure or the politics of the self-employed and/or small-and medium-business owners in the global South are nuanced and manifold. But part of the explanation is surely similar to the reason for the dearth of class analyses of the middle classes in advanced countries that Erik studied: it is often assumed that they are unlikely to sympathize with working-class struggles for emancipation and reduced inequality. Similarly, in recent years,

---

1   Erik Olin Wright, "Class and Occupation: Special Issue on Work and the Working Class," *Theory and Society* 9, no. 1 (1980): 188–9.

some scholars have argued that self-employed workers and small-business owners (who, like middle classes, sit in CCL) form the primary support base for the growing tide of fascist, right-wing nationalist leaders in countries such as Brazil, Turkey, and India.

Lloyd and Susanne Rudolph are among the few scholars to have examined Indian workers sitting in CCL. Writing in the 1980s (that is, before India turned to its version of neoliberalism in the 1990s), the Rudolphs examined India's agrarian sector under its postcolonial economic paradigm of Fabian Socialism. Specifically, they shed light on small and middle peasant farmers, who they famously termed "bullock capitalists." As the name implies, bullock capitalists had access to some capital (in the form of bullocks or tractors) and thus employed workers, paid wages, invested and sold in markets, and reaped profits. But bullock capitalists were also forced to sell their own labor (or that of their family), thereby self-exploiting and working their own farms at subsistence wage rates. Although they were a minority class in rural India (especially relative to the mass class of landless laborers), the bullock capitalists in the Rudolphs' view were a significant class actor that would "be at the center of political events and constellations of power."[2] They went on to write, "Bullock capitalists are advantageously placed by their objective circumstances to become the hegemonic agrarian class."[3] Although they acknowledged Bullock capitalists' existence in the class structure, the Rudolphs underplayed their class politics. They argued that bullock capitalists' early and intermittent successes in political organization were rooted in a cross-class mobilization effort that *subsumed* the importance of class inequalities and exploitation and instead highlighted "sectoral" inequalities and urban India's exploitation of rural or "traditional" India.[4] Such arguments no doubt deflected subsequent scholars writing in the 1990s and 2000s from examining the politics of Indian workers in CCL as a potential pathway to transformation.

---

2   Lloyd Rudolph and Susanne Rudolph, "Determinants and Varieties of Agrarian Mobilization," *Agrarian Poverty and Agricultural Productivity in South Asia*, ed. Meghnad Desai, Susanne Hoeber Rudolph, and Ashok Rudra (Berkeley: University of California Press, 1984), 315.

3   Lloyd Rudolph and Susanne Hoeber Rudolph, *In Pursuit of Lakshmi: The Political Economy of the Indian State* (Chicago: University of Chicago Press, 1987), 342.

4   Rina Agarwala and Ron Herring, "How Does Class Matter in Politics? Rethinking Conditions and Reasons," in *Interpreting Politics: Situated Knowledge, India, and the Rudolph Legacy*, ed. John E. Echeverri-Gent and Kamal Sadiq (New Delhi: Oxford University Press, 2019).

But this depiction of those in CCL as uniformly unable to offer a more emancipatory future belies empirical reality. As James Scott famously argued, agrarian revolts were triggered by middle peasants experiencing culturally unacceptable downward mobility: a violation of the "moral economy" common to rural society.[5] And, as I have written elsewhere, some urban self-employed workers have collectively organized in recent years to demand legal recognition, and protection, as members of the working class.[6]

Contrary to common depictions of the occupants of CCL as problematic participants in working-class movements, Erik suggested in the mid-1980s that those inhabiting CCL might "potentially pose an alternative to capitalism."[7] Although Erik continued to repeat this suggestion, including in his book *Classes*, he never expanded on it. Nevertheless, he gives us reason to empirically examine the potential and constraints of the politics of those who occupy CCL. Drawing from Erik's early work, and guided by his suggestions on the potential implications of these actors for transformative movements, I ask in this paper: *Under what conditions can (and do) those who inhabit CCL organize as a class-for-themselves to erode the decommodifying vigor of contemporary capitalism?*

There are several reasons this is an important question to examine empirically. First, as already noted, the number of people who find themselves in CCL is expanding throughout the world. Yet our understanding of these people's position in capitalist production, their experience with exploitation therein, and their relationship to those in other classes remains thin. Examining the politics of those operating in CCL forces us to address these gaps. Second, Erik's Real Utopias Project has been criticized for omitting class and class struggle and evading the agent of change.[8] But Erik's own work can help us close that gap: his early work gives us tools with which to analyze the inhabitants of CCL

5 James C. Scott, *The Moral Economy of the Peasant: Rebellion and Subsistence in Southeast Asia* (New Haven, CT: Yale University Press, 1976).

6 Rina Agarwala, "Redefining Exploitation: Self-Employed Workers' Movements in India's Garments and Trash Collection Industries," *International Labour and Working-Class History* 89 (2016): 107–30.

7 Erik Olin Wright, "A General Framework for the Analysis of Class Structure," *Politics and Society* 13, no. 4 (1984): 402.

8 Michael Burawoy, "A Tale of Two Marxisms: Remembering Erik Olin Wright (1947–2019)," *New Left Review* 121 (January–February 2020): 67–98. Reprinted in this volume as chapter 1.

as a new class agent, one which could help create the very future that Erik envisioned—that is, one that is democratic, fair, and community-oriented. Finally, by addressing this question, we can envisage the expanding number of people operating in CCL as a historical force, connecting the concept to a theory of capital accumulation.

In his last book, *How to Be an Anticapitalist in the Twenty-First Century* (2019), Erik expressed a lack of faith in the ability of the working class to serve as a collective agent for change, arguing that it had become too fragmented and complex. Drawing on the case of India, however, I argue that contemporary forms of exploitation have inadvertently forced a mass, complex, and extremely heterogeneous subsection of workers (commonly referred to as "informal workers") to share several lived experiences, forge a common identity, and articulate common interests. The result has been the construction of organizations that hold the state accountable for recognizing their productive labor and providing state welfare that can decommodify their labor—efforts which evoke Erik's notion of "taming" capitalism to neutralize its harms and reflect instances of "dismantling" capital by institutionalizing some elements of socialism at the state level.

Despite the increasing fragmentation of the working class, informal workers have forged a collective solidarity across class categories that include workers employed by capital as well as workers sitting in CCL, such as the self-employed. While these movements are still in an infant stage, they have already forced the Indian state to value nonstandard types of work, to recognize workers who have long been super-marginalized because of their gender or caste, and to begin some redistribution from capital to labor in the form of welfare. In doing so, these movements are expanding our understanding of "productive labor" to include a broader citizen base, thereby exemplifying the empowerment of civil society and reflecting the emancipatory values that Erik insisted on in his last book. If real utopias offer a unifying vision for a transformed and emancipated society, I wonder if those in CCL might serve as one set of agents spearheading that change.

First Comes Structure: Contradictory Class Locations and Exploitation

Contrary to many Marxist class analysts writing in the 1970s and 1980s, Erik highlighted the persistently growing, but woefully ill-defined, group of what was commonly referred to as the middle classes, a group that did not neatly fit into either the bourgeoisie or the proletariat. Rather than addressing the politics of the middle classes, he focused on defining their structural position in class relations. But this effort should not be read as a deflection of class politics, but rather as a stepping stone to ensuring a more precise and rigorous analysis of class politics, class conflict, and social change. In 1980, Erik wrote, "Without a rigorous account of the structure of class relations, a theory of social conflict or social change would be radically incomplete."[9] And in an article written in 1987 and republished in 1994, he reiterated, "My intuition has been that I could not effectively embark on the task of confronting in a serious way the explanation of class formation [i.e., politics] until I got the conceptual apparatus used in those explanations [i.e., class structure] straightened out."[10]

To this end, Erik taught us how to more precisely redefine the increasingly complicated class structure of capitalist societies. First, he usefully countered many neo-Marxists' attempts to wish away what he called the "embarrassment of the growing middle class," which in turn was undermining the bipolar basis of Marxists' capitalist class map. Neo-Marxists at the time offered three conceptualizations of the middle classes: (1) an illusion that was, in fact, the same as the working class; (2) a subsegment of the bourgeoisie (i.e., the "new petty bourgeoisie") or a subsegment of the working class (i.e., a "new working class"); or (3) a new third class known as managerial professionals.[11] But Erik refuted all three of these, instead offering a fresh conceptualization of the nebulous group *not* as a single class, but as an entity that simultaneously operated within the two classes (i.e., the bourgeoisie and proletariat) and shared material interests with both of them—hence their "contradictory" character. In doing so, Erik forced us to engage, rather than ignore, the so-called "middle classes," and the constantly evolving nature of the structure of class

---

9   Erik Olin Wright, "Varieties of Marxist Conceptions of Class Structure," *Politics and Society* 9, no. 3 (1980): 325.

10   This excerpt first appeared in the exchange Erik had with Michael Burawoy in the *Berkeley Journal of Sociology*. Wright, "Reflections on Classes"; Wright, "Reply to Burawoy's Comments on 'Reflections on Classes,'" *Berkeley Journal of Sociology* 32 (1987).

11   Wright, "Varieties of Marxist Conceptions of Class Structure"; Erik Olin Wright, *Interrogating Inequalities* (London: Verso, 1994), 250.

relations. He also exposed the misleading nature of the term "middle classes," since this group did not sit in between the two classes; rather, it was mutually constitutive of those classes.

Second, and a few years later, Erik explained the complicated heterogeneity that marked this group of so-called middle classes. Influenced by the work of John Roemer, Erik pinpointed exactly what defined middle classes' contradictory location—namely, the existence of *multiple* pathways of exploitation. "Exploitation," of course, referred to one person's ability to profit off another's labor, which in turn created relationships of interdependence on one hand and opposing material interests on the other. But it was Erik's (eventual) willingness to highlight a multipronged material and relational basis of the ability to exploit (versus be exploited) that made his conceptualization of CCL so appealing, even in spaces outside advanced industrial economies and beyond the population of professionals and managers. Inequalities in exploitation, Erik argued, lay in the unequal ability to own or control a variety of productive assets—including (1) capital assets or means of production, (2) labor assets or labor autonomy, (3) organization assets or production processes, and (4) skill assets or human credentials.[12] Ownership and control of these assets, in turn, determined people's varying relationships to means of production, hired labor, authority, and expertise. And such varying relationships led to varying levels of power. While many capitalists may control all four types of assets, and many workers may lack control over all four, a large group of people sitting in CCL control some of these assets (and thus exploit along some axes), but lack control over others (and are thus exploited along other axes). By pinpointing these varying relations of asset control and the resulting relations of exploitation, we could begin mapping the opposing material interests of those sitting in a range of emerging class locations under evolving structures of capitalism.

Specifically, Erik depicted a revised class map to represent those sitting in the CCL of advanced capitalist societies (see Figure 10.1). Erik was always clear that such mapping and categorizing efforts never

---

12 Wright, *Classes* (London: Verso, 1985); Wright, "A General Framework for the Analysis of Class Structure"; Wright, *Class Counts: Comparative Studies in Class Analysis* (Cambridge: Cambridge University Press, 1997).

perfectly match the nuances of reality. Instead, he called on us to ask: "Do these categories, however crude they might be, enable us to identify interesting puzzles?"[13] I argue here that articulating the various class location categories operating in the contemporary era is essential to addressing the puzzle of class politics today. To this end, Erik defined multiple subcategories of workers sitting in CCL. The first category comprises managers, supervisors, and experts. Some are "expert managers" who control labor, exert authority, and possess skills, but do not own or control means of production or organization/production processes. Other managers lack credentialed skills, but still control labor and exert some authority. Still others are "experts" who possess skill, but do not control labor or exert authority.

Most important for scholars studying the global South, Erik delineated three additional CCL subcategories (which I update in this article). First, in his early work, he defined the "petty bourgeoisie" as neither exploiters nor exploited through capitalist relations, since they work for and by themselves and do not hire wage labor or exert authority, nor are they hired by capital.[14] As shown in Figure 10.2, Erik later refined this category to acknowledge the petty bourgeoisie's other relations to exploitation through their ownership of means of production, control over the production process, and some skills (which may or may not be credentialed).[15] Although in his early work he emphasized that the petty bourgeoise do not sit in CCL, he is less clear about their location in his later work. Second, in his early work, Erik highlighted small employers, who (like the petty bourgeoisie) are directly engaged in production processes and own their own means of production. But (unlike the petty bourgeoisie and similar to capitalists) they employ and exploit wage labor (generally less than ten employees). Third, Erik noted semi-autonomous wage earners, who (like traditional workers hired by capital) are employed and exploited by capital, but (like the petty bourgeoisie) retain control over certain aspects of the labor process, such as *what* they produce (not just *how* they produce). Unfortunately, he dropped further discussion of these latter two categories from his later works.

---

13   Wright, *Class Counts*, 44.
14   Wright, "A General Framework for the Analysis of Class Structure."
15   Wright, *Class Counts*.

Although Erik's discussion of these CCL subcategories remained underdeveloped, he gave us a powerful foundation upon which to build. Most importantly, he insisted that class categories should not be defined by simplistic, gradational status markers—such as income, occupation, and cultural penchants. Rather, Erik urged us to highlight the multiple axes of exploitation that differentiate categories of class relations, which in turn force our attention to the diverse relationships of simultaneous interdependence and antagonism that bind classes to one another in various ways. It is this double-edged relationship, of course, that lays the seeds for class conflict and, in some cases, political organization. And, finally, Erik underscored the importance of subjective understanding: if these multiple axes of exploitation as a transfer from one social group to another are "deemed unjust or illegitimate," how (if at all) will the different actors sitting in different subcategories of CCL organize to fight this unjust and illegitimate relationship?[16]

Figure 10.1. Wright's Basic Map of Class Relations in Advanced Capitalist Societies

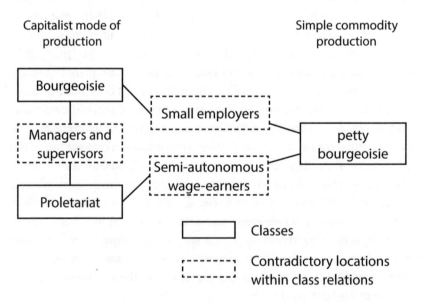

Source: Erik Olin Wright, "Varieties of Marxist Conceptions of Class Structure," Politics and Society 9, no. 3 (1980).

---

16 Wright, Interrogating Inequalities, 239.

Figure 10.2. Wright's Expanded Map of Class Relations to Exploitation

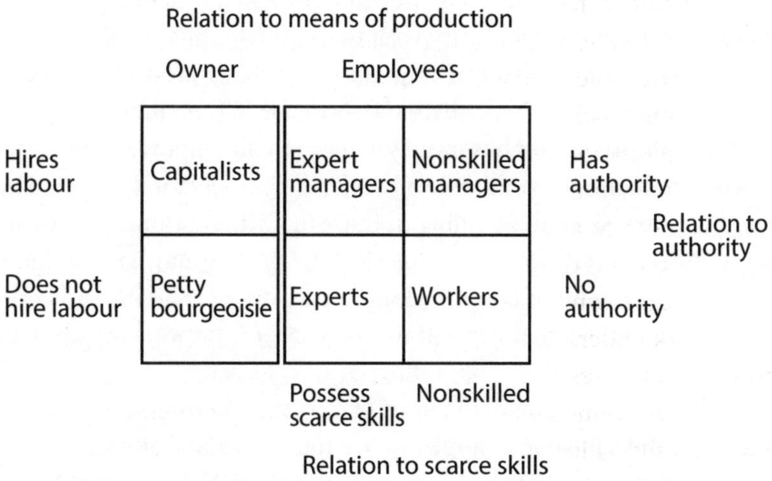

Relation to means of production

	Owner	Employees		
Hires labour	Capitalists	Expert managers	Nonskilled managers	Has authority
				Relation to authority
Does not hire labour	Petty bourgeoisie	Experts	Workers	No authority

Possess   Nonskilled
scarce skills

Relation to scarce skills

Source: Erik Olin Wright, *Class Counts: Comparative Studies in Class Analysis* (Cambridge: Cambridge University Press, 1997).

And Then Comes Politics: Potential and Constraints

While real utopias offer us a lens into how an egalitarian, democratic, and solidarity-based economic order can sustain itself, Erik's early analyses on class structure gave us a road map to analyze how such an order might be built in the first place. His efforts to expand the bipolar class structure to include contradictory class locations laid the foundation on which to examine the potential and the constraints that those in CCL pose for social change.

Unfortunately, Erik did not delve into empirical analyses on actually existing struggles among those in CCL. However, he did usefully highlight possible pathways and outcomes for struggle. For the traditional working class, he argued, the number of people in CCL matters. Erik wrote, "When a large proportion of wage laborers sit in contradictory locations within class relations, it may be much more difficult to organize the working class itself into a class party (either a revolutionary or reformist party), since it will be more difficult for individual workers to see the class structure as a polarized, antagonistic structure."[17] As I

---

17   Wright, "Varieties of Marxist Conceptions of Class Structure," 197.

discuss below, I do not find evidence for this in India. But Erik also notes that if the working class tries to question the capitalist mode of production, capital might unify with those in CCL against the working class; by contrast, if the working class organizes around immediate demands and interests, capitalists and those in CCL are more likely to be divided. This prediction has more salience in contemporary India.

Erik also highlighted the role of working-class electoral parties. Here he again emphasized the number of those in CCL, cautioning that when that number is large, working-class electoral parties may have an incentive to deflect attention from working-class interests and instead appeal to broader interests that can attract the votes of the working class and those in CCL.

Finally, he highlighted the role of capital, offering some hope of potential solidarity. For example, Erik wrote, "If capital attempts to deal with economic crisis through a general assault on the living standards of all wage-earners, this may increase the possibilities of class alliances between the working class and contradictory class locations." But he also went on to caution that "if on the other hand (capital) concentrates the effects of crisis on the weakest segments of the working class" and favors those in CCL, the latter might abandon the working class.[18]

India's Class Structure: The Petty Bourgeoisie, Gender, Caste and State Regulation

Erik's class structure map enables us to delineate the relations those in CCL have with other classes. But to apply it to India, three tweaks are necessary. The first involves a reconceptualization of the "petty bourgeoisie" and its location in contemporary class relations. The second involves the articulation of an additional class category: unpaid family labor. And the third introduces an additional aspect of exploitation: access to state labor regulation and recognition.

As shown in Figure 10.2, Erik placed an important spotlight on the petty bourgeoise—as distinct from capitalists, managers/supervisors, (non-managerial) experts, small shopkeepers, semi-autonomous wage earners, and traditional workers employed by capital. Following his own

---

18   Ibid., 197.

forceful call to distinguish classes on the basis of their relationship to exploitation and *not* on the basis of income or occupation, Erik defined the petty bourgeoise as those who own means of production, but who are also direct producers and (most importantly) do not hire waged labor. Some may make a profit, while others may generate only a subsistence wage. They can be involved in manufacturing, services, agriculture, or trade, and their activities can span occupations. In this way, Erik's conceptualization of the "petty bourgeoisie" loosely echoes what some scholars studying the global South call "petty commodity producers," as well as what some scholars engaging in "mode of production" debates call the "self-employed" (a term I use in this article).[19]

However, Erik's conceptualization of the petty bourgeoisie left many questions unanswered. For example, he rarely provided examples of those who comprise this class category and interchangeably called them the "artisan petty bourgeoisie," the "agrarian petty bourgeoisie," and the "retail trade petty bourgeoisie"; he also sometimes mentioned shop-keepers. But, as Erik himself insisted, class and occupation are not equivalent. Artisans, retail traders, and small shopkeepers, therefore, could just as easily be categorized as "small employers" and "semi-autonomous wage earners" rather than as "petty bourgeoisie."

The most glaring problem with Erik's conceptualization of the petty bourgeoisie is that it absolves them of responsibility for exploitation, arguing they operate outside capitalist relations of exploitation (and thus outside CCL) simply because they do not hire paid labor (see Figure 10.1).[20] But this conceptualization invisibilizes the petty bourgeoisie's self-exploitation and their heavy exploitation of their unpaid family members' productive labor. In the agrarian and non-agrarian sectors, historically and today, the petty bourgeoisie relies on this direct labor to assist in production and profitability; often, this labor determines their ability to survive another day.

Self-exploitation and unpaid family labor also characterize the productivity/subsistence earning of small employers and semi-autonomous wage earners. This labor is distinct from and in addition to the

---

19 Note that the similarity between these categories is based on their relationship to the multiple axes of exploitation, *not* on income (which may range within each category). Utsa Patnaik, ed., *Agrarian Relations and Accumulation: The "Mode of Production" Debate in India* (Bombay: Oxford University Press, 1990).

20 Although Erik's conceptualization of CCL evolved over time, this conceptualization of the petty bourgeoisie remained consistent even in his later work.

reproductive labor of family members. It includes, for example, the wife who stacks the shelves, cleans the floors, and manages all the accounts of a small shop that is owned by her husband, or the daughter who assists her mother in rolling cigarettes in the basement of her father's local cigarette kiosk. It includes the daughter-in-law who collects the cloth scraps and sews the embroidery patterns for her father-in-law's tailoring business, as well as the young Dalit migrant boy who cleans the workshop and delivers the finished clothes for the tailor in return for housing and food in the tailor's home.[21]

Like paid workers, unpaid family laborers are exploited by those profiting (or even earning a subsistence wage) off their labor. Unlike paid workers, however, they are tied to their exploiters by blood or marriage.[22] Most unpaid family labor in India (and elsewhere), therefore, is performed by females and children; in some cases, low-caste or racialized domestic workers are also classified as "family members" and thus are unpaid. Their exploitation is exacerbated by the denial of paid wages, and normalized by axes of exploitation based on the unequal control over sexuality and/or social constructions around gender, age, caste, ability, and worth.

Therefore, defining the petty bourgeoisie as those who do not exploit because they do not hire paid labor hides ascriptive power relations and suggests that women and child laborers are not "exploited" simply because they are tied to the exploiter by blood or marriage. I think we can do better.

Reconceptualizing the Petty Bourgeoisie

Instead, I argue the petty bourgeoise should be reconceptualized to describe those who own their own means of production, control part of the production process, and do not hire paid labor, but who do *exploit the unpaid labor of themselves and their family members*. This reconceptualization allows us to retain Erik's call to distinguish them from capitalists and small employers (who hire paid *and* unpaid labor) and from

---

21   Although such domestic workers are not technically family members, they are often counted in the Indian census as "family members" and thus omitted from legal labor protections.

22   For many domestic workers, they are tied through a false claim to family membership.

semi-autonomous wage earners (who do not own their own means of production). But it also redefines the petty bourgeoisie as another subcategory of those in CCL, thereby acknowledging the petty bourgeoisie's exploitation of unpaid labor and their growing involvement in modern, capitalist economies. This is an important corrective to Erik's conceptualization of the petty bourgeoise as pre-capitalist, non-exploitative, agrarian, and "contracting" or declining.[23] And it enables us to expose the petty bougeoise's clear involvement in capitalist production and exploitation.

Bringing in Gender and Caste

By reconceptualizing the petty bourgeoisie as exploiters of "unpaid productive labor," we bring women, children, and low-caste domestic workers, as well as the power structures of gender, age, caste, and race (i.e., structures based on ascriptive characteristics) out of the shadows, making them more visible in our understanding of contemporary class exploitation. We also correct our understanding of small employers and semi-autonomous wage earners, who similarly rely on such marginalized groups and power hierarchies. In contrast to Erik's later suggestion that we should look at class locations as "mediated" by household class,[24] this schema views unpaid family laborers as linked to the class structure, not simply through familial relations, but rather through their "job," which makes them direct producers. Moreover, their control over various productive assets differs from others in CCL, and from that of capitalists and traditional paid workers. Acknowledging unpaid family labor in this way forces us to broaden our conceptualization of "jobs" to include production that is not remunerated in the form of wage payments, but which is nonetheless implicated in capitalist forms of exploitation.

---

23 Wright, *Classes*; Wright, "A General Framework for the Analysis of Class Structure"; Wright, *Class Counts*.
24 Wright, *Interrogating Inequalities*, 252.

Introducing a New Axis of Exploitation: Access to
State Labor Regulation and Recognition

Finally, I argue we must add an additional axis of exploitation to Erik's map of class relations in Figure 10.2—that is, access to state regulation and recognition of labor and production. Such regulation and recognition decommodify exploited labor (thereby increasing the value of labor power and labor's ability to reproduce), while subjecting capital owners to greater costs (thereby altering the core characteristics of capital). Laborers who do not own any means of production or hold credentialed skills, but who do have access to state regulation and recognition, tend to earn higher wages, enjoy greater job security, and cover more of their reproductive costs (such as health care, housing, and education). Acknowledging this axis of exploitation makes important corrections to our class relations map.

One further correction occurs among paid workers. Erik depicted paid workers in a single category as those who are hired by capital, do not own means of production, have little control over the production process, and have low to no credentialed skills. But when we add "access to state labor regulation" to potential axes of exploitation in India, we can further categorize paid workers into the following subgroups: (1) "formal workers" (who are recognized, regulated, and protected under state labor laws and have a labor contract that secures their minimum wages, job security, and benefits); (2) "regular informal workers" (who receive a finite contract from capitalists guaranteeing the number of workdays but receive no non-wage benefits or other labor rights); and (3) "casual informal workers" (who have no contract, benefits, or other labor rights) (see Figure 10.3). Formal workers are declining in number throughout the world. In India they represent 4 percent of the total labor force and only 30 percent of the non-agricultural workforce.[25] From 1999 to 2011, the share of regular informal workers accounted for much of the growth in working-class

---

25 NSS, "National Sample Survey on Employment and Unemployment, 68th Round, 2011–2012," ed. Ministry of Statistics (New Delhi: National Sample Survey Organisation, Government of India, 2012); PLFS, "Periodic Labour Force Survey (PLFS), 2017–2018" (New Delhi: National Statistical Office, Government of India, 2019).

jobs in the public and private sectors.[26] By 2018, regular informal workers accounted for 70 percent of all regular salaried workers in India.[27]

Another correction occurs among those in CCL. As per Erik's schema, one subcategory of those in CCL—namely, managers, supervisors, and experts—generally enjoy access to state labor recognition and regulation. But other subcategories of those in CCL—such as small employers, the petty bourgeoisie, and semi-autonomous wage earners—do not enjoy such access. In India (as in many countries) production regulation is limited to specific spaces, such as the factory. But many workers in CCL do not operate in such spaces; rather, they work in private, unregulated spaces (such as their own home, the employers' home, or unregistered work sheds) or in public spaces that are unregulated for work (such as the street or a park). Second, India (like many countries) limits production regulations to "large" enterprises, which the government defines by the number of formally employed paid workers (which can range from six to one hundred for different laws); small employers and petty bourgeoisie remain unregulated. Finally, in India (as in many countries), capital avoids labor regulation by claiming to "buy" its finished products or services from other businesses, even though those products or services are produced and designed directly for the so-called buyer. Semi-autonomous wage earners and the petty bourgeoisie are the sellers of such products or services, and they are paid on a piece-rate basis (in the form of a "consumer price"), rather than a time-based wage. Although they resemble mislabeled proletarian workers, they hold some autonomy in *how* and *when* they produce, even if they lack autonomy on *what* they produce. Erik emphasized the latter, but in my interviews with Indian women workers, they emphasized the importance of the former two aspects of production (i.e., how and when) as key to balancing their reproduction obligations at home with their production requirements and to grappling with their scarce time.

These corrections (depicted in Figure 10.3) expose a set of shared interests that can potentially bind some workers in CCL with those in

26   Rina Agarwala, "The Politics of India's Reformed Labor Model," *Business and Politics in India*, ed. Christophe Jaffrelot, Atul Kohli, and Kanta Murali (New York: Oxford University Press, 2019), 95–123.

27   PLFS, "Periodic Labour Force Survey."

the other classes. For example, informal workers (who do not sit in CCL) may share an interest with semi-autonomous wage earners (who do sit in CCL) in more state recognition and protection for laborers. Meanwhile, capitalists (who do not sit in CCL) may share an interest with small employers (who do sit in CCL) in less state recognition and protection for laborers. Small employers, the petty bourgeoisie, and family laborers (who all sit in CCL) may favor greater state recognition and provision to assist the family unit, or they may fear that such recognition would threaten the gender and caste hierarchies of control and power that shape family units. These interests may be shared with workers and/or capitalists (who do not sit in CCL).

Figure 10.3. Building on Wright to Map the Basic Class Relations in India

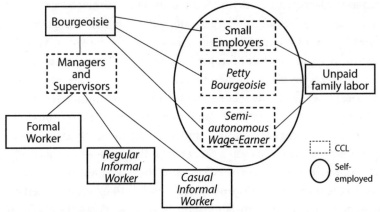

In India, the term "informal workers" is used to denote all classes of workers who are unrecognized or unregulated under labor and production laws. This includes those who do not sit in CCL, such as so-called regular informal workers (who are hired on a contract but lack many legal benefits), and casual workers (who usually lack a formal contract), as well as those who do sit in CCL, such as small employers, petty bourgeoisie, and semi-autonomous wage earners. As I have argued elsewhere, although informal workers are unregulated by laws based on the standard employment relationship with capital, they *are* regulated by numerous other state laws. Moreover, while some value the ability to operate under minimal state regulation and control, some are fighting for increased state recognition and protection for their nonstandard labor relationships.[28] As a result of their struggles, different groups of informal workers have attained different gradations and types of labor and production regulations. Let us now examine these struggles in greater depth.

Indian Politics from Above: Unpacking the "Self-Employed"

Following Erik, I argue that having a precise class structure map that illuminates different subcategories of workers in CCL helps improve our understanding of contemporary class relations and class politics from above and below.

From above, the Indian government since 2010 has tried to expand what it calls "self-employment." Self-employment has been promoted as a rural and urban job-creation strategy for those who have not been directly absorbed into capitalist production (as a formal, regular informal, or casual informal worker). The term "self-employment" dovetails perfectly with the Indian government's currently favored market logic of self-sufficiency and entrepreneurship. And self-employment has been heralded for operating purely in the sphere of market exchange, outside relations of capitalist exploitation and production. The Indian state's support of self-employment follows a long history in the field of international development. In the early 1970s, Keith Hart drew on Accra fieldwork to highlight how urban migrants who were not absorbed into formal employment generated alternative income sources through self-employment.[29] Shortly thereafter, the International Labour Organization (ILO) incorporated urban self-employed workers into its poverty-alleviation programs.[30] In the late 1980s, self-employed workers reemerged in the development literature as a beacon of hope for modern, unfettered markets. Using data on Lima, Peru, Hernando de Soto

---

28   Rina Agarwala, *Informal Labor, Formal Politics, and Dignified Discontent in India* (New York: Cambridge University Press, 2013).

29   Keith Hart, "Informal Income Opportunities and Urban Employment in Ghana," *Journal of Modern African Studies* 11 (1973): 61–89.

30   S. V. Sethuraman, "The Urban Informal Sector: Concepts, Measurement and Policy," *International Labour Review* 114, no. 1 (1976): 69–81; John Weeks, "Policies for Expanding Employment in the Informal Sector of Developing Countries," *International Labour Review* 111, no. 1 (1975): 1–13.

famously argued that self-employment enables workers to avoid governments' mercantilist regulations, which he depicted as rent-seeking mechanisms for Latin American bureaucracies and ruling classes.[31] By the late 1990s, the World Bank had reversed its exclusive focus on formal workers and joined the ILO in promoting self-employment as a beneficial option for those squeezed out of formal labor markets.[32]

At first glance, the Indian state's efforts to expand self-employment seem successful. According to the Indian government, self-employed workers currently constitute 58 percent of its rural labor force and 35 percent of its urban labor force.[33] But Figure 10.3 forces us to ask: Who comprises this group of "self-employed"? When promoting self-employment, the Indian government, and development institutions such as the World Bank and the ILO, equate the "self-employed" to "small employers." India's previous (interim) finance minister, Piyush Goyal, for example, went so far as to say job losses are a good sign, as today's youth "prefer to be job creators rather than job seekers."[34] And India's current prime minister, Narendra Modi, famously answered an interviewer's question about job creation in the economy by referring to *pakoda* sellers (*pakoda* is a popular snack) ahead of the 2019 Lok Sabha (parliamentary polls). To support the growth of small employers, the Indian government has extended countless loans, skills-training programs, and incentive schemes to start one's own business.

Despite this support, however, small business owners comprise less than 5 percent of those officially classified as "self-employed." The remaining 95 percent occupy the two other subcategories of those in CCL (see Figure 10.3). The petty bourgeoisie includes small tailors, trash collectors, and street vendors (such as pakoda sellers). And semi-autonomous wage earners include domestic workers and home-based garment and cigarette manufacturers. Workers in both these subcategories sit at lower levels of power and resources than do small business

---

31 Hernando de Soto, *The Other Path: The Informal Revolution* (New York: Harper and Row, 1989).

32 World Bank, *World Development Report 2004: Making Services Work for Poor People* (New York: Oxford University Press: 2003); World Bank, *World Development Report 1995: Workers in an Integrating World* (New York: Oxford University Press, 1995).

33 PLFS, "Periodic Labour Force Survey."

34 Jahnavi Sen, "Lost Your Job? Piyush Goyal Thinks That's a 'Very Good Sign,'" *The Wire*, October 6, 2017, thewire.in/economy/piyush-goyal-india-jobs.

owners. Neither offers the paid jobs the government is heralding through its promotion of self-employment. And both exacerbate hidden forms of capitalist exploitation and production through their reliance on unrecognized and unpaid family members. Both enable capitalist employers to pose as "buyers" of their products, thereby absolving capital of any responsibility for workers' labor conditions, security, and social reproduction. And both meet capitalists' interests in escaping costly labor obligations, while still enabling capital to benefit from workers' provision of the goods and services needed for production and profitability.

Much more work is needed to measure and refine the three subcategories of the self-employed in different countries. Following Erik's work in the US and Sweden, we might require qualitative surveys asking people about their work conditions, levels of autonomy, and labor organizations. And, as Erik underscored, the boundaries between these categories will always be imperfect. But acknowledging the extensive and varying levels of exploitation occurring among the different subcategories of workers classified as "self-employed" is vital to exposing the hollowness of the state's promotion of "self-employment" as a solution to unemployment.

At the same time, by lumping these three subgroups of workers together in a single category of the "self-employed," the Indian state has inadvertently shed a useful spotlight on their shared experiences. For example, workers in all three subgroups lack a clear employer-employee relationship since they all rely on self-exploitation and unpaid family labor. Therefore, the question of who (if anyone) is profiting from their labor is complex. All three are intricately involved in capitalist production—offering cheap inputs to capital (such as auto parts, transport, or products manufactured on order); goods and services to middle- and upper-class capital owners (such as cleaning, elderly care, gardening, and waste collection); and goods and services to low-wage workers (such as food, clothing, and haircuts). And all three sit in CCL, having some ownership or control of production assets—be it physical capital, labor (either wage or unpaid), organization, process, or skill—while being simultaneously dependent on the value of their own labor.

These shared experiences raise a key question: Have they led to an articulation of shared interests, identities, and joint class struggles among the self-employed?

Indian Politics from Below: Self-Employed Struggles for Recognition and Decommodification

Scholars often assume that workers in CCL, and particularly those in the CCL subgroup known in India as the "self-employed," cannot organize as a class because they operate outside of state regulation and are their own employers. But we know that such predictions are neither theoretically nor empirically supported. Theoretically, class structures help shape class interests, but whether or not class members organize and act upon them is historically and politically contingent and cannot be predetermined. The conflicting interests of those in CCL offer obstacles but also potential for class consciousness and mobilization. Empirically, India's self-employed workers support capitalist accumulation and thus hold structural power vis-à-vis state actors that support such accumulation. Therefore, we might expect them to draw on this power to organize.

Drawing from my interviews with Indian domestic workers, trash collectors, street vendors, and home-based garment and cigarette manufacturers (all of whom are categorized as self-employed workers sitting in CCL), I argue that the two largest subgroups (i.e., the petty bourgeoisie and semi-autonomous wage earners) are organizing. These efforts began in the 1970s, grew in the 1980s, and won some victories in the 1990s and 2000s. These movements are at an infant stage and cannot be compared to advanced social democracies. However, they lend significant insights into *the making of* a newly mobilized and swelling class identity among self-employed workers in India's non-agrarian, "modern" sectors. They also reflect instances of cross-class alliances (highlighted in Figure 10.3 in *red*) between self-employed workers in CCL and regular-informal and casual informal workers (who are not in CCL) in the form of joint organizations, strikes, and institutionalized state programs.

Underlying the budding cross-class alliance between India's self-employed and casual workers (which I have written about elsewhere) is a shared axis of exploitation among those whose production is controlled by capital but who are unrecognized and unregulated by the state's labor laws.[35] To overcome this axis, these workers are demanding (1) state recognition as legitimate economic actors *despite* their complex

---

35   Agarwala, "Redefining Exploitation."

employer-employee relationship and (2) state welfare and peer-to-peer support that can decommodify their labor. Given the elusive relationship that self-employed workers have to capital, it is not surprising that they target the state. To attain their demands, self-employed workers employ *non-class identities*, such as caste, gender, citizenship, and strata (such as "the poor"). These trends suggest that the most important effects of India's pro-business, liberalization turn has been to alter the rhetoric of class politics along non-class lines in ways that include those in CCL.

It is noteworthy that despite the Indian government's claim that the self-employed are small employers, India's self-employed have mobilized around their interests as "workers" (rather than as entrepreneurs or business owners) who have been left out of the post-reform state's promise of prosperity from market-led growth. As capital owners themselves, some small-business owners and petty bourgeoisie were at first happy to be absolved of responsibility toward labor. But over time, as laborers in their own units, they have enjoyed neither the legal right to welfare nor basic income. Therefore, they have increasingly demanded from the state new economic policies and labor regulations that support, rather than punish, their livelihoods.

By the 1990s, self-employed workers were officially counted (as individual workers, rather than solely as enterprises) in the government's National Sample Survey on Employment and Unemployment. They were also invited to serve as advisers and partners in numerous government committees and policy discussions. These victories indicated state recognition for a population that has long been excluded from India's class-based protective regulations. In addition, some self-employed workers successfully organized to win new regulations that promise access to welfare programs. Implementation has been unsurprisingly low, and these workers have not established their own political party to represent themselves. Nevertheless, their struggles have expanded the number and types of beneficiaries of state regulation and recognition to include more diverse employment relationships, as well as occupations such as domestic work, street vending, waste-picking, and home-based manufacturing, many of which are dominated by excluded minorities, such as women and members of the lowest castes.

Domestic workers' movements represent one of the newest groups of self-employed workers to organize as a class. Although Indian domestic workers have been organizing since the 1950s, their organizations have grown since the ILO passed Convention 189 on Domestic Work in 2011. Today, there are sixty-nine registered domestic workers' organizations in India; 83 percent of these are unions and nearly all of them are exclusively female.[36] Following the model of construction workers, domestic workers are fighting to attain comprehensive legislation to regulate their work and provide them with social benefits through welfare boards.[37] Their fight for labor legislation is as much a demand for state recognition of their status as workers as it is a demand for protection and the decommodification of their labor. In a context where labor law enforcement is increasingly waning, domestic workers express their demands for legislation as a counterweight to the power of their employers. They have won some legislative victories at the state level and secured the creation of welfare boards in four states (although these boards were created with no funding mechanism). Most recently, the national government agreed to accept the registration of their unions. These victories are striking, as the government continues to deny recognition of their employment relationship. Interestingly, the cumulative failures in securing national legislation for domestic workers have galvanized unions into joint action at the national level.

In recent years, self-employed recycling and waste collectors, most of whom are members of the lowest castes, have begun to organize. Like domestic workers, trash collection workers have tried to expand the definition of the "working class" by broadening the concept of "exploitation" beyond the standard employment relationship, to also include exploitation by state officials (such as municipal offices responsible for trash collection or the police who demand bribes from workers), and by middle-class residents who employ informal trash collectors or who control public spaces.[38] In this way, waste collectors have fought for (and, in many cases, obtained) state-certified identity cards that help them access existing government health and pension programs and obtain voter identity cards and ration cards for the public food distribution system—all of which require residence documentation (which

36   Rina Agarwala and Shiny Saha Saha, "The Employment Relationship and Movement Strategies among Domestic Workers in India," *Critical Sociology*, online publication first (2018).

37   Agarwala, *Informal Labor*.

38   Agarwala, "Redefining Exploitation."

these workers usually lack). They have also formed innovative cooperatives to ensure their access to income, such as SWaCH in the city of
Pune, through which they negotiated a municipal contract to serve as
the city's official household trash collector and sorter. Although households claim to "buy" the service of door-to-door trash collection for a
"user fee," waste collectors have redefined the exchange as "wages." They
have also demanded that NGOs that hire waste collectors to clean public
toilets as a public service pay them fair and timely wages for their work
rather than categorizing them as "volunteers."

Finally, self-employed home-based garment workers have become
organized. Indian garments constitute 30 percent of export earnings,
indicating the high value–added component of the industry.[39] In the
state of Gujarat, all home-based garment workers and headloaders (who
transport garments from homes to wholesalers and retailers by carrying
the loads on their heads or via handcarts) have obtained identity cards
from the state government. They have also won the establishment of a
state-level welfare board that offers both productive capital and reproductive welfare: a sewing box with scissors, a table, and other tools; skills
training; and 1,200 rupees for medical needs. In some cities, they have
negotiated collective wage/fee agreements with shop owners, who claim
to "buy" the finished garment pieces or the transport service. They have
also redefined the unit of minimum wages to be on a piece-rate basis,
rather than a time basis, and have secured a seat on the minimum wage
advisory committee at the national level.

Self-employed workers also view themselves as being exploited by
urban formal workers. Formal workers' protections and benefits, self-
employed workers argue, are subsidized by the unprotected and unregulated goods and services that self-employed workers provide. Self-
employed workers not only provide inputs for formal employers and
workers; they also enable underpaid formal and informal workers to
reproduce themselves.

---

39   Ibid.

Potential Agents for an Emancipatory Future?

Under what conditions have India's self-employed workers in CCL organized and forged class alliances with regular and casual informal workers who are not in CCL? Given the massive number of poor self-employed workers who are *not* well-resourced, privileged small business owners, we might see class organization among India's self-employed as an instance where capital has gone too far, squeezing labor enough to force those in CCL to join forces in a collective struggle with traditional workers. But in the case of India, the state and formal workers also provided conditions for this new collective struggle.

From the 1920s to the 1950s, when Indian independence movement leaders were fighting to structure India's own social contract, organized formal workers and the state joined forces to both give the state an enormous role in managing capital-labor relations and limit labor legislation to big businesses. At the time, there was a deep faith that democratic pressures could force the state to hold capital responsible for labor. In addition, working-class movements and parties agreed to hold only big business accountable for decommodifying labor, on the assumption that the petty bourgeoisie and small employers could not afford to comply with protective labor legislation, and that they would eventually disappear with development.

But these efforts merely gave capital an incentive to keep self-employment alive. Most large businesses created small, unregulated subsidiaries (which in turn could hire unregulated regular and casual workers). Many businesses turned to "buying" and "selling" inputs from semi-autonomous earners and petty bourgeoisie, rather than directly hiring wage workers. In the meantime, the self-employed (as well as workers in unregulated small businesses) remained invisible. For decades, they were not counted in labor force surveys, their interests were not counted in labor policies, and labor organizations and unions did not recognize them as "workers." Over time, casual and self-employed workers shared a resentment not just of capital, but also of formal workers. It was in this context that the Indian state and capital could join forces to further undermine formal workers' class struggles by yielding to some of the demands for recognition and decommodification by self-employed and informal workers. Far from invisibilizing the self-employed, the Indian state valorized self-employment as an ideal solution to the nation's notorious "jobless growth," offering (at least the promise of) an employment option for the masses who were not being absorbed by India's booming economy.

In his early work, Erik insisted that "class alliances" require a class compromise on differences and antagonisms and thus differ from a "multi-class movement" against a common enemy.[40] But as he showcases in his later work on real utopias, a more just and egalitarian future will rely on the combination of diverse countermovements that together can slowly "erode" the unjust features of unfettered capitalism.[41] Such movements, therefore, will not only build progressive power, but sustain it with a unifying vision for a more just future. In this vein, India's self-employed workers' movements and their attempts to join forces with other informal workers must be viewed as some of the many contemporary agents of transformation. I wish I could ask Erik what he thinks of this suggestion.

40   Wright, *Interrogating Inequalities*.
41   Erik Olin Wright, *How to Be an Anticapitalist in the Twenty-First Century* (London: Verso, 2019).

11

The Class Basis of Anticapitalism: Labor Politics in Contemporary Argentina
Rodolfo Elbert

As Michael Burawoy has pointed out, Erik Olin Wright's work moved "from a class analysis without utopia to utopia without class analysis."[1] One way of transcending this tension is to explore the political ramifications of class divisions that affect transformative agents who are also capable of taking up the tasks of anticapitalism (i.e., resisting capitalism while at the same time prefiguring a socialist pathway to transcend it). In this chapter, I bring Erik's early class analysis into conversation with his later oeuvre on anticapitalist strategies, exploring the ways in which the socioeconomic fragmentation of the working class in Latin America affects the capacity of the labor movement to become an agent for progressive social change and, potentially, an anticapitalist social force.

I first engage in what Erik defined as the task of "diagnosis and critique" of capitalism. Using statistical analyses of survey data and

I want to thank Michael Burawoy and Gay Seidman for their guidance in the formulation of the argument for this chapter and for their extremely helpful comments on previous versions of this manuscript. I also want to thank the other participants of the conference "Engaging Erik Wright: Between Class Analysis and Real Utopias." Their questions and comments helped me improve the ideas presented in this chapter. Finally, I want to thank my friend and colleague Dr. Pablo Pérez Ahumada for his feedback and help on parts of the statistical analysis.

1   Michael Burawoy, "A Tale of Two Marxisms: Remembering Erik Olin Wright (1947–2019)," *New Left Review* 121 (January–February 2020): 69. Reprinted as chapter 1 in this volume.

ethnographic material from fieldwork, I explore the links between formal and informal workers in Argentina's contemporary labor movement, focusing on the complex relations between class identity and class interests in the collective action of a fragmented working class. In the final part of the chapter, I explore the implications of these dynamics for Erik's theory of anticapitalism in the Latin American context. I argue that grassroots unions that seek to overcome the socioeconomic fragmentation of the working class can be understood as "agents of transformation" that could help undermine capitalism from within. A strong, unified labor movement would be a prerequisite for progressive social change in the context of crisis and permanent austerity and simultaneously a potential platform for anticapitalist strategies.

The Class Analysis of Informality: The Standard Approach and the Marxist View

Erik proposed his class schema in the early 1970s to provide a Marxist explanation for the persistence and growth of the middle class in developed capitalist societies. This was considered an "embarrassment" for Marxist theory, which had long argued that over time, the class structure of capitalist societies would be increasingly polarized. On the contrary, the golden age of Western capitalism generated the growth of managerial and professional occupations based on the increasingly complex organizational structure of multinational companies and the state.

Faced with this empirical anomaly, Erik developed his concept of "contradictory class locations," which explained that individuals located in those positions simultaneously occupied two class locations.[2] One brought them closer to working-class interests (because they did not own the means of production), and the other was similar to that of the capitalist class (because they were in control of the labor process). The contradictory character of these locations was expressed in the ambiguity of their class interests because these were not related strictly to a fundamental interest in maintaining capitalism (like the bourgeoisie) nor replacing it with socialism (like the working class). Instead, these interests could shift according to the proximity of individuals to each of

2   Erik Olin Wright, *Class, Crisis and State* (London: New Left Books, 1978).

the polarized positions (in terms of authority and/or skills) as well as the changing dynamics of the class struggle.

Erik's class schema can be understood as one of the main contributions to sociological Marxism since the 1970s. His concept of contradictory class locations addressed an empirical anomaly that raised questions about a core prediction of classical Marxism. In this theoretical move, Erik developed a "conceptual belt" for a Marxist view of class centered on the notion of exploitation, and he generated new predictions that advanced our scientific knowledge of capitalist societies.[3] For the next twenty years he then pursued quantitative research to test the main predictions of his class theory. Some of those predictions fared better than others, but all in all, he contributed to the emergence and consolidation of quantitative class analysis in the contemporary social sciences, as well as to the revitalization of Marxist social sciences in the context of the collapse of existing socialism around the world.[4]

Faced with the options of either embracing alternative social theories or moving to some type of post-Marxism, Erik stubbornly maintained that an exploitation-centered concept of class was more appropriate for explaining middle-class positions in capitalist societies. In this chapter, I argue that Latin American societies present a similar dilemma for Marxist sociologists, although in this case the anomaly is not the persistence of the middle class, but the heterogeneity of the working class. The social fragmentation of the working class in the region is a consequence of the fact that a significant proportion of workers are persistently employed or self-employed under informal employment arrangements. What are the implications of this fragmentation for a class analysis of Latin American societies?

Under Erik's supervision, my doctoral dissertation tackled this puzzle. At first, I thought that I might need to approach this problem much as Erik had approached the persistence of the middle class in advanced capitalist societies—that is, through a theoretical and empirical exploration of the objective class interest of informal workers. However, from the very beginning Erik made it clear that in this case we had to do "less" instead of "more." Instead of creating a new concept to define the class position of

---

3   From this perspective, Erik's work can be understood as part of what Burawoy defines as the Marxist research program in sociology. Michael Burawoy, "Two Methods in Search of Revolution: Trotsky versus Skocpol," *Theory and Society* 18 (1989): 759–805.

4   Erik Olin Wright, *Class Counts: Comparative Studies in Class Analysis* (Cambridge: Cambridge University Press, 1997).

informal workers, he suggested I should follow the class boundaries of the Marxist class schema and propose a research agenda to explore the similarities and differences between formal and informal workers at a subordinated theoretical level.[5] Empirical analysis would deliver the answer to my puzzle: Can we maintain a classical concept of the working class in the context of the deep socioeconomic fragmentation that has separated formal and informal workers?

The standard view of informality is that formal and informal workers form two distinct classes with different structural locations, interests, identities, and lived experiences.[6] Consequently, authors suggest that class analyses of Latin American societies need to incorporate informality as a new class cleavage, resulting in the following class schema: capitalist class, petty bourgeoisie, middle class, formal proletariat, informal proletariat, and informal self-employed. The rationale behind the new schema is that "social classes such as the 'proletariat' can be defined as relatively homogeneous entities in the advanced societies, while in the periphery, they are segmented by their limited incorporation into the fully monetized, legally regulated economy."[7]

---

5   I was lucky enough to have Gay Seidman as a co-adviser (in practice) for my dissertation research. With respect to this core issue in my dissertation, Gay fully agreed with the strategy of retaining the Marxist class schema and exploring the relations between formal and informal workers at a subordinated level. Gay oriented me toward the analysis of the way unions and activists in the field were dealing with the problem. This is, instead of assuming class differences between formal and informal workers, ask activists what they think and what they do to overcome this divide. Gay Seidman, *Manufacturing Militance: Workers' Movements in Brazil and South Africa, 1970–1985* (Berkeley: University of California Press, 1994).

6   Alejandro Portes, "Latin American Class Structures: Their Composition and Change during the Last Decades," *Latin American Research Review* 20, no. 3 (1985): 7–39.

7   Portes and his colleagues made an important breakthrough in the literature on class and informality because they overcame perspectives that considered that informal workers were isolated from the formal economy and thus were not part of the class structures of Latin American societies. Instead, Portes suggests that individuals employed in the informal economy are fully integrated to the class structure of Latin American societies, and he has inaugurated a line of research that focuses on the links between informal workers and the formal economy. Paradoxically enough, this research program was based on the assumption that there is a class schism that divides formal and informal workers. In my opinion the paradox resides in the fact that the standard view was the first to research the links between formal and informal workers, but the guiding assumption in that research was that these two groups represent distinctive social classes particular to Latin American societies. And this assumption led to

An alternative perspective based on the legacy of Erik's class analysis considers formal and informal workers as significant segments of the same class because they share similar experiences of exploitation and domination in production.[8] From this perspective, formal and informal workers share the same class position, although informality adds complexity to Latin American class structures at a subsidiary level since it does generate class segments. The alternative view challenges the idea that the contrast between the formal and informal proletariat has the same conceptual status as other class divides and rejects the notion that informality is a deep cleavage dividing Latin America's working class. Instead, despite the socioeconomic fragmentation that affects the working class, formal and informal workers belong to the same social class because they share a fundamental class interest, defined by the range of actions and strategies of social change that affect their material well-being.[9]

The working class, as defined by Erik, is thus divided into three segments: the formal proletariat is composed of wage earners in working-class locations whose employers make retirement contributions (that is, workers registered in the social security system), while informal workers are unregistered wage earners. A third segment of the working class is composed of the informal self-employed—mainly unskilled individuals, usually self-employed in subsistence jobs.[10] Throughout this chapter, I explore the patterns of class formation in contemporary Argentina, focusing on the relationship between class identity and class interests of a fragmented working class. Instead of assuming that informality is a class cleavage that

---

exaggerations in their conclusions about the socio-fragmentation that affects the working class in Latin America and the impossibility of a unified class mobilization of Latin American labor movements. Alejandro Portes and Kelly Hoffman, "Latin American Class Structures: Their Composition and Change during the Neoliberal Era," *Latin American Research Review* 38, no. 1 (2003): 41–82; Tamar Diana Wilson, "Approaches to the Informal Economy," *Urban Anthropology and Studies of Cultural Systems and World Economic Development* 40, no. 3–4 (2011): 205–21.

8   Erik Olin Wright, *Understanding Class* (London: Verso, 2015), 173.

9   Ibid., 166.

10   The class position of the informal self-employed in Latin America might present a different challenge to Marxist class analysis. Can we include self-employed individuals in the working class? I had long conversations with Erik about this. We concluded that the informal self-employed should be given a similar theoretical treatment as the informal proletariat because they mostly had survival jobs that put them in the working class in terms of living conditions. In addition, a significant proportion of unskilled self-employed in Latin America are in fact quasi-employees and thus subject to direct exploitation and domination.

divides workers, empirical research should study the specificity of the social relations that link (or separate) formal and informal workers.

Informality, Fragmentation, and Class Identity in Argentina

In this section I explore the relationships between objective class position, informality location, and class identity. Recognizing that the working class in Argentina is objectively fragmented, I will explore the effects of this fragmentation on patterns of class self-identification of workers. Both the standard view of informality (Portes) and the alternative view (Erik) would expect a statistically significant difference between the privileged classes and working classes in terms of class self-identification. The theoretical expectation in both frameworks is that individuals in the formal proletariat, informal proletariat, or informal self-employed locations would have consistently higher levels of working-class self-identification when compared with the privileged class locations (contradictory locations, formal petty bourgeoisie, and capitalist class).

But then the two perspectives part ways. The expectation of the standard view is that there should also be statistically significant differences in the rates of working-class self-identification in the comparison between the formal proletariat and the informal locations. Based on Portes's class analysis, one would expect that formal workers should have lower rates of working-class identity because they have a "privileged" location in the class schema of Latin American societies. On the contrary, if we follow the intuition behind Erik's class analysis, we would expect no significant differences between the different segments of the working class.

To test these hypotheses, I analyze data from a survey study carried out by the research team of the Programa de Investigación sobre Análisis de Clases Sociales at the Instituto de Investigaciones Gino Germani, Universidad de Buenos Aires, consisting of 1,065 cases (245 from Buenos Aires City and 820 from Greater Buenos Aires) based on a stratified, multi-stage sample design, with random selection at all stages.[11]

11   The survey study was directed by Ruth Sautu, Pablo Dalle, Paula Boniolo, and Rodolfo Elbert and funded by the PICT 2012-1599 project awarded by the Agencia Nacional de Promoción de la Investigación, el Desarrollo tecnológico y la Innovación, Argentina. *El análisis de clases sociales: Pensando la movilidad social, la residencia, los lazos sociales, la identidad y la agencia* (2020): 1–391.

The objective of the analysis in this section is to explore the statistical relationship between objective class location, informality location, and subjective class self-identification.

The questionnaire used in the survey included a question about class self-perception, with the following wording: "Newspapers, TV, politicians, some people, talk about social classes. Do you consider yourself as belonging to a social class?" Eighty-four percent of survey respondents answered affirmatively to this question and were subsequently presented with a list of five possible class locations to choose as their own: Upper, Upper-middle, Middle, Working, or Lower. This produced an initial class self-perception distribution, which can be regarded as "spontaneous," for it includes all survey respondents who claimed to belong to a social class when faced with the first question. Sixteen percent of survey respondents, who replied they did not see themselves as having a class location or who refused to answer the question, were asked the following question: "Many people say that they belong to a certain class. If you had to choose, you would say you belong to . . ." And they were shown a flashcard with the same class options. Adding up "spontaneous" and "induced" survey respondents, slightly more than 99 percent of them chose a class location.

In Table 11.1, we can see the relationship between the class-and-informality objective position and the class self-identification variable:

Table 11.1. Class Self-Perception of Individuals by Class-and-Informality Location (Buenos Aires, 2016)

	Class self perception					
	Upper	Upper-middle	Middle	Working	Lower	Total
Capitalists	0.0	5.0	85.0	10.0	0.0	100(20)
Petty bourgeoisie	0.0	9.6	67.5	20.5	2.4	100(83)
Contradictory locations	0.3	6.6	69.7	18.8	4.6	100(304)
Formal proletariat	0.0	0.5	34.0	58.5	7.1	100(212)
Informal proletariat	0.0	0.4	29.8	55.7	14.2	100(282)
Informal self-employed	0.0	1.5	35.9	55.7	6.9	100(131)
Total	0.1	3.2	47.3	41.7	7.8	100 (1032)

Source: Own elaboration base of PI-Classes 2016.

The data presented in Table 11.1 allow us to descriptively confirm the general trend toward a consistency between objective class location and subjective self-identification. In the aggregate, 71 percent of survey respondents chose a class category that is consistent with their objective location. The remaining third is divided into 20 percent of people from working-class locations who self-identified with the middle class and 10 percent of people from privileged classes who self-identified with the working class or the lower class. Within the privileged classes, it is worth stressing that almost a quarter of those in the formal petty bourgeoisie chose a working- or lower-class self-identification (the contradictory locations show a similar percentage), while only 10 percent of the employers show this lack of consistency. Furthermore, within the working class, about a third of those surveyed in each segment self-identified "upward," choosing the middle class or the upper-middle class. This phenomenon is mostly expressed among the self-employed in the informal sector, with 37.4 percent of survey respondents making this type of selection. The percentage is slightly lower in the formal proletariat (34.5 percent) and the informal proletariat (30.2 percent).

This data provides proof of the methodological consistency of the class self-identification variable required to conduct the statistical test for our two hypotheses.

If the formal proletariat, the informal proletariat, and the informal self-employed are indeed segments of the same social class, one would expect small or no differences in terms of their class self-identification. In order to conduct a statistical test of both hypotheses (one about the differences between privileged locations and working-class locations and the other about the differences between formal and informal locations in terms of class self-identification), I performed a logistic regression that uses class identity as its dependent variable, the results of which I present below.

One of the requirements of logistic regression is that the dependent variable must be dichotomous. Consequently, we grouped the self-identification categories as follows: those self-identified with the upper, upper-middle, and middle classes were categorized as "middle class," while those self-identified as working or lower class were categorized as "working class." Those who did not provide an answer (nine individuals) were excluded from the analysis. After this recategorization, the dependent variable is assigned the value of 0 for those self-identified with the middle class and a value of 1 for those self-identified with the working class. It is important to bear this in mind when reading the regression coefficients since a positive value indicates that this class category is related to an increase in the chance of identification with the working class with respect to the reference category.

The main independent variable in the analysis is the class-and-informality schema, to which we added a series of relevant socio-demographic controls. In the regression (displayed in Table 11.2), we used an abbreviated class schema as the independent variable, taking "privileged classes" as the reference category (includes individuals in the capitalist class, petty bourgeoisie, and contradictory locations). An analysis of the regression coefficients tells us what effect each class-and-informality location has on people's class identification compared with the privileged classes. We expect a positive coefficient for the working-class locations (formal proletariat, informal proletariat, and informal self-employed) compared to the reference category, since the chances of self-identification with the working class in these locations should be higher than the chances of class self-identification with the privileged classes.

Table 11.2. Determinants of Working-Class Self-Identification (Buenos Aires, 2016) (logistic regression, standard errors in parenthesis)

Class location (reference: Privileged classes)	Coeficientes (EE)
Formal proletariat	1.87***
	(0.188)
Informal proletariat	2.14***
	(0.180)
Informal self-employed	1.75***
	(0.218)
Socio-demographic controls	
Gender (ref. male)	-0.287**
	(0.143)
Cohort (ref. born 1950–60)	-0.074
	(0.063)
Likelihood Ratio χ^2	209.69
DF	
Pseudo R^2	0.1466
N	1032

Source: Own elaboration base of PI-Classes 2016. Note: omitted categories are Contradictory Locations (social class variable), Male (gender variable), Born 1950–60 (cohort variable). Response variable was categorized as 0 (middle class) and 1 (working class). Positive coefficients means that a greater proportion of cases in that group self-identify as working class when compared to the reference category.

Regression analysis confirms our hypotheses regarding the relationship between objective class, informality location, and subjective class self-identification, controlling for a series of significant socio-demographic variables. First and foremost, the regression confirms that self-identification with the middle class prevails among the privileged sectors of the social structure, regardless of the fraction to which they belong. On the other hand, the working-class locations are associated with greater likelihood of self-identification with the working class compared with contradictory locations. In all cases, these results render statistically significant coefficients. The strongest effect is present in the informal proletariat (in this location the chances of self-identification with the working class are doubled compared with the reference category) followed by the formal proletariat (1.87) and the self-employed in the informal sector (1.75). What is relevant in this case is that all the categories display significant differences with respect to the privileged classes in terms of our first hypothesis.

Our second hypothesis contrasts Portes's expectation that there would be significant differences between formal and informal workers' class self-identification, to Erik's expectation that there would be no differences between these groups. Do formal and informal workers have similar patterns of class self-identification? Is there a statistically significant difference between these groups? To answer these questions, the best way to represent the coefficients resulting from a logistic regression is through the method of *predicted probabilities*, which consists of estimating the probability of a result from the category changes in the main predictive variable, controlling for the effects of other independent variables. Put differently, a constant value is defined for the control variables (in our case, gender and cohort), and we estimate the changes in the probability of an event associated with changes in the categories of the selected independent variable. In our study, we will estimate the probability of a working-class self-identification for the different class locations, controlling for gender (the estimate presupposes the female gender) and birth cohort (the first cohort includes those individuals that were born between 1950 and 1960).

Graph 11.1 broadly summarizes the relationship between objective class, informality location, and class self-identification resulting from the logistic regression. The advantage of the predicted probabilities method is that it allows us to determine whether there are statistically significant

Graph 11.1. Predicted probability of working-class identity by class location (95% Cls)

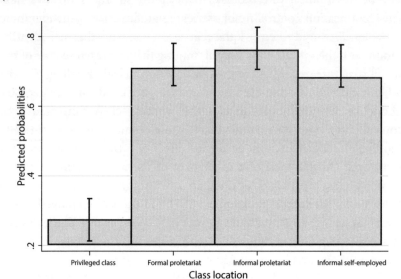

differences in class self-identification between all categories of the independent variable. The graph shows the predicted probabilities of identification with the working class for different class-and-informality locations, including the confidence interval estimated based on the logistic regression.

First and foremost, the results reveal a significant gap between the privileged classes and any of the working-class locations. While the probability of self-identification with the working class for the privileged classes is 27 percent, all working-class locations show an estimated self-identification above 60 percent. Additionally, it supports Erik's expectation that there would be no differences between the formal and the informal locations in terms of class identity. The overlapping confidence intervals suggest that there are no significant differences in class self-identification of different segments of the working class.

Organizing Against Fragmentation in the Industrial Workplace (and Beyond)

So far, we have analyzed the patterns of class self-identification of the Argentine working class, showing that there are no significant differences between formal and informal workers in terms of class identity. However, the fact that formal and informal workers all identify as working class does not necessarily translate into unified collective action and a unified collective identity at the workplace. Even if the socioeconomic fragmentation of the working class might not result in conflicting identities, it could translate into divergent material interests for the different subgroups.

As Erik pointed out in his last work on class analysis, the precariat should be considered a segment of the working class because it shares the same fundamental material interests with other groups of workers.[12] The long-term interest of all workers is to replace the capitalist "game" with a socialist "game" based on democratic production processes and equal distribution of the social product. This new "game" would benefit both formal and informal workers and would harm the capitalist class, whose interest is to maintain the capitalist game of exploitation and domination. However, there could be differences in the immediate material interests of different groups of workers at the level of the "rules of the game" or "moves within these rules."[13] This means that we can define informal and precarious workers as "significant segments" of the working class because although they share the fundamental material interests of the formal working class, there could be instances in which particular changes of the rules of the game or moves within the capitalist game would benefit one group of workers over others.

If we want to understand the complicated relationship between class structure, class identity, and class interest, we need to move beyond statistical analysis and into an analysis of the factory politics of a fragmented working class. What are the patterns of collective action of a working class that is subjectively unified but objectively fragmented? Are there organizing strategies oriented at unifying the socioeconomic interests of the different sectors? Or do unions deploy exclusionary politics that reinforce the division? More broadly: Can a fragmented working class be the leading force for progressive social change and, ultimately, be at the center of anticapitalist strategies in Latin America?

---

12   Wright, *Understanding Class*, 168.
13   Ibid., 171.

In order to address these questions, I will discuss evidence from qualitative research that I conducted on the Argentine labor movement since 2010, with a specific focus on the industrial workplace. The focus of the research was to compare union strategies of formal workers from three factories located in a city in Northern Gran Buenos Aires region: V-Car (automobile production), K-Foods (food processing), and FR-Meat (meat packing). This area has been one of the most industrialized regions in the country since the 1970s, when multinational companies established production north of Buenos Aires city along the Pan-American Highway (its Spanish name is Autopista Panamericana). The contemporary landscape of the region includes factories that mostly employ formally employed skilled workers, located near precarious neighborhoods where most residents are informal and unemployed workers. This region provided an interesting scenario for qualitative research on the way unions dealt with the fragmentation of Argentina's working class. Based on non-participant observation and in-depth interviews, I studied union strategies to deal with precarious work inside the factory and union strategies regarding the informal working class living near the factory.

During this period, I identified two prevalent union strategies in industrial workplaces. One strategy, developed by Peronist unions with a top-down tradition, consisted of the subordinated integration of informal and precarious workers. A second strategy, proposed by left-oriented unions as part of a grassroots union movement, sought to unify the different segments of the working class on an equal standing. I observed the first strategy in the automobile factory V-Car. Inside its workplace, the Peronist union endorsed precarious contracts, although in some instances, it did help informal workers organize for higher salaries—for example, helping outsourced janitors campaign for better salaries and working conditions and, potentially, gain union contracts. However, the same union quickly dismissed the opportunity to include janitors in the autoworkers' union contract, and instead it worked to demobilize the janitors.

The union at V-Car thus followed a monopolistic organizing pattern that excluded informal workers from the nearby neighborhoods. In the absence of an organizing strategy linking the workplace to neighborhood communities, union activism was channeled through national Peronist politics. Despite efforts by the party leadership to encourage links across the formal-informal divide, the bureaucratic union failed to generate any meaningful solidarity with informal workers.

A very different strategy, involving grassroots solidarity aimed at uniting formal and informal workers, was present in the two other factories I studied: K-Foods and FR-Meat. In both factories, union renewal in the late 2000s resulted in left-leaning grassroots unions winning union elections. In both cases unions sought to organize precarious workers, supporting their demands for formal standard contracts.

The success of this organizing strategy depended on many factors, including the type of factory regime, the structural power of precarious workers, and the associative power of the union at the time of the struggle. The most successful campaign involved a group of subcontracted forklift drivers at K-Foods—key workers hired on a precarious basis. The grassroots organizing began with weekly meetings of union activists, formal workers, and subcontracted workers from the night shift, meetings that spilled over into community gatherings. The campaign's original goal was to match the wages of informal workers to the wages of formal workers. However, after achieving this goal, the company threatened to end the contract with the subcontractor. In response, the forklift drivers, with the support of formal workers, committed to a strike action, demanding the company employ them directly. As a result, management agreed to formalize the status of informal workers—a shift that transformed the balance of power in the factory, especially as it affected the employment of precarious workers.

In contrast to V-Car, the unions at K-Foods and FR-Meat were heavily involved in the politics of the surrounding community. But the success of their organizing strategy depended on how the employees' homes were distributed in the community. The situation at FR-Meat was particularly favorable as most of the workers lived nearby the factory, building strong links between the union and neighborhood organizing. The union supported community soup kitchens for the destitute and, most spectacularly, a two-month land occupation that extended to road blockades and a sit-in in the mayor's office. The main organizer of this local campaign for social housing was a union representative from the plant and, indeed, the union was essential to the campaign's success.

Labor Politics, Class Interests, and Anticapitalism in Contemporary Argentina

The Argentine labor movement faces the paradoxical reality of a work-ing class that is subjectively unified but objectively fragmented. In the previous section I explored different types of organizing strategies deal-ing with this fragmentation at the industrial workplace and in relation to the community. One noteworthy development of the late 2000s was the emergence of a grassroots union movement that, under certain conditions, could successfully unify different segments of the working class. In this section I will explore the ways in which this experience of union renewal at the factory level can contribute to building the labor movement as an agent of anticapitalist transformation.

First, grassroots unions can be considered real utopias in as much as their novel democratic designs have challenged the more typical bureau-cratic unionism that had dominated union politics for the previous forty years. Grassroots organizing has led to the inclusion of rank-and-file members in decision-making processes, and to open democratic elec-tions involving competition between different groups, representing alternative constituencies.

Although unions are purely capitalist institutions in the sense that they provide the mechanisms to represent the interests of workers in the capital-ist workplace, studying the democratic innovations of grassroots unions is necessary if we want to understand the role of the labor movement in a broader anticapitalist strategy. Since Erik's vision of democratic socialism includes democratic decision-making in the sphere of production, we must pay attention to the conditions and possibilities of union democracy.

A second way in which grassroots unions can contribute to social trans-formation is through the development of solidarity across different segments of the working class. In *How to Be an Anticapitalist in the Twenty-First Century*, Erik maintained that the labor movement remains one of the key progressive social forces in challenging capitalism. However, he also noted that the collective organization of the working class is more complicated today than in the past because economic struggles over immediate class interests could intensify divisions among different groups of workers.[14]

---

14 Erik Olin Wright, *How to Be an Anticapitalist in the Twenty-First Century* (London: Verso, 2021), 64.

This study of organizing strategies in the contemporary industrial workplace in Argentina shows how the fragmentation of the working class can be overcome. When the lower strata organized themselves independently, it was possible to build unity across different sectors of the working class. In the absence of such grassroots organizing, top-down unionism was likely to consolidate a labor aristocracy. Traditional unions in Argentina have prioritized the demands of their members, rather than addressing the needs of informal and precarious workers. Alternative grassroots unions have been successful in building solidarity across different segments of the working class when they have connected their workplace struggles to the interests of local communities beyond the factory. The success of strategies to win formal contracts for precarious workers depended not only on both the structural and associative power of the union, but on a conscious political commitment to building solidarity.

Finally, the experience of grassroots unionism in Argentina highlights the relevance of the labor movement for debates regarding anticapitalism. The dominant political orientation of the labor movement in Argentina is still the Peronist strategy, which emphasizes the need to domesticate capitalism in order to secure certain social rights for specific groups of workers, without questioning the socioeconomic fragmentation of the working class. We see this in the industrial workplace, where Peronism leads to the subordinated integration of informal and precarious workers. In some instances, bureaucratic unions have allowed precarious workers to fight for their demands, but the unions made sure that these struggles did not challenge the persistence of precarious labor arrangements. At the national level, these unions supported the center-left Peronist strategy of precarious hegemony as a way out of neoliberal collapse.[15] The main feature of this regime was a paradoxical combination of a limited redistribution of wealth and persistent working-class fragmentation.

On the other hand, the grassroots union movement has been led by leftist groups with an explicit anticapitalist orientation. In this case, a ruptural strategy was favored over other types of anticapitalism. In fact, the most radical attempts to unify a fragmented working class (union

---

15   Ruy Braga, *A política do precariado: Do populismo à hegemonia lulista* (São Paulo: Boitempo, 2012).

struggles to get formal contracts for informal workers and strategies to take over bankrupt companies during the economic crisis) were led by left-oriented unions that also supported a sustained anticapitalist strategy. In summary, labor politics in Argentina are also about confrontations between anticapitalist strategies: Peronists aim to resist and tame capitalism (by building a social pact that improves the living conditions of workers but sustains fragmentation), while the left maintains a ruptural strategy (by organizing at the workplace for the unification of the working class but also attempting to sustain a narrative of the necessity of smashing capitalism).

Final Considerations

As Erik has noted, the fragmentation of the class structure in contemporary capitalism represents a major challenge to the construction of politically robust anticapitalist collective actors.[16] In particular, Latin American societies present an extreme case of working-class fragmentation, including formal, precarious, and informal workers, as well as the informal self-employed. In Argentina, the experiences of grassroots union movements at the end of the 2000s represent an example of how workers can creatively overcome socioeconomic divisions at the workplace and in the community. The movement demonstrated important successes at the factory level but faced great difficulties when it tried to scale up its organizing. Even at the peak of its influence, the grassroots movement was unable to win the leadership of national unions. In this context, workers and activists debated which type of organizing strategy would allow the formation of a robust anticapitalist social force. Should the labor movement be at the center of an anticapitalist strategy in Argentina? Or should we focus on organizing those who are excluded from the formal economy? How can we develop solidarity links between these sectors? What type of anticapitalist strategic orientation should the movement have?

In 2015 Erik visited Argentina as part of his global trip to present his proposal on *How to Be an Anticapitalist in the Twenty-First Century*, and took part in the debates around these strategic issues. I particularly

---

16 Wright, *How to Be an Anticapitalist in the Twenty-First Century*, 63.

recall his presentation to a group of activists and workers at the Madygraf factory, a recovered enterprise located in the Northern Gran Buenos Aires region. As usual, Erik started his presentation with a statement that the ruptural strategy had to be rejected because historical evidence suggests that the most viable path toward a democratic-socialist society is not to smash capitalism, but to erode it. This generated an intense reaction from the public, mostly composed of workers and political activists, who defended the ruptural pathway.

The criticism from the audience revolved around the implausibility of a long-term strategy of reforming capitalism because, at some point, it would generate a violent response from the bourgeoisie. In particular, activists mentioned the example of Allende's Chile, where the attempt to build socialism without smashing capitalism was dramatically disrupted by a military coup. Activists felt that Erik did not take into account this historical evidence, or that of other Latin American countries where dictatorships violently repressed the radicalization of labor movements in the 1970s. One of Madygraf's leading activists insisted that the historical evidence points to cooperatives as a way to build working-class power in the context of a long-term ruptural anticapitalist strategy.

Erik politely rejected the criticism. Instead, he highlighted the importance of the experience of recovered enterprises for the long-term strategy of eroding and taming capitalism. Furthermore, he insisted that a combination of non-ruptural strategies was the only plausible way forward to anticapitalism if we wanted to achieve a socialism organized around equality, democracy, and solidarity. He reiterated the argument that smashing capitalism does not produce human emancipation, so that even if it were possible to destroy capitalism, the result would not be emancipatory socialism.[17] In summary, he tried to convince activists that the factory takeover and its organization under cooperative principles was already an optimal anticapitalist strategy, arguing that it was not necessary to link this strategy to a ruptural agenda. In the end, there was no resolution to the debate. Erik maintained his position, and activists left the room still skeptical about his proposal that socialism could be built without smashing capitalism first.

---

17 The reconstruction of this conversation is based on Erik's personal notes of the trip, which he shared with me after he came back to the United States.

This story is perhaps the best illustration of Erik's understanding of the role of the intellectual in public debate, and it is an example we should follow. As a scholar, he opened up spaces in academia to discuss and debate visions of a socialist future. He questioned the idea that "there is no alternative" to capitalism, developing a systematic and rigorous analysis of strategies that might allow us to end capitalism and build a democratic-socialist alternative. But he did not stop there. He traveled around the world presenting his ideas to diverse audiences and engaged in passionate debates with activists about the potential and limitations of his proposal. In this way he contributed to building strong popular movements that could advance an anticapitalist agenda. Now it is up to us to continue his legacy.

12

From Class Analysis to Real Utopias and Back Again: Erik Olin Wright in Conversation with Left Populism
Peter Ramand

> *Utopia lies at the horizon.*
> *When I draw nearer by two steps,*
> *it retreats two steps.*
> *If I proceed ten steps forward, it*
> *swiftly slips ten steps ahead.*
> *No matter how far I go, I can never reach it.*
> *What, then, is the purpose of utopia?*
> *It is to cause us to advance.*
>
> —Eduardo Galeano

Who has the power to systematically transform society? Classical Marxism's answer to this question was elegant and simple: capitalism exploits workers, and therefore socialism is in the material interest of the proletariat; workers create value in society and have the capacity to halt production and profit. On this basis, the working class was a collective actor uniquely well positioned to transform society.

Additionally, Marx offered theories of capitalist development and social formation: capitalism's contradictions would tend toward intensifying economic crises, and societies were expected to gradually polarize into two increasingly homogeneous class blocs. The long-term systemic instability caused by these tendencies, according to Marx's theory, would eventually lead to a working-class takeover of power.

Marx, however, never elaborated a theory of politics to inform socialist strategies of transformation. And as Dylan Riley discusses in a 2020 essay, the strength of Marx's theory lay primarily in its explanation of the rhythms of capitalism rather than its sociology of class formation.[1] What Marxism needed was a framework for analyzing complexity within the class structure of modern capitalist societies and, in particular, a way of understanding the growing number of intermediate locations that had developed between the capitalist and proletarian classes. This was the project that primarily occupied the early years of Erik Olin Wright's career.

There were many reasons for Wright's interest in class analysis, discussed throughout this volume. One of the less-cited motivations, and I believe a principal concern, was his desire to develop a framework that could assist in thinking about how to build radical class-based coalitions in ways that account for fragmentation and complexity within the class structure. "Class consciousness is knowing which side of the fence you are on," a poster Wright displayed in the Havens Center (now the Havens Wright Center) reads. "Class analysis is figuring out who is there with you." For Wright, this meant developing a theoretically informed, empirically rigorous framework for mapping the class structures of modern capitalist societies.[2]

In this regard, Wright found the results of the Comparative Class Analysis Project (CCA) unsatisfying. He never felt that the analysis contributed substantively to political projects aiming to challenge exploitation and oppression. It was for this reason, among others, that Wright established the Real Utopias Project (RUP) and began to wind down the large-scale international surveys that defined his investigations of class. The RUP, he felt, could more directly contribute to thinking about projects of radical transformation.

As Michael Burawoy has pointed out, however, there is a sharp disjuncture between these two projects. The former never truly seemed to inform the latter, leading Burawoy to conclude that Wright "moves from a class analysis without utopia to utopia without class analysis."[3]

---

1 Dylan Riley, "Real Utopia or Abstract Empiricism? Comment on Burawoy and Wright," *New Left Review* 121 (January–February 2020): 99–107.

2 Erik Olin Wright, *Class Counts: Comparative Studies in Class* Analysis (Cambridge: Cambridge University Press, 1997). See chapters 13 and 14.

3 Michael Burawoy, "A Tale of Two Marxisms," *New Left Review* 121 (January–February 2020): 69. Reprinted in this volume as chapter 1.

The challenge, he proposes, is to find a way of reintegrating Wright's "scientific" and "critical" Marxisms. I will argue that a direct unification of Wright's RUP and class analysis projects is possible through an engagement with Wright's investigation of agency and collective action in *How to Be an Anticapitalist in the Twenty-First Century* (HBA).[4] Although the book's final chapter, titled "Agents of Transformation," is less developed than Wright hoped, having been written only after his cancer diagnosis, it is arguably the book's most unique contribution. The framework is rich and nuanced and points to the cluster of questions that could have animated the next phase of the RUP.

There have been numerous attempts to rethink the problem of collective agency on the radical left. Wright chose not to engage these while writing the final chapter of HBA. This, he said, would come later. Initially, he wanted to think through the conceptual and theoretical problems involved in constructing collective actors without being overly influenced by other schools of thought. While he was in hospital, we spoke about some of the similarities and differences between the framework he had developed and those proposed by others. When I first read a draft of "Agents of Transformation," I was immediately struck by similarities between Wright's conclusions and those reached by advocates of "left populism." Some critiques of left populism also applied to his arguments. This, Wright promised, was something we would explore after he got out of the hospital. This chapter is an attempt to honor that commitment in some small way.

In what follows, I will outline the points of convergence between Wright's thinking and two leading proponents of left populism, Ernesto Laclau and Chantal Mouffe, who have had considerable influence on recent left projects. I break down Wright's and the left populists' theses on "collective agency" formation into what I consider to be their core propositions, comparing these and exploring parallel critiques that can be applied to each account. Both frameworks, I argue, are limited by similar factors—namely, a lack of testability and inattentiveness to class dynamics at play in collective actor formation. These limitations can be overcome, however, by directly incorporating Wright's framework for investigating class into a holistic research project. Not only could this

---

4   Erik Olin Wright, *How to Be an Anticapitalist in the Twenty-First Century* (London: Verso, 2019).

provide a basis for extending Wright's project, but also, I argue, it could provide a sounder grounding for other studies of political articulation. To illustrate how this might be done, I conclude the chapter with a discussion of populist mobilization in the UK: the Scottish independence referendum, Brexit, and Labour's electoral fortunes under the leadership of Jeremy Corbyn. Using survey data from the British Election Study (BES), I demonstrate how Wright's class analysis could inform progressive mobilizing strategies and how it could be used to "test" the efficacy of political articulation.

The Peculiar Convergence of Wright, Laclau, and Mouffe

"Left populism" has undergone something of a renaissance in recent years.[5] Syriza in Greece, Podemos in Spain, and La France Insoumise have all openly self-identified as populist, and their leading cadre cite Ernesto Laclau and Chantal Mouffe as chief theoretical influences.[6] Synthesizing insights from post-structuralism and a rereading of Gramsci's *Prison Notebooks*, Laclau and Mouffe argued for a shift in the way socialists think about agency and social subjectivity. The mission of the left should be reformulated as a project for "radical plural democracy," and the language of "workers versus capitalists" should be abandoned in favor of a new friend/enemy distinction: the "people" versus the "oligarchy."

A comparison of Wright and the left populists is all the more interesting because their intellectual biographies are so different. Wright's

---

5   For ease of comparison, when discussing the post-Marxist contribution to the study of populism I will refer almost exclusively to writing by Laclau and Mouffe, eschewing discussion of contributions from their collaborators. Throughout the chapter I refer to Laclau and Mouffe as the "left populists" or "post-Marxists." I do so solely as shorthand for purposes of readability. The chapter also omits discussion of the now substantial literature on populism within the social sciences. Two excellent reviews of academic literature on populism are Rogers Brubaker, "Why Populism?," *Theory and Society* 46 (2017): 357–85; and Bart Bonikowski and Noam Gidron, "Varieties of Populism: Literature Review and Research Agenda," in Weatherhead Working Paper Series No. 13-0004, 2013.

6   Íñigo Errejón and Chantal Mouffe, *Podemos: In the Name of the People* (London: Lawrence & Wishart, 2016), 72–3; Perry Anderson, *The H-Word: The Peripeteia of Hegemony* (London: Verso, 2017), 95.

analytical neo-Marxism, on the face of it, could hardly be more dissimilar to the post-Marxist "anti-essentialism" espoused by Laclau and Mouffe.[7] Indeed, in *Hegemony and Socialist Strategy* Wright is cast as a "class essentialist" on a "Diogenes-like search for the 'true' working class."[8] Despite this, Wright and the left populists arrive at similar conclusions, albeit via contrasting routes.

How to Be an Anticapitalist

How to Be an Anticapitalist in the Twenty-First Century was initially intended as a pithy abbreviation of the arguments presented in *Envisioning Real Utopias*. Wright had, over time, become more and more interested in speaking to non-academic audiences, and he wanted to provide a distillation of the RUP for activists less familiar with academic verbiage. This alone would have been a valuable contribution, but the book quickly developed a life of its own. In it, Wright makes original arguments that partially reflect his changing concerns: "My focus of attention had shifted from establishing the credibility of a democratic-egalitarian alternative to capitalism to the problem of strategy."[9] Wright had previously engaged this topic,[10] but in HBA he reformulated, refined, and systematized his arguments. He also engaged a related problem for the first time: how to construct and connect collective agents capable of transforming capitalism.

Wright was unsatisfied with the final chapter of HBA, having had little time to work on it, but it contains more than I think he realized. In part it elaborates much that remained unsaid in previous writings on the RUP. But more than that, in clear and precise language it outlines the conceptual issues involved in building a movement. It is a fresh intervention into an old debate that deserves to be interrogated as rigorously as the rest of Wright's work, not least because it might have been the first statement in what could have formed a rich new vein of research for the RUP.

---

7   Chantal Mouffe, *For a Left Populism* (London, Verso: 2019), 62.

8   Ernesto Laclau and Chantal Mouffe, *Hegemony and Socialist Strategy: Towards a Radical Democratic Politics* (London: Verso, 1985), 83.

9   Wright, *How to Be an Anticapitalist*, xi.

10   For example, Erik Olin Wright, "Working-Class Power, Capitalist-Class Interests, and Class Compromise," *American Journal of Sociology* 105, no. 4 (2000); Wright, *Envisioning Real Utopias*, 273–375.

The central propositions of Wright's thesis on agency in HBA can be reformulated and summarized as follows:

1. Robust collective actors anchored in political and civic society are required to transform society in a progressive direction.

2. Due to increasing complexity and fragmentation within the class structure, class identity no longer provides a universalizing basis for solidarity, if it ever did; labor unions and other traditional class-based actors have insufficient capacity to transform capitalism by themselves.

3. Identities play a critical role in the formation of collective actors, especially when rooted in forms of socially imposed inequality or domination.

4. Interests are also a powerful mobilizer, and every identity group has interests associated with that identity. For example, women have "identity-interests" in ending gender-based oppression, and racial minorities have "identity-interests" in policies that mitigate racial discrimination.

5. However, individuals hold multiple potentially salient identities, and interests associated with one identity can often be in tension or even incompatible with another.

6. Values constitute a potential basis for overcoming these barriers and could allow political unity across diverse identities to be constructed, even if identity-interests between groups are in tension.

7. Three clusters of values are particularly important in this regard: equality and fairness; community and solidarity; and, most importantly, freedom and democracy.

Comparing Wright and the Left Populists

In the following section I break down the left-populist thesis into what I consider to be its fundamental propositions as they relate to constructing collective agency, and compare them with Wright's framework.

1) The working class is no longer the agent of social change

Laclau and Mouffe's first core argument is that the working class is not *the* agent of social transformation. The left, they argue, adopted a "class essentialist" epistemology, which assumes political interests are defined by an individual's position within the relations of production. This stems from the concept of "objective interests," which, they say, "lacks any theoretical basis whatsoever, and involves little more than an arbitrary attribution of interests by the analyst."[11] Instead, the left should oppose different forms of subordination without attributing any a priori centrality to any of them.[12]

Wright would reject Laclau and Mouffe's ontology and their assertion regarding objective interests. Nevertheless, he reaches similar conclusions regarding working-class agency. While noting that class is still "at the very heart of strategic thinking about eroding capitalism," Wright acknowledges that transformations in advanced capitalist societies have undermined working-class capacities. In particular, fragmentation within the class structure has limited the possibilities of forging a common class identity. Contrary to the process of social homogenization predicted by Marx, "the class structure has become more complex in ways that undercut the shared sense of fate and life conditions." Wright continues, "While it may be true that income distributions . . . have become considerably more polarized in recent decades . . . there is a pervasive fragmentation of lived experience that makes a common class identity difficult to forge."[13]

2) Collective agency can be forged among disparate subjectivities by appealing to identities, values, and interests

If we accept the first proposition—that the proletariat is not the subject of radical social change—then a new framework for thinking about collective actor formation is needed. Laclau contends that populism emerges from the failures of elites to satisfy the demands of different

---

11   Laclau and Mouffe, *Hegemony and Socialist Strategy*, 83.
12   Mouffe, *For a Left Populism*, 3.
13   Wright, *How to Be an Anticapitalist*, 136.

social groups.[14] A new language needs to be constructed, he argues, to unite these groups and express their separate grievances, "articulating" them together. To do this, the left should evoke *identities* and *values*. Interests do not give rise to ideologies, according to this view; rather, discourses create subject-positions. Identities are fundamental in this process because populists aim to unite particularistic groups—defined, for example, by their position within gender, race, and sexual relations—with the aim of constructing a new identity frame, that of "the people."

Wright does not evoke discourse as the means to cohere individuals and groups, but he deploys some of the same concepts to develop his framework. Identities, he suggests, play a particularly important role in the process of forming emancipatory collective actors because they can facilitate the solidarity needed for sustained collective action. Wright explains the process of identity formation as follows:

> Social structures are characterized by multiple forms of intersecting inequality, domination, exclusion and exploitation. These generate experiences of real harms in the lives of people . . . These experiences get transformed into shared identities through cultural interpretations, which . . . are themselves objects of contestation. The . . . social bases of emancipatory social movements—class, race, gender, ethnicity, and so on—are deeply connected to these kinds of identities.[15]

Wright argues that each identity group has an interest associated with that identity. While formulated differently, this is more or less consistent with the logic of the post-Marxists.

Wright then introduces a tension. Individuals hold multiple identities, and interests associated with one identity are often in tension or even incompatible with others.[16] He cites the example of racial minorities, who have identity-interests in ending discrimination in the hiring process. Sometimes, he notes, "there are tensions between the identity-interests of racial minorities and the identity-interests of workers, as

---

14   Ernesto Laclau, *On Populist Reason* (London: Verso, 2007), 118–21.
15   Wright, *How to Be an Anticapitalist*, 128–29.
16   See also Laclau, *On Populist Reason*, 139–56.

when struggles against racial discrimination affect the immediate conditions of labor market competition for white workers."[17]

How can this be overcome? "Values," Wright argues, "constitute a potential basis for overcoming these barriers and could allow political unity across diverse identities to be constructed, even if identity-interests between groups are in tension."[18] This is because, in reference to the example cited above, even if the material identity-interests of white and Black workers may conflict under certain circumstances, the egalitarian values associated with the interests of both groups overlap substantially.

One final point of comparison between Wright and the left populists is required in relation to our discussion of identity. As previously noted, Laclau and Mouffe believe that heterogeneous subjectivities must be forged into a collective actor named "the people." This is, for them, a fundamental objective of populist discourse. Wright does not name the collective actors with which he engages, nor does he give primacy to discourse in their formation. Nevertheless, he makes a parallel argument which, I think, more concisely engages the process of populist subject formation.

> One way that [identities] change is through the effects of social struggles. The lived experience of participating in social movements and other forms of collective action can change a person's sense of who they are . . . Partially this is simply a spontaneous result of the shared experience of struggle, but of course it is also a result of the wide range of cultural and ideological practices that occur within social movements designed to cultivate changed identities.[19]

In practice, Laclau and Mouffe's framework implies a top-down process. If the construction of "the people" is predicated on discursive articulations that properly fit the situation, a privileged agent of sorts is needed to formulate the articulation. "For relations of subordination to be transformed into sites of antagonism," writes Mouffe, "one needs the presence of a discursive 'exterior' from which the discourse of subordination can

---

17   Wright, *How to Be an Anticapitalist*, 138.
18   Ibid., 138.
19   Ibid., 129.

be interrupted."[20] Thus, in Spain, critiques of Podemos have highlighted the role played by intellectuals and party leaders in formulating "correct" discourses, which rank-and-file members have been expected to unquestioningly accept.[21] Wright's formulation is a more holistic account of the process of subject formation within contentious political processes. Ideological practices, discursive or otherwise, can transform people's perceptions of identity and can encourage the formation of new salient collective identities, but this takes place within a process that involves an array of contextual cultural factors and the direct effects of participation in social struggles. Subjectivity, then, is formed through the democratic civic interaction entailed in social movement activity.

3) The centrality of radical democracy

Wright and the left populists again converge in their conclusions that deepening democracy should be the central demand of left movements.

Laclau and Mouffe argue that democracy is the most important "floating" or "empty" signifier in populist struggle. What does this mean? Within their theoretical system a "chain of equivalence" is formed by the articulation of various unfulfilled, particularistic demands among groups within a society. This leads to one demand, Laclau argues, "stepping in and becoming the signifier of the whole chain."[22] For the left populists, "democracy" is the floating signifier *par excellence*; enhanced democracy is desirable for all subordinated groups and the meaning of democracy can be reinfused with values of equality and popular sovereignty. This is crucial because "the objective of a left populist strategy is the creation of a popular majority to come to power and establish a progressive hegemony."[23]

Wright makes no reference to semiotics but nevertheless reaches the same conclusion regarding the centrality of democracy to the left project:

---

20 Mouffe, *For a Left Populism*, 42.

21 Luke Stobart, "From *Indignados* to Podemos," in *Europe in Revolt Mapping the New European Left*, ed. Bhaskar Sunkara and Catarina Príncipe (Chicago: Haymarket Books, 2016); Josep Maria Antentas, "Iglesias, Errejón, and the Road Not Taken," *Jacobin*, February 11, 2017.

22 Laclau, *On Populist Reason*, 131.

23 Mouffe, *For a Left Populism*, 50.

The value of democracy ... should be given particular emphasis in articulating the concrete program of progressive politics. A deeper democracy ... is in the interests of a very broad part of the population beyond the working class ... Efforts to restore and deepen democracy ... constitute a unifying objective for people who may be less sympathetic to the overall anticapitalist agenda.[24]

Radical democracy, then, becomes a central pivot in the tactical formulations of both Wright and the left populists. Because of its majoritarian appeal, it is a powerful mobilizing tool, capable of unifying a variety of identity-interests or subject-positions.

4) An enemy must be forged

The starkest differences between the frameworks developed by Wright and the left populists involve their contrasting approaches to social conflict. Laclau and Mouffe draw heavily on Schmittian theory, which emphasizes the construction of friend/enemy distinctions. Wright, conversely, is a proponent of deliberative democratic processes of which the left populists—especially Mouffe—are skeptical.[25] For Laclau and Mouffe, it is unthinkable that a radical social subject could be constructed without this being done explicitly in relation to an "enemy" because, they argue, antagonistic conflict is *definitional* of both politics and democracy.[26]

Wright's proposed method of "eroding capitalism" involves two central processes: the steady expansion of egalitarian non-capitalist institutions within the interstices of capitalist society, and the development of political projects capable of using the state to incubate these real utopias. "The basic problem with this," according to Dylan Riley, "is that Wright tells us nothing about what is still the central task of any viable strategy for winning socialism: destroying the entrenched political and economic power of the capitalist class."[27] Without challenging ruling class power, the expansion of real utopias could be crushed as soon as they start to encroach on capitalist profitability.

---

24   Wright, *How to Be an Anticapitalist*, 143.
25   Chantal Mouffe, *The Democratic Paradox* (London: Verso, 2009); Mouffe, *For a Left Populism*, 69.
26   Mouffe, *The Democratic Paradox*, 36–60.
27   Dylan Riley, "An Anticapitalism That Can Win," *Jacobin*, January 7, 2016.

Wright's answer to this challenge rests in the contention that class relations do not, under all circumstances, necessitate a zero-sum game. Some corporatist social democratic regimes achieved a form of class compromise that was, according to Wright, relatively beneficial to all sides. High levels of working-class associational power, under certain circumstances, can both protect the interests of workers and help capitalists solve collective action and coordination problems in the production process. Wright calls this a "positive class compromise."[28] The same "symbiotic" logic can be applied elsewhere. Wright acknowledges that reforms and emancipatory institutional designs are liable to be dismantled, but this can be avoided if reforms solve problems for capitalists while simultaneously expanding possibilities for emancipatory alternatives.[29] He suggests that universal basic income (UBI) grants could operate according to this logic:

> [UBI] can help solve a range of real problems within capitalism and contribute to the vitality of capital accumulation ... On the other hand, it has the potential to help unleash a dynamic that expands the space for democratic-egalitarian interstitial transformations ... [UBI] could both erode the dominance of capitalism within the overall economic system and strengthen conditions for capital accumulation within the reduced spaces where capitalism operates.[30]

This logic may, however, not play out in practice. The Meidner plan, which Wright has written about, operated according to a similar logic.[31] This was a "share levy" system proposed in the late 1960s by Swedish social democratic economist Rudolf Meidner as an alternative to taxing corporations. Rather than paying taxes on profits, corporations would issue shares to a "wage-earner fund" controlled by trade unions. Over time the accumulation of shares in the fund would shift the balance of ownership and, after several decades, would result in majority ownership of a corporation. It was assumed this would be accepted by company executives and their shareholders, as they would keep all profits. Instead,

---

28 Wright, *Envisioning Real Utopias*, 343 and 361–4.
29 Ibid., 110–11.
30 Ibid., 111.
31 Ibid., 230–4.

however, the policy provoked a backlash from the Swedish capitalist class, resulting in the Social Democratic Party losing control of government for the first time in four decades.

Parallel Critiques of Wright and the Left Populists

There have been numerous critical engagements with the work of both Wright and the left populists in recent years. Because many of the core propositions formulated by both in relation to agency are similar, parallel critiques can be made of both.

Social and Associational Power

Wright and the left populists agree that robust collective actors must involve people outside the traditional working class. Mouffe is explicit about the implications of this: "The second wave of feminism, the gay movement, the anti-racist struggles and issues around the environment . . . transformed the political panorama, but the traditional left parties were not receptive to those demands."[32] The project of left populism, then, was to suture together a coalition of these movements alongside traditional working-class organizations.

But there have been profound transformations within these movements. When Laclau and Mouffe initially formulated their arguments, these movements represented emergent radical forces who disrupted existing power and authority relations. Since then, however, most have gone through a Michelsian process, developing organizations run by professional personnel who often become disconnected from the lived experiences of the people they represent. These organizations face funding issues that encourage de-radicalization, and attempts to lobby the state have brought many into the orbit of elite networks. In short, they have increasingly been embedded in corporate and state power structures. Meanwhile, the working class has been largely disembedded. In this sense, the left-populist challenge has been flipped relative to the 1970s. This shifting relationship is recognized by Mouffe:

---

32   Mouffe, *For a Left Populism*, 2.

When Ernesto Laclau and I wrote *Hegemony and Socialist Strategy*, the challenge for left-wing politics was to recognize the demands of the "new movements" and the need to articulate them alongside more traditional workers' demands. Nowadays the recognition and legitimacy of these demands have significantly progressed and many of them have been integrated into the left agenda. In fact it could be argued that the situation today is the opposite of the one we criticized thirty years ago, and that it is "working-class" demands that are now neglected.[33]

The implications of this acknowledgment are not considered further by Mouffe, but they pose problems for the left-populist project. Identity politics has become the discourse of contemporary left "insiders," and the "new movements" have not only been integrated into the left, but also increasingly into the economic, political, and cultural "establishment." It will be impossible to build robust collective actors unless the left can incorporate individuals from peripheral geographies that previously formed the bases of social democracy and trade unionism. This needs to be accounted for if we hope to build robust collective actors, and it seems unlikely that a discursive blueprint taken from the 1980s will achieve this. The construction of collective agency, therefore, requires a class analysis of associations.

Dylan Riley's critique of Wright's arguments has similar implications. In *Envisioning Real Utopias*, Wright defines socialism as a system in which "the means of production are socially owned and the allocation . . . of resources . . . is accomplished through the exercise of what can be termed 'social power.'"[34] The path to socialism, then, involves gradually increasing "social power" over the economic and political realms. But what is social power? And how is it exercised? For Wright, social power is rooted in the collective mobilizing capacity of civic organizations. "Civil society," Wright argues, "is the site of a form of power . . . rooted in the capacity of people to form associations to advance their collective goals."[35] Yet the basis of social power lies in the civic associations where cultural elites presently predominate. What

---

33   Ibid., 59.
34   Wright, *Envisioning Real Utopias*, 121.
35   Ibid., 145.

guarantee is there that a collective agent constructed out of civil society would wield its social power in the service of a socialist project?

This is the basis of Riley's critique: "Whether the subordination of economic to social power leads to 'economic democracy' depends heavily on who wields social power." "Wright," he argues, "reproduces one of the main weaknesses of the Tocquevillian tradition: an uncritical embrace of 'civil society' without an adequate specification of the way that class power shapes its political valence."[36]

The Unmooring of Articulation from Reality

Laclau and Mouffe's incorporation of post-structuralism allowed them to break with materialist constraints, but it also introduced weaknesses associated with the linguistic turn in social theory. Objects of discourse require no fixed referents, or, as Laclau writes, "the language of populist discourse is always going to be imprecise and fluctuating." Constructions of "the elite" and "the people" need not refer to sociological categories, as populist discourse is "not statistical, but performative."[37] As Perry Anderson notes, for political practitioners the vagueness of left populism can be an asset since to "specify . . . too accurately or realistically risks casting the net of hegemonic interpellations too narrowly, exposing the rhetorical percentages as the fiction they are."[38] This may be fine for politicians, but it casts doubts on the framework as a theoretical system. Anderson reflects on the "aporia":

> The result has been to detach ideas and demands so completely from socio-economic moorings that they can in principle be appropriated by any agency for any political construct. Inherently, the range of articulations knows no limit. All is contingency: expropriation of the expropriators could become the watchword of bankers, secularisation of church lands a goal of the Vatican . . . Not only can anything be articulated in any direction: everything becomes articulation.[39]

---

36   Riley, "An Anticapitalism That Can Win."
37   Errejón and Mouffe, *Podemos*, 105.
38   Anderson, *The H-Word*, 97.
39   Ibid., 96.

From Class Analysis to Real Utopias

This critique cannot be leveled at Wright. The articulation of collective agency in his work does not rely on discursive gymnastics. It is fundamentally connected to identity-interests anchored in an implicit analysis of social reality, implying objective limits to articulation strategies. By returning to Wright's work on class, this can be made explicit.

Bringing Class Back In

In *Class Counts*, Wright lays out a general framework for studying class formation with respect to class structure and class struggle. By "class formation" he means the construction of "collectively organized social forces within class structures in pursuit of class interests."[40] For the most part this involves creating organizations that link individuals within and across class locations. These could be political parties or labor organizations, but could also include social clubs, neighborhood associations, or even informal social networks. Class formation, for Wright, includes "any form of collectively constituted social relations which facilitate solidaristic action in pursuit of class interests."[41] With the exception of the reference to class interests, this definition is consistent with the discussion of collective agency formation in HBA.

Wright develops a macro model of class formation elaborating the relationship between class structure, class formation, and class struggle (see Figure 12.1) in which class structure "limits" class formation.[42] Three mechanisms are identified: first, processes of exploitation powerfully shape material interests; second, lived experiences in a class structure produce class identities; third, the distribution of resources in a society influences the attractiveness of potential alliances. These three mechanisms combine to determine the probability that a given class formation could emerge.[43]

---

40 Wright, *Class Counts*, 379.
40 Wright, *Class Counts*, 379.
41 Ibid., 380.
42 Ibid., 373–405.
43 Ibid., 397.

Figure 12.1. Macro Model of Relations between Class Structure, Class Formation, and Class Struggle

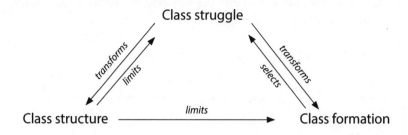

This is consistent with the arguments Wright develops in HBA and demonstrates how his framework avoids the pitfalls of post-Marxist unmooring. It also elaborates the relations between structure and agency implicit in "Agents of Transformation." And yet, class analysis is strangely absent from Wright's RUP.

Integrating Class Analysis and Real Utopias

Wright's class analysis investigated the structural dynamics of class, while HBA focused on political articulation. To integrate the "scientific Marxism" of Wright's early career with the "critical Marxism" of the RUP, I propose the following strategy: rather than study *either* discourse *or* structure, we can investigate the *relations* between the two. Class analysis can be used to test the efficacy of articulation strategies pursued by collective agents.

It may be useful, at this point, to recap Wright's approach to mapping the class structure. Wright specifies two dimensions within employment: relations to authority within the production process, and levels of skill and expertise. On the authority dimension he distinguishes between managers, who are involved in strategic and organizational planning in the workplace; supervisors, who possess some degree of power over other workers; and those with no authority over others. On the skill dimension, Wright differentiates between expert occupations that ordinarily need an advanced degree, skilled occupations that require a lower level of specialized training, and occupations that don't necessitate significant training. This produces a map of "contradictory locations within class relations," "privileged appropriation locations within exploitation relations," and "polarized locations within capitalist property relations," which can be seen in Table 12.1 below.[44] Wright's framework can then be operationalized and used to test hypotheses using survey data.

Table 12.1. Wright's Twelve-Location Class Matrix

Owner	Employee		
Capitalist	Expert manager	Skilled manager	Non-skilled manager
Small employer	Expert supervisor	Skilled supervisor	Non-skilled supervisor
Petty Bourgeoisie	Expert	Skilled worker	Non-skilled worker

Relation to Authority

Relation to Scarce Skills

This approach conceptually privileges class-based forms of domination. The matrix can be seen as a map of the "degree of inherent antagonism of material interests of people located in different places in the structure."[45] From the perspective of working-class locations (the lower right of the matrix), as you move toward the upper left, interests become increasingly antagonistic. Other identity distinctions and forms of domination can be explored within this framework, but always in relation to class. However, there is no reason this cannot inform intersectional understandings of subject formation. If, for example, an organization wanted to mobilize low-paid, Black women and developed discourses accordingly, the efficacy of the approach could be tested by including interactions in the model. To reduce the intricacy of intersectional analysis to interaction effects in statistical models may be a step too far for some, but if the

44   Ibid., 19–26.
45   Ibid., 395–6.

data collected is sensitive to these concerns, there is no reason insights cannot be gleaned.

Case Studies: The UK Labour Party and the Scottish National Party (SNP)

To illustrate how to bring class analysis and articulation together into a holistic research project, I will review two cases. First, I discuss the articulation strategy adopted by Jeremy Corbyn's Labour Party in the 2017 UK general election. The discussion of Corbynism is intended as a rough illustration of how Wright's class analytic framework could be used by organizers to develop and refine their strategies. Second, I assess the SNP's political articulation before and after the Scottish independence referendum of 2014. This example illustrates how the efficacy of articulation could be tested.

The following sections draw on data analysis of the British Election Study (BES), waves 1–13. This is a nationally representative sample for England, Wales, and Scotland, conducted each year by YouGov. Each wave contains between 18,864 and 27,682 respondents. Wright's class matrix is reconstructed from National Statistics Socio-economic Classification (NS-SEC) operational categories. This recategorization is complicated by several factors. First, it was difficult to ascertain within the data which managers oversaw strategic decision-making and which had a primarily supervisory role. On this basis, supervisors and managers have been collapsed into a single category within the authority vector. Likewise, capitalists and small employers have been collapsed into a single category as the sample contained few, if any, proper capitalists. This produces a matrix of eight locations rather than twelve (see Table 12.2). Logit regressions are used, although in this chapter I present descriptive findings alongside significance tests rather than β coefficients.

Corbynism

The UK Labour Party, during the leadership of Jeremy Corbyn, is an example of a collective actor discussed by both Wright and the left populists. Corbyn's Labour is a central focus of Mouffe's most recent investigation of populism, and Wright suggests his strategy for eroding capitalism could find particular resonance among young Labour Party members inspired by the party's left turn.[46]

The snap general election of 2017 presented a problem for the Labour Party. Labour's support was split—more so than its rivals'—among Brexit-supporting working-class voters in peripheral areas and pro-European professionals and students in the cities. Opposition to Brexit was highest among experts (40 percent support) and students (19 percent), while non-skilled workers were among the most supportive (62 percent).[47]

How could this fractured electoral coalition be articulated? Labour's strategy was to de-emphasize the European question, instead focusing on domestic policy that could, in Wright's formulation, "tame" capitalism. Policies for state-led job growth, the nationalization of railways, and increased social spending were framed in terms of the values Wright advocates: equality, democracy, and solidarity. Additionally, Corbyn and his representatives attempted to mobilize identity-interests, arguing that proposed policy would reduce the gender pay gap for female workers, the cancellation of university fees would benefit students, and building social housing would be in the interest of renters.

The Labour Party narrowly lost the general election but secured its single largest increase in vote share in nearly a century. Table 12.2 shows support for Labour by class location. For organizers and activists this moment represented a breakthrough: social-democratic articulation had secured a sizable vote among diverse class positions, with the biggest gains coming from working-class and expert locations. However, support later fell across all class locations as the salience of Brexit reasserted itself, a sustained campaign against Corbyn and his allies was carried out in the media, and Labour became embroiled in accusations of antisemitism. Could the decline have been arrested? It is impossible to say. But a method of linking messaging and mobilization tactics to an objective class analysis could have aided activists in their attempts to maintain momentum from the election.

---

46   Mouffe, *For A Left Populism*; Wright, *How to Be an Anticapitalist*, 63.
47   British Election Study (BES), wave 13.

Table 12.2. Support for Labour by Class Location, 2017 General Election

Employer	Expert manager/ supervisor	Skilled manager/ supervisor	Non-skilled manager/supervisor
18%* (N=252)	28%*** (N=660)	29%*** (N=2303)	41% (N=605)
Petty bourgeoisie	Expert	Skilled worker	Non-skilled worker
30%*** (N=1658)	37%* (N=1952)	41%* (N=6116)	43% (N=3050)

Note: Data is from BES, wave 13, collected between June 9 and 23, 2017. Significance tests refer to a logit regression model of class location predicting Labour vote, with non-skilled workers as the reference category, controlling for age, gender, race, and education.

There is, I believe, evidence to suggest that sustained populist articulation may have been more effective in holding Labour's electoral bloc together than attempts to overturn the Brexit referendum result, which in many respects became the party's key objective. Labour's coalition remained split on the EU, attitudes toward globalization, and a host of other indicators. For example, a majority of individuals in middle-class locations (experts and expert managers) think that globalization has done "more good than bad," compared with only 25 percent of unskilled and 32 percent of skilled workers. Common ground could, however, have been found over left-populist demands. Fifty-eight percent of experts agree or strongly agree that management will "always try to take advantage of employees," as do 74 percent of unskilled workers and 63 percent of skilled workers. For comparison, only 44 percent of expert managers hold this view. A similar trend holds when respondents are asked about attitudes regarding redistribution—whether there is "one law for the rich and one for the poor," and a number of other variables associated with left-populist attitudes. In short, a continuation of left-populist mobilization might have been more successful in maintaining Labour's coalition than the approach pursued. Wright's agentic framework would serve organizers well in formulating strategy and tactics, especially when connected to a systematic class analysis.

Scottish Independence

The efficacy of discursive articulation can be tested, in part, via a similar strategy to that discussed above. I will examine this in relation to the Scottish independence referendum of 2014.

The campaign for Scottish independence was narrowly defeated in that year's referendum. This campaign is another example of the left populism discussed by Wright, Laclau, and Mouffe: independence was framed as an opportunity to redistribute wealth and break with a neoliberal consensus imposed by an out-of-touch Westminster establishment. Advocates of independence argued for a civic nationalism that would be more welcoming of migrants than the British Home Office, and the referendum was notable for high voter turnout, with large numbers of working-class voters registering to vote for the first time.[48] The populist nature of the campaign climaxed in the final months before the vote, as polls narrowed and the debate became increasingly contentious. The structure of the campaign maps onto Wright's framework. Multiple groups framed the case for sovereignty in terms of identity-interests, such as "Women for Independence," "Scots Asians for Independence" and even "Whiskey Drinkers for Yes." These emerged alongside groups like National Collective, a pro-independence artist collective, and the left-wing Radical Independence Campaign, of which I was a founding member.[49] These organizations were united, to varying degrees, by egalitarian values: an independent Scotland could be a fairer society, with a government more representative of the democratic will of the people.

Following the referendum, leaders of the Scottish National Party (SNP) evaluated the campaign, concluding that they had secured working-class support, but had lost because they failed to convince middle-class voters of the case for sovereignty. To win in the future, they concluded, they would need to win over "Middle Scotland." The party reoriented its approach, gearing policies, speeches, and adverts

---

48   James Foley and Peter Ramand, "In Fear of Populism: Referendums and Neoliberal Democracy," *Socialist Register* 54 (2018).

49   See James Foley and Peter Ramand, *Yes: The Radical Case for Scottish Independence* (London: Pluto, 2014).

toward the new target demographic. The transformative potential of independence was downplayed in favor of discourses emphasizing stability and continuity. In short, the SNP developed articulation strategies prior to and after the referendum. The initial left-populist articulation gave way to a "centrist" strategy, which aimed to suture together an electoral bloc incorporating professionals alongside working-class voters.

We can deploy an illustrative test of the efficacy of both articulation strategies. Table 12.3 shows support for independence by class location at the time of the referendum. The class location most supportive of independence is unskilled workers, with 54 percent favoring constitutional change. Moving along the skills dimension, there is a monotonic decline in support. A similar relationship holds on the authority dimension: whether unskilled, skilled or experts, managers and supervisors are less favorable toward independence. The petty bourgeoisie is the location second most supportive of Scottish sovereignty, with nearly half favoring the breakup of the union. This provides a baseline from which we can examine changing levels of support.

Table 12.3. Mean Support for Independence by Class Location, 2014

Employer	Expert manager/supervisor	Skilled manager/supervisor	Non-skilled manager/supervisor
41.4% (N=89)	34.2%** (N=120)	41.2%*** (N=502)	45.1% (N=137)
Petty Bourgeoisie	Expert	Skilled worker	Non-skilled worker
49.5% (N=316)	41.2%*** (N=475)	45.8%** (N=1336)	54.1% (N=621)

Note: Data is from BES, wave 3, collected between September 19 to October 17, 2014. Significance tests refer to a logit regression model of class location predicting "Yes" vote, with non-skilled workers as the reference category, controlling for age, gender, race, and education.

The discussion regarding articulation can be reformulated into the following hypotheses:

H1: The SNP's articulation strategy is effective, but there is no observable class dynamic. Average support for independence increases uniformly across class locations.

H2: The SNP's articulation strategy is effective, but there *is* an observable class dynamic. Average support for independence increases among *either* middle-class locations (expert, expert manager/supervisor, and skilled manager/supervisor) or working-class locations (non-skilled worker, skilled worker, unskilled manager/supervisor).

Przeworski has argued that when political parties primarily representing working-class voters attempt to expand their support among the middle classes, working-class support will decline.[50] On this basis:

H3: The SNP's articulation strategy is partially effective. There is an *inverse* relationship between support for independence among middle- and working-class locations. As support for independence among expert, expert manager/supervisor, and skilled manager/supervisor locations increases, it will fall among skilled worker, unskilled worker, and unskilled manager locations, or vice versa.

Table 12.4 shows support for independence by class location at five different time points. It presents data from waves 1, 3, 4, and 9 of BES. Data for wave 1 was collected between February and May 2014. The same individuals were surveyed immediately after the referendum (W3, see Table 12.3), six months after the referendum (W4), and immediately after the Brexit referendum (W9). The differences between the time points can be imputed, in part, as the effects of the articulation strategies deployed by the SNP and the independence movement. This data is presented for illustrative purposes. There are countless intervening variables that would bias the results of any modeling strategy. Therefore, I present descriptive averages without significance tests, and all inferences should be treated with a degree of suspicion.

50   Adam Przeworski, *Capitalism and Social Democracy* (Cambridge: Cambridge University Press, 1986), 23–42.

Table 12.4. Mean Support for Independence by Class Location, 2014–17

Employer				Expert manager/ supervisor				Skilled manager/ supervisor				Non-skilled manager/supervisor			
W1	W3	W4	W9	W1	W3	W4	W9	W1	W3	W4	W9	W1	W3	W4	W9
41%	41%	48%	48%	34%	34%	47%	46%	40%	44%	48%	54%	48%	45%	52%	49%
Petty bourgeoisie				Expert				Skilled worker				Non-skilled worker			
W1	W3	W4	W9	W1	W3	W4	W9	W1	W3	W4	W9	W1	W3	W4	W9
47%	49%	50%	50%	39%	41%	49%	54%	38%	46%	48%	48%	45%	54%	55%	52%

Note: Data is from BES waves 1, 3, 4 and 9. Data for W1 was collected between February 20 and May 9, 2014, W3 between September 19 and October 17, 2014, W4 between March 4 and March 30, 2015, and W9 between June 24 and July 4, 2017.

In the months prior to the referendum, the populist strategy deployed by the movement for independence appears to have been effective, with support for a "Yes" vote increasing among most class locations, and declining only among unskilled managers/supervisors. Gains were largest among skilled and unskilled workers and modest among middle-class locations.

The change between W3 and W4 indicates that the SNP's new strategy after the referendum was moderately successful. Support among experts increased by 8 percent in this six-month period, and by thirteen points among expert managers and supervisors. Support among employers also increased by 7 percent. Backing among working-class locations largely plateaued during this time, neither increasing nor decreasing. However, support for independence among non-skilled managers/supervisors grew by 7 percent, following the trend of middle- rather than working-class locations.

For sections of the middle class, Brexit represented a disjuncture. Support for independence increased a further six points among experts and skilled managers/supervisors. This could be an independent effect of the Brexit phenomenon, or it could be that the SNP's continuity message only resonated with some after the ruptural threat of leaving the EU became apparent. To the extent that this data can be used to adjudicate between hypotheses, it suggests that the SNP's articulation strategies were effective before and after the referendum, and changing support had a noticeable, non-inverse class dynamic (hypothesis 2).

Conclusion

The problem of collective agency could have marked the beginning of a new vein of investigation for Wright and the Real Utopias Project. Wright increasingly saw questions of socialist strategy as central to his intellectual project. As he writes in the preface to HBA, his focus had shifted from examining democratic-egalitarian alternatives to the problem of transformative strategies, or "how to get from here to there," as he puts it.[51]

While preliminary, Wright elaborated the conceptual building blocks from which we can engage questions of agency, subjectivity, and class formation. I have argued that his conclusions on this topic share many similarities with the arguments of Ernesto Laclau and Chantal Mouffe, prominent proponents of left populism. Both frameworks provide insights about collective actor formation but also suffer from similar shortcomings related to their application to concrete cases. Wright, however, provides a way out of the impasse: integrating his class analytic and agentic frameworks allows us to test the efficacy of articulation strategies. I have applied this approach to recent examples of populist mobilization in the UK. Further research in this vein could test, refine, and extend Wright's formulations in HBA. It could also provide a sounder basis for scholars working in the left-populist tradition to anchor and test their formulations.

I can think of no greater way to honor Erik than to use the tools he left us to investigate and support the development of emancipatory movements across the globe.

---

51   Wright, *How to Be an Anticapitalist*, xi.

13

Fifteen Dollars and a Revolution: Building Anticapitalist Workers' Movements
Stephanie Luce

I began graduate work in sociology at the University of Wisconsin–Madison almost by accident. I had been working as an economist at the US Department of Labor, feeling that all my economics training taught me very little about how the economy worked, let alone how workers could best improve their labor conditions. I decided I needed to study more so I could return to the world of fighting for worker rights.

It was through a class with Erik Olin Wright that I first began to see how the economy really worked. A Marxist analysis gave me a framework for analysis and praxis.

I got involved in a living wage campaign in Milwaukee, which succeeded in getting the city to pass an ordinance mandating higher wages, but I began to wonder whether the city was enforcing the policy. I was afraid to study the issue—what if I found all the hard work organizers had done around the country to pass living wage ordinances was in vain?—but Erik pushed me, arguing that this was exactly the kind of thing we needed to know. If there is a reason labor campaigns were not working, organizers needed to know and redirect their efforts. Through his mentorship, I learned that I could combine my desire to organize

Acknowledgments to my colleagues Mimi Abramowitz, Sofya Aptekar, Kafui Attoh, Deepak Bhargava, Josh Freeman, Penny Lewis, Ruth Milkman, John Mollenkopf, Samir Sonti, and Joel Suarez, as well as the other authors in this volume, for comments on earlier drafts of this article.

around worker rights and take on the hard questions, always striving to learn more and do better.

I continue to straddle the world of scholarship and labor organizing and rely heavily on what Erik taught me, which was to keep asking hard questions, conduct rigorous research, and never lose sight of the ultimate goal: a postcapitalist real utopia.

Erik's final book, *How to Be an Anticapitalist in the Twenty-First Century* (2019), helps us keep a sharp focus on that goal. It is timely, as capitalism appears on shakier grounds than it has been in a while and anticapitalist movements are growing around the world. But unlike earlier periods of anticapitalist movement growth, this period is unusual, as union density and labor power are at historic lows in most countries. In this chapter I attempt to apply lessons from *How to Be an Anticapitalist* to the labor movement. As unions attempt to rebuild and gain power, they can do so in ways that are more anticapitalist. I also discuss dimensions of labor campaigns that reflect Wright's concept of real utopias.

Despite their weaknesses, unions continue to fight for and win workplace campaigns. But can they move from these to transformative change? For example, can they move from fighting for a $15 minimum wage to building unions to eroding capitalism? This is not a new question: theorists and activists have long debated the role of labor movements in anticapitalist struggles and, of course, there are plenty of unionists who have fought to defend and expand capitalism. Some on the left argue that unions are too reactionary to challenge capitalism. But others see a unique role for trade unions and worker struggles in bringing about a new system.

There are opportunities and limits to the role labor unions can play in a revolutionary struggle, but Wright's analysis, along with the changing nature of work and capitalism, may offer some new perspectives on how the labor movement and anticapitalist movement might intersect. This includes his ideas on anticapitalist strategies, anticapitalist values, constructing a collective agent, and real utopias.

In *How to Be an Anticapitalist*, Wright argues that capitalism can be eroded by a combination of strategies that are complementary and exist at different "levels of the game." The strategies include resisting, escaping, taming, dismantling, and smashing capitalism. Labor unions are a way to *resist* the worst impacts of capitalism. By organizing, striking, and engaging in workplace action, they fight for higher wages and better working conditions.

Workers can *escape* capitalism to some extent by forming worker co-ops. Even though few co-ops can exist truly outside of capitalist markets, they can be building blocks for an alternative economic system. Resisting and escaping are both "moves in the game."

In this chapter I focus on two strategies that aim to change the rules of the game: taming and dismantling capitalism. Workers can *tame* capitalism when they come together to lobby, vote, and apply pressure for laws that improve conditions, guarantee workers' rights, or regulate capital. They can *dismantle* capitalism by taking commodities or sectors out of the market altogether, expanding the public good. Labor campaigns can adopt these strategies to build anticapitalist movements.

I then argue that labor campaigns can be more anticapitalist by grounding their analysis and solutions in egalitarian values. I show how campaigns with similar demands can take different forms depending on their underlying values.

Next, I consider one of the major puzzles Wright grappled with in his work: "how to create collective actors with sufficient coherence and capacity for struggle to sustain the project of challenging capitalism."[1] I argue that current campaigns that are expanding labor struggles beyond the workplace, based on an intersectional analysis and approach, offer the potential for labor campaigns to be more anticapitalist.

Finally, I suggest that some of the cases discussed in the chapter contain elements of Wright's real utopias in that they are based on egalitarian values and contain features that would exist in a future non-capitalist society.

Anticapitalist Strategies: Taming Capitalism

One way that labor campaigns can be more, rather than less, anticapitalist is by focusing on strategies to change the rules of the game. Wright notes that anticapitalist movements must include efforts to neutralize

---

1   Erik Olin Wright, *How to Be an Anticapitalist in the Twenty-First Century* (New York: Verso, 2019), 119.

the harms of capital through resistance (such as workplace strikes against wage cuts) or taming capital (such as campaigns for minimum wage laws).

Workers are often stuck in moves in the game that neutralize the harms of capital. They try to form unions, strike against wage cuts, and resist attacks against employers. While this is important, to move toward taming capitalism and changing the rules of the game requires that workers build capacity as a class.

In recent decades, we have seen a proliferation of city and state laws that give workers new rights: citywide minimum-wage policies, paid sick leave, paid family leave, "ban the box" employment ordinances, equal pay, and even a handful of innovative regulations against irregular scheduling. At first glance, these laws may appear to be expressions of labor strength. But as political scientist Daniel Galvin notes, most of these new employment laws cover issues that would be governed by collective bargaining if unions were stronger and their density greater. He identifies "the emergence of new employment laws at the subnational level designed to address the same problems labor law no longer effectively addressed, but in different forms and through different mechanisms."[2] Without labor power in the workplace, many of the new employment laws will be poorly enforced. Workers might not even know about their new rights, or they may fear retaliation for demanding their due. In the end, the fundamental problem remains: workers have unequal power that legal changes alone won't fix. Anticapitalists within labor movements must go beyond passing laws to changing the rules of the game in ways that build class capacity.[3]

For example, living wage and minimum wage activists in some cities won higher wages along with securing the creation of new agencies to monitor, investigate, and enforce those wage laws. The Los Angeles living wage campaign fought for, and won, the right for city employees and nonprofit organizations to visit workplaces and educate workers about their rights under the new law. In San Francisco and New York,

---

2   Daniel J. Galvin, "From Labor Law to Employment Law: The Changing Politics of Workers' Rights," *Studies in American Political Development* 33, no. 1 (2019): 50–86.

3   Political scientists describe this process as the establishment of "policy feedback loops." See, for example, Alexander Hertel-Fernandez, "How Policymakers Can Craft Measures That Endure and Build Political Power," Roosevelt Institute, June 17, 2020, rooseveltinstitute.org.

labor activists ensured the establishment of new city agencies focused on enforcing a host of municipal labor ordinances.[4]

Perhaps the most expansive effort to date is in Seattle, Washington. After the city passed its $15 minimum wage, a task force composed of unions, community groups, business, and government created a plan for a new city agency that would enforce the law and other local ordinances. That agency, the Office of Labor Standards, was created in 2014 and now has twenty-three staff members.[5] The office uses city funds to contract with local nonprofits to conduct education and outreach with workers, ensuring that the information they are provided about their rights comes from worker-friendly labor organizations rather than government officials.[6] Workers receive training and get assistance filing complaints. The agency has developed new approaches to monitoring that don't rely on surprise visits from a limited number of government inspectors or waiting for workers to file complaints.[7] Instead, the community organizations develop ongoing relationships with workers to maintain knowledge about industries and workplaces.[8]

Scholars have argued that what is more effective than complaint-driven enforcement is "strategic enforcement": targeting high-violation industries, conducting company-wide investigations, and more. This can increase the capacity of the state itself to be more responsive to workers' rights, and push it to use its own resources more effectively and democratically in enforcing the laws on the books.

The "co-enforcement" model goes even deeper. It brings workers' rights organizations in to work as long-term partners with state agencies. This increases the state's capacity to investigate and monitor

4 Stephanie Luce, *Fighting for a Living Wage* (Ithaca, NY: Cornell University Press, 2004).

5 Virginia B. Garcia and David G. Jones, "Seattle Minimum Wage Enforcement Audit," Seattle Office of City Auditor, December 16, 2019, seattle.gov.

6 Teri Gerstein, "State and Local Workers' Rights Innovations: New Players, New Laws, New Methods of Enforcement," *Saint Louis University Law Journal* 65, no. 2 (2020).

7 Janice Fine et al., "Strategic Enforcement and Co-enforcement of U.S. Labor Standards Are Needed to Protect Workers through the Coronavirus Recession," Washington Center for Equitable Growth, January 14, 2021, equitablegrowth.org.

8 Janice Fine and Tim Bartley, "Raising the Floor: New Directions in Public and Private Enforcement of Labor Standards in the United States," *Journal of Industrial Relations* 6, no. 2 (2019): 252–76.

workplaces, and at the same time it builds the capacity of worker organizations.[9] Such a model is important because it can improve enforcement but also because it can build working-class capacity for further organizing beyond a specific law, which is necessary for building anticapitalist movements.

Anticapitalist Strategies: Dismantling Capitalism

A second group of labor campaigns that are more anticapitalist are those that work to decommodify institutions or sectors of the economy, moving them from private to public ownership or control. These efforts involve what Wright describes as *dismantling* capitalism, which requires changing the rules of the game in a way that transcends capitalist structures. These are difficult campaigns to win and therefore not common in labor history. But two new efforts suggest hope for anticapitalist labor campaigns.

Taking on the Banks

Since the 2008 financial crisis, unions, community organizations, research centers, and allies have launched several campaigns to hold large commercial banks accountable for the damage they have done to workers, customers, and the economy.

In 2013 the Communications Workers of America (CWA) launched the Committee for Better Banks, a bank worker organizing project with financial assistance from experienced bank worker unions in Brazil.[10] In partnership with Jobs With Justice and community organizations like New York Communities for Change and Make the Road, they began outreach to workers in the finance sector. Through organizing, they learned that bank workers faced unreasonable sales goals. Frontline bank workers in branches and call centers had to collect so much debt per hour, pushing customers to open new accounts and take out more

---

9   Fine et al., "Strategic Enforcement and Co-Enforcement of U.S. Labor Standards Are Needed."

10   E. Tammy Kim, "Workers of the (Finance) World Unite—and Unionize," Al Jazeera, December 13, 2013, america.aljazeera.com.

loans. Bank workers resented the pressure and felt they had to put sales goals above customer needs. According to Erin Mahoney of the CWA, "Frontline workers want to be advocates and financial advisers for their customers." But with extreme sales goals, they could not always provide the best options for customers. "Maybe the customer is calling about their checking account, but bank workers have to push a credit card on them to meet a certain amount of those credit card sales every day or every hour," explains Mahoney. "Customers don't like this, and frontline bank workers don't either."[11]

The organizers built a committee at Wells Fargo, helping workers circulate petitions and conduct actions at branches against the sales goals. For years, frontline bank workers had been blowing the whistle on Wells Fargo for the way the bank pushed its staff to set up fake accounts, but only after they began to work collectively, and with community allies, did they manage to get Wells Fargo in 2016 to agree to end sales goals.

In California, the bank workers partnered with consumer groups and research organizations like Action Center on Race and the Economy (ACRE), Alliance of Californians for Community Empowerment, and other groups fighting against Wells Fargo on several issues, including the fake accounts scandal as well as discriminatory lending, profiting from private prisons and immigrant detention centers, and financing the Dakota Access Pipeline. ACRE named Wells Fargo "America's Most Racist Bank."[12] In 2018, advocates got the Los Angeles City government to pass an ordinance designed to reduce high-pressure sales goals to protect workers and customers. Per the ordinance, the city will only deposit its money in a bank if it can prove that it does not link employee pay or employment status to selling products customers might not want or need. The CWA has also worked with bank workers in support of $15 minimum wage legislation and a $20 wage at Wells Fargo. In 2020, bank workers at Beneficial State Bank won the right for CWA to represent them.

All of this work happened alongside an effort to establish public banks in multiple cities and the state of California. In 2018, Ballot Measure B in Los Angeles, which would have established a city public

---

11   Erin Mahoney, interview with the author, September 8, 2020.
12   ACRE, acrecampaigns.org.

bank, failed with 44.15 percent of the vote, but the following year, the state of California passed AB 857, legalizing public banking for the first time in the state's history. Implementation has slowed due to the pandemic, but advocates continue to push the effort forward, including raising proposals to establish municipal public banks.

The work I describe here is not all driven by unions, and rather than one sole campaign, it involves a combination of efforts by a range of organizations working to transform the banking industry. This multi-pronged effort aims to resist and tame capitalism, and the latest moves to establish public banks suggests it has real potential to dismantle at least some aspects of capitalism. Public banking activist Pamela Haines considers these campaigns a revolutionary reform strategy because they allow us to ask questions such as, "Why don't we have control over our common wealth?"[13]

Health Care Is a Human Right

Another arena where unions are participating in broader struggles to resist, tame, and possibly dismantle capitalism is health care. In particular, National Nurses United (NNU) and the New York State Nurses Association (NYSNA) have taken a bold approach to combining strong workplace organizing with broader campaigns to transform the health care industry. "Nurses see firsthand that people have not been properly cared for, and don't have good access to quality health care," explained Judy Sheridan-Gonzalez, president of NYSNA. "Equity in health care becomes an issue that nurses can easily understand and embrace."[14]

Nurses must take classes to maintain their credentials, and NNU offers courses with a strong political economy foundation. Nurses learn about the ways in which racial capitalism shapes health care systems through courses like "Just-in-Time Management and the Factory-Hospital," "Fighting the Monopoly Epidemic," and "Confronting Institutionalized Racism in Health Care."

NNU has made Medicare for All a key goal and has devoted resources to building support inside and outside the union. Before the pandemic,

13   Pamela Haines, "Public Banking Has the Potential to Truly Revolutionize Our Economy," *Truthout*, November 21, 2021, truthout.org.
14   Judy Sheridan-Gonzalez, interview with the author, March 25, 2021.

nurses volunteered to do door-knocking and utilize "deep organizing" methods to have conversations with people about their health and health care concerns. The union sees the fight for public health care as a "non-reformist reform," as Michael Lighty, director of public policy for the California Nurses Association/NNU explained. "Single payer is the reform that establishes health security and enables greater equality and freedom—values worth fighting for."[15] NNU is part of a broader coalition of organizations fighting for single-payer health care based on the principle that health care is a human right: "Everybody in, nobody out," goes the coalition's slogan.[16]

NYSNA also supports the call for single-payer Medicare for All. As Sheridan-Gonzalez explains, a lot of NYSNA members were hit by Hurricane Sandy in 2012 and saw firsthand how our health care system was completely inadequate to address people's needs. NYSNA created the New York Relief Program to send volunteers to help in natural disasters, such as Hurricanes Irma and Maria and the typhoon in the Philippines in 2017. NYSNA observes the links between climate justice work, health care reform, and strong shopfloor unionism. Sheridan-Gonzalez says that some nurses get active in the union because they want something for themselves (higher wages, better working conditions), while others are motivated by a moral imperative to provide care and look out for others. That second instinct often leads to charity work, but the union has tried to enlist these nurses into a more politicized effort, engaging in solidarity work rather than charity.

As with public banking, the fight for single-payer health care is not the work of one union or one campaign, but a joint effort of organizations, of which NNU is a driving force. NNU sees the fight for public health care as a direct confrontation with racial capitalism.

Anticapitalist Values

In addition to prioritizing anticapitalist strategies that tame and dismantle capitalism, labor campaigns can be more anticapitalist by grounding

---

15   Michael Lighty, "Liberals Strike Back ... Against Single Payer," *Common Dreams*, August 8, 2017, commondreams.org.
16   Medicare For All, medicare4all.org.

their work in anticapitalist values. Wright argues that there are three sets of values that lay the foundation for a critique of capitalism: equality/ fairness, democracy/freedom, and community/solidarity. He notes that all "have hotly contested meanings," and in fact, some values can be posed against each other and create contradictions. For example, the values of community and solidarity can have a dark side, where within a group they can lead to building barriers to others even as the group maintains some strong inclusive tendencies.[17] And the meaning of values is contingent on time and geography.[18] But discussing, developing, and centering anti capitalist values can help anticapitalist movements select the kinds of reform campaigns they should engage in, and shape them to be their most effective.

We can apply Wright's anticapitalist values to labor in several ways. First, we can look at the core values that unions or labor campaigns promote in their main work through their bargaining demands or policy campaigns. Second, we can analyze the values the unions or labor organizations promote through their actions—how they function and how they organize.

From a methodological standpoint, both can be difficult. Take a large national union like the Communication Workers of America or the International Brotherhood of Teamsters. We could evaluate the rhetoric on their websites, look at the speeches made by their leadership, or analyze the content of their bargaining demands. There could be great variation from local to local, sector by sector.

Or take a labor movement campaign, like the fight for a living wage. Living wage campaigns have been enormously popular in the United States and several other countries. But part of why they are so popular is that the basic demand for higher wages can be motivated by a variety of

---

17 The contradictory nature of these values can be seen throughout labor history. Many labor unions have been built on a strict notion of solidarity with union brothers within the craft that is maintained by excluding immigrants or Black workers or women, for example. Alex Gourevitch has written about the different ways the value of "freedom" was interpreted by labor movements in the nineteenth century, from the more libertarian understanding of "freedom of contract" to the more radical view of freedom as self-governance in all aspects, including the workplace. See Gourevitch, *From Slavery to the Cooperative Commonwealth: Labor and Republican Liberty in the Nineteenth Century* (Cambridge: Cambridge University Press, 2014).

18 Joel Suarez, *The Labor of Liberty: Work and the Problem of Freedom in American History*, forthcoming.

reasons. Historically, the Catholic Church has played a big role in the living wage movement using moral grounds: it is unjust, it is immoral, for employers to hire workers and not pay them a wage high enough to support themselves and their families.

Others have promoted living wages to bolster the economy. In fact, in the UK, many of the more vocal advocates of the London Living Wage come from the business community. They speak of the ways in which paying higher wages is good for business and employee morale. In 2015, the Tories surprised many when they announced they would raise the national minimum wage to a living wage, in part to cut back spending on social programs. Still others have pushed for living wages as a strategy to build worker power, such as the US Fight for $15 movement that has sought to raise wages and establish unions.

How should we measure the values of a campaign? In my interviews with living wage supporters, including representatives from unions, business, government, and foundations, there was an emphasis on equality and fairness. Citizens UK, the main community group behind the London Living Wage, emphasized community and citizenship, and thus indirectly engaged the ideas of what it takes to engage in democracy. But even in the unions, very few listed democratic control of society or the freedom for self-rule among their goals. None of Wright's six values appears explicitly on the London Living Wage website. The dominant messaging is about the benefits that paying a higher wage offer to business.

The US Fight for $15 website suggests a very different campaign than that of the London Living Wage, with an emphasis on workers, structural racism, and worker power. Interviews indicate a complex movement that is diverse in terms of geography and coalition partners, but most Fight for $15 activists highlight equality and fairness. Solidarity is also central, including solidarity across sectors and occupations. The Fight for $15 campaign started with fast-food workers, but even from the start, it was a campaign of workers, community activists, faith-based organizations, unions, and even a few high-profile employers. The $15 concept soon spread to other sectors, and the "days of action" included childcare providers, airport workers, domestic workers, adjunct professors, and more.

Fight for $15 also emphasizes solidarity with the Movement for Black Lives. SEIU, the union behind Fight for $15, launched an internal Racial Justice Task Force to study structural racism and develop proposals for union functioning. It sought out contact with Black Lives Matter organizers and related organizations and asked them to endorse Fight for $15. Charlene Carruthers, founding national director of the Black Youth Project 100, told *Jacobin* magazine why her group decided to endorse the campaign: "Black and brown workers are at the forefront of the Fight for $15. We wanted to make sure their narrative was representative. We tried to shift the messaging and make sure that the Fight for $15 was more squarely centered in racial and gender justice."[19]

The alliance between the movements continued to grow, helping to bring a racial justice component to the wage fight and an economic justice analysis to Black Lives Matter. For example, on April 3, 2017, activists held teach-ins and demonstrations around the country on the theme "Fight Racism, Raise Pay." An organizer from the Movement for Black Lives, Chelsea Fuller, stated:

White supremacy and corporate greed have always been linked in America. The fast-food workers who are going on strike for $15 an hour and the right to a union are resisting the same institutional racism and oppression that fuels police violence across the country. We are stronger when we stand together, and so our movements are going to keep fighting back against the twin evils of racial and economic inequality that continue to hold back black and brown people.[20]

Beyond these alliances, Fight for $15 has spread across international borders. The historian Annelise Orleck writes about McDonald's workers from the United States, Brazil, South Korea, and Japan all meeting at a Fight for $15 international gathering and realizing they all shared identical burn marks from working on the fryer. Fight for $15 activist Bleu Rainer describes the moment as unforgettable, realizing the global connections he had with workers around the world.[21]

19   Brendan McQuade, "A United Front," *Jacobin*, September 2, 2015.

20   Justin Miller, "Fight for 15 and Black Lives Matter Join Forces on Anniversary of MLK's Death," *American Prospect*, April 4, 2017.

21   Annelise Orleck, *"We Are All Fast-Food Workers Now": The Global Uprising against Poverty Wages* (Boston: Beacon Press, 2018).

At the same time, the Fight for $15 is not monolithic, and there are critics who say the campaigns have been top-down, run by union leaders and lobbyists with little to no worker input. In this sense the movement may have a democratic message, but the campaign itself may be anything but.[22]

This highlights the challenges of measuring the values of a movement: there are the values stated in movement literature and speeches, but there are also the values embodied in the organizing and institutions behind and within the movement. There are the values that go into education around the campaign, but they may have little to do with the values of the voters who approve the legislation.

The methodological challenges raise political questions about how factions operate within movements. These examples show that whereas the dominant value within the UK movement might highlight moral arguments for higher wages and business stability, others in the movement prioritize other values. In fact, the majority appear to see the living wage as a tool to save capitalism rather than abolish it. That is not the case in the United States; nonetheless, the Fight for $15 includes everyone from billionaires who worry about economic and political stability, to socialist city council members like Kshama Sawant in Seattle.

Wright's work may provide a framework for the kinds of values anticapitalists should promote, but the on-the-ground reality of making those more universal demands within a movement is the subject of decades of debate and strategizing on the left. How do anticapitalists find space for their counternarratives within a broader movement? And how might they ensure that the values of the narrative are also fully embodied, in the ways that the organizations function and the campaigns are run?

Can Wright's values provide a North Star for anticapitalists working within unions or labor campaigns? Rather than shaping the fight around obtaining a living wage, anticapitalists should work to build unity within the movement around fundamental values. Those values should be used to evaluate the direction of the campaign, messaging, and the structure and functioning of campaign organizations.

---

22 Jonathan Rosenblum, *Beyond $15: Immigrant Workers, Faith Activists, and the Revival of the Labor Movement* (Boston: Beacon Press, 2017).

Of course, the meaning of values is contested, and it may be particularly difficult to apply values across international borders. But the fact that the values are contested and possibly contradictory does not mean they have no meaning at all or cannot be a foundation of a campaign. We can apply a dialectical approach to the meaning of values just as we use dialectical methods in other aspects of anticapitalist organizing. Historian Joel Suarez shows how work itself can be both a source of exploitation and a source of liberation. Wright's approach pushes activists to go beyond the content of the demand (living wages) and consider the values that motivate the demand, and if that requires debate, education, and collective meaning-making, so much the better.

Creating Collective Actors: Intersectional Campaigns

Wright wrote that perhaps the most vexing challenge for eroding capitalism is how to organize a collective agent to lead the struggle. Unions historically are hampered by a narrow workplace or sectoral consciousness and thus focus on gains for their members rather than the broader working class. Also, capitalists have frequently succeeded in developing methods to divide the working class.

Labor movements must find ways to unite the working class despite traditional divisions, often based on identity. As theorists from Antonio Gramsci to Stuart Hall to Kimberlé Crenshaw have written in various forms, people are never just one identity. They are not *just* workers, or women, or parents. They have identities based on their race, gender, ethnicity, age, occupation, hobbies, and more.

Wright builds on this idea in *How to Be an Anticapitalist*, which may come as a surprise to those who know of Wright's historical focus on class. The book's last chapter points out that people do not just have class interests, but many interests, some of which follow from their identities.[23] Labor unions cannot assume all workers see their class identity as central, and not all workers will choose to act based on their class interests. Some may prioritize other identities and interests; some may be motivated to act based on their values more than their interests.

---

23   Wright, *How to Be an Anticapitalist*, 133.

This approach pushes us to go beyond the traditional notion of union organizing that is rooted in workplace issues and class identity. One way to do that is through labor-community group alliances. For the past several decades, progressive unions have worked in coalition with community organizations under the notion that "I'll be there for your struggle, and you'll be there for mine." This builds community and reciprocity and is important for building power. But it is still based on the premise that people are either "labor" or "community," and thus Wright's approach suggests going even deeper. For example, unions might organize around workers' other identities as well, or organize with community allies around shared values.

In other words, Wright argues that constructing collective agents should be centered on anticapitalist values, and done in a way that connects values to interests. For example, labor movements based on class interests share the same values of equality/fairness and democracy/freedom as racial justice and other emancipatory movements. Rather than trying to place race and class in a hierarchy, anticapitalist movements must connect them explicitly through their campaign demands. This approach also fosters a more expansive and inclusive use of community/solidarity values.

Let's return to some of the opportunities and limits of labor union organizing in capitalism. Marx argued that capital helps sow the seeds of its own destruction by bringing workers together in the first place. Workers come together in factories and meet one another, discuss, learn that they have shared interests as a class, and find that they can have power if organized as such. In this sense, capital helps organize labor.[24]

But capital can also disorganize labor. Employers saw the power workers could have by coming together, and over the years they have created divisions between workers, often based on race or ethnicity or immigration status or gender. Sometimes they physically divided workers, including the effort to create smaller, decentralized factories starting in the 1950s and 1960s.[25]

---

24 Though in some industries, it is the other way around, such as in the coal industry (John R. Bowman, "When Workers Organize Capitalists: The Case of the Bituminous Coal Industry," *Politics and Society* 14, no. 3 [1985]: 289–327), or the garment industry (Steve Fraser, *Labor Will Rule: Sidney Hillman and the Rise of American Labor* [Ithaca, NY: Cornell University Press, 1993]).

25 Mike Davis, *Prisoners of the American Dream: Politics and Economy in the History of the US Working Class* (London: Verso, 1986).

And, as Cedric Robinson argued, workers come into capitalism through different, racialized, modes of production, and the legacy of these different modes have sometimes fragmented rather than homogenized the working class.[26] While states have assisted and enabled these processes, workers have divided themselves as well: racism, patriarchy, and nationalism are tools not exclusively imposed from above. Workers themselves can accept, promote, and enforce white supremacy and patriarchy. So how can a shared collective anticapitalist project be crafted?

As the modern factory has broken down and become fissured, and with the rise of contingent work and the gig economy, it becomes harder to identify the new kind of "factory." Workers may struggle to see their common class interests. But could this work to labor's advantage? Some organizers have worked to expand the notion of the workplace to include communities and to show the way in which capital has brought together a much broader set of actors. It is not just the "boss" that we see daily that organizes our daily work lives, but the investors who own the company, and who also might own the mortgages on our homes or be pushing to privatize our children's schools. It can be the state that employs workers, regulates access to public services, and controls the police. The following two cases from Minnesota and Connecticut highlight this perspective.

Bargaining for the Common Good in Minnesota

In 2014, unions and community organizations launched the Bargaining for the Common Good (BCG) network. Building off successful strikes in recent history, particularly the Chicago teachers' strike of 2012, and indeed, a longer history of labor-community traditions, the BCG network advocates an approach utilizing the leveraging power of collective bargaining to win gains for union and community members. It aims to broaden the organizing beyond dues-paying union members, and to win gains that benefit other stakeholders which, importantly, would be hard for the union to win on its own.

Greg Nammacher, president of SEIU Local 26, describes how such common struggle developed for his union and its community allies in

---

26 Cedric Robinson, *Black Marxism: The Making of the Black Radical Tradition* (Chapel Hill, NC: University of North Carolina Press, 1983).

Minneapolis–St. Paul. The union represents janitors who work for subcontractors for large companies. "We were clear that we wanted to take on some of the biggest companies in the Twin Cities to win our contracts, to raise wages and benefits for our members," he says. "We were also clear that we were not going to be able to win that by ourselves. These companies were too big and too powerful to cough up what we wanted if it was just the workers going after them."[27]

The union reached out to allies in the environmental movement and first held a meeting at the leadership level to compare demands and do a power map. They realized that the large building owners in the downtown Twin Cities were responsible both for keeping janitors' wages low (via subcontractors) and also for a significant amount of pollution.

The union surveyed their membership and found that many were concerned about climate change and worried about the chemicals they were required to use, often without training. Some members also spoke about climate justice from their perspective as climate refugees. Nammacher tells of a woman from Ecuador who said the land where she grew up was no longer usable due to climate change, which pushed her to migrate to the United States. She was excited by the chance to fight on an issue impacting her relatives back home. Members had already connected the climate issue to their work. "It was really us at leadership that had not thought about how to bridge these things that kind of live in different activist silos in our country," says Nammacher. "But for them it was obvious."

Union stewards helped educate members and build a contract campaign that included environmental demands as well as the usual ones concerning wages and working conditions. They invited community allies to open bargaining sessions. As negotiations continued, the union continued to work with members and allies and prepare for a strike. When the union finally did strike, "half of the people that were on the picket lines were community activists primarily around climate issues and half the people were striking workers," explains Nammacher.

The final issue holding up the contract was the demand for green cleaning rules. "Literally the issue that prevented us from getting the settlement on the last night from 9:00 p.m. until 4:00 a.m. was down to this question," says Nammacher. "It was just very interesting how hard

---

27   Greg Nammacher, interview with the author, September 11, 2020.

the companies fought it, which gets to how much they will push against expanding worker voice to issues outside traditional wages and benefits that intersect with deeper needs in the community." The union was ready to go back out on strike, but in the end the company agreed to the green cleaning demands, including a fund for the use of green cleaning products, increased recycling, and moving to daytime cleaning to reduce energy use in large buildings. This was in addition to gains in the traditional areas of wages and benefits.

Class and Race in Connecticut

On June 11, 2020, members of the health care union 1199 SEIU walked off the job to kneel for eight minutes and forty-six seconds of silence in memory of George Floyd and Breonna Taylor. This was the amount of time Police Officer Derek Chauvin knelt on Floyd's neck (later reports showed the actual time was even longer). The union joined the nationwide Walkout for Black Lives in support of the larger movement against police brutality and for racial justice.

Rob Baril, president of SEIU 1199 New England, explains that the walkout was just an extension of what has already been happening for the nursing home worker union in Connecticut and Rhode Island. "There are a lot of ways in which Black Lives don't matter," said Baril, explaining that the COVID-19 pandemic had made clear the ways in which Black and brown people experience significant health disparities compared with white people, as well as how they served on the front lines as essential workers. For Baril, the pandemic was a form of apartheid not seen in this country since Jim Crow, given the scale of suffering, sickness, and death among Black and brown people.[28]

Working with community partners, the union has pushed to integrate racial justice demands into its upcoming contract negotiations. Members see firsthand the impact of a racist system on their ability to do their jobs. For example, social workers in the union have seen the state cut mental health services over the years, which means it is more likely that not them, but police, will be dispatched to deal with mental health crises. The union has included a bargaining proposal to expand the mobile health crisis units and the number of social workers so that

28   Rob Baril, interview with the author, July 2020.

911 calls are more likely to be handled by trained medical professionals. It is also demanding more resources for reentry programs for people released from prison.

KB Brower, organizing director for the BCG network, explains that the democratic structure of the union helped facilitate the process of bringing in community demands to bargaining: "1199 has a really active engaged membership that is used to being fully involved in the bargaining process," she says. "They had a whole structure for members helping write the contract language, decide on the contract language, a really kind of deep democratic process where members have real ownership of writing contract language, so adding in the community piece actually felt very natural and right to the existing members." Brower says union staff could not have developed these kinds of demands: "It was the members themselves who are living it every day who understand where the holes are, and the community members who say, 'This is what resources are necessary, this is what's missing.'"[29]

Real Utopias

The campaigns I describe above show how labor organizing can contribute to anticapitalist movements. They also reflect some elements of Wright's concept of real utopias. As Harry Brighouse writes in chapter 5 of this volume, a real utopia is an existing or viable policy, project, or institution that is built on a set of anticapitalist principles and prefigures something that would exist in a future egalitarian society.

In addition to the Fight for $15 movement, several other of the campaigns described here are based on anticapitalist values. SEIU 1199 New England leaders built an intersectional campaign not just because it made for better strategy, but because they thought it was the right thing to do. In 2020, as health care workers put their lives on the front lines and police killed Black people at random, the union stepped in to fight for basic human rights. Baril asks, "How do we change the terms of the debate and stop articulating, 'This is what . . . we think we can win,' and start articulating, 'This is what we think we deserve.'" Capitalism makes certain human lives expendable; the union said, "No more."

---

29   KB Brower, interview with the author, December 15, 2020.

The Bargaining for the Common Good approach has been adopted most expansively by teachers' unions, and it is easy to see why, as most workers go into teaching because they want to help students. A traditional union approach that focuses on winning wage increases and pension plans may not sit well with teachers who might be told their gains come at the expense of students. The BCG approach allows them to integrate their power and needs as workers with student needs, as well as other political interests they may have, such as racial justice. In my own experience organizing university teaching assistants, I found that many workers were reluctant to put their time into winning gains for themselves, but were willing to step up and take risks to build a union that would fight to make the university more democratic.

Like teachers, some nurses have at times been reluctant to engage in workplace organizing because it can put those they serve at risk. Nurses are trained in solidarity; their job is almost by definition based in anti-capitalist values. Medicare for All is a natural extension of this. In fact, one of the other big campaigns that nurses' unions have pushed, "safe staffing," is also based on solidarity and community. As Judy Sheridan-Gonzalez explains, "Safe staffing is the rallying cry for all of our members because it has a community orientation, because you can care for your community."[30]

A real utopia also includes elements we would want in a future egalitarian society. Certainly, public goods such as healthcare and banking fit in a real utopia. But we might also include co enforcement and BCG as models for egalitarian decision-making and implementation.

As one of several stakeholder governance models, Co-enforcement is, to borrow the title of a volume in the "real utopias" book series, a way to deepen democracy.[31] It democratizes a state function by bringing stakeholders in to help review the law, monitor workplaces, and evaluate progress. In a future egalitarian society, we will need mechanisms to monitor conditions of work and develop solutions when problems arise.

A postcapitalist society won't necessarily remove the need to bargain. Even in a society of worker cooperatives, there still would need to be mechanisms to deliberate how to balance workplace and community

---

30   Judy Sheridan-Gonzalez, interview with the author, March 25, 2021.
31   Archon Fung and Erik Olin Wright, eds., *Deepening Democracy: Institutional Innovations in Empowered Participatory Governance* (New York: Verso, 2003).

issues, such as teacher working conditions and the student learning environment. Like co-governance, BCG can bring all stakeholders to the table to make democratic decisions about priorities based on solidarity and fairness.

Conclusion

Labor organizing can be a way to prop up capitalism and keep it running smoothly, but it can also be the foundation of anticapitalist movements. Any union might have such contradictory tendencies within it. Wright's framework suggests that even a simple reform like a minimum wage law can support capitalism and help erode it at the same time. In this chapter I described ways that labor campaigns can be more anticapitalist through the strategies they pursue and the values they adopt.

Some unionists have attempted to build anticapitalist labor campaigns for decades, so some of what I described here is not new. There have been ambitious efforts to win workers' rights alongside civil rights, access to housing, and public goods. While those failed in the goal of transforming capitalism, today's labor markets may have begun to evolve in ways that unexpectedly allow for a way past some of the limitations unions have faced historically. The massive consolidation of corporate power means more workers are ultimately working for the same boss—and those same corporations control ever more of our housing, schools, and access to everything from clean water to credit. At the same time, many local and national states have adopted policies that enable this consolidation.[32]

Wright's framework can be used to shape collective agents beyond the workplace. Capital, aided by states, brings us together in our many identities, but it is up to organizers to shape the ways in which we develop shared narratives about our interests and values. Wright's emphasis on democracy applies not just to the content of the reforms

---

32   This is not to stay all states are similar or that all have necessarily "converged" into one model. There are important distinctions between varieties of capital, and states have taken different paths (David Soskice and Peter A. Hall, *Varieties of Capitalism: The Institutional Foundations of Comparative Advantage* [Oxford: Oxford University Press, 2001]). This is in part what makes Wright's argument that there are contradictory spaces within states, and space for leftists to pursue inside/outside strategies.

we should demand, but also to the assessment of the organizations themselves.

Union leaders cannot just assert these values: a union is in theory a democratic organization. There are plenty of examples of unions with leaders on the left who pass the correct political resolutions and issue statements of solidarity with other struggles, but creating a collective agent must go beyond resolutions and the correct political line; it must go deep into the membership. These efforts may not start as explicitly anticapitalist, but as Alex Han, an organizer with the Chicago Teachers Union, found, it is almost impossible to talk about multiple worksites and common targets without eventually talking about capitalism.[33]

Although socialists were pushed underground or out of the labor movement altogether in the 1950s, today more and more unionists openly identify as socialist or anticapitalist. Some who had a more pragmatic approach now see that it is impossible to win basic labor demands without addressing capitalism as a system. Longtime labor organizer Stephen Lerner explained that for most of his career he fought for "specific winnable demands," believing that over time these would add up to larger change. But in the last decade it has become clear that this pragmatic strategy is not powerful enough to address massive inequality in wealth and power, and it won't inspire workers to take the kind of dramatic action that is necessary. Shortly before helping found the BCG network, he explained, "Times of crisis create movement-building moments that make it possible and necessitate raising bigger questions about how capitalism operates and what are alternatives that offer the hope of a better and more just world. We are in such a moment now."[34]

More labor leaders are also seeing racial justice as fundamentally intertwined with the fight for economic justice. Certainly, some unionists in the past made similar arguments, but many of those more radical voices were lost in the postwar labor movement.[35] By 2021, even mainstream leaders had made a shift. For example, Marty Walsh, former head of the Boston Building Trades Council, spoke of the need to

---

33 Alex Han, interview with the author. October 23, 2020.

34 Stephen Lerner, email to the author, April 29, 2012.

35 Ellen Schrecker, "The Legacy of McCarthyism," in *American Labor and the Cold War: Grassroots Politics and Postwar Culture*, ed. Robert W. Cherny, William Issel, and Kieran Walsh Taylor (New Brunswick, NJ: Rutgers University Press, 2004).

address systemic racism in his confirmation hearing as US secretary of labor.[36]

Whether these shifts toward a more expansive understanding of labor movements reflects a real transformation or just a temporary shift in strategy remains to be seen, but it seems unlikely labor unions can exist much longer in their current form. And as the demographics of the labor market change, workers themselves will likely push for change from the inside.

The labor force is changing in other ways as well. Marx and other labor theorists wrote about the division between "hand labor" and "head labor," between managers who think and workers who do, and between workers and intellectuals. At the time they were writing, capitalists were working to deepen the division of labor and break tasks into more and more parts, deskilling the work and alienating workers from the fruits of their labor. Only 21 percent of the world's population was literate in 1900, and even though rates were higher in the United States and some European countries, access to higher education was limited.[37] For most, books were a luxury.

But in this aspect, too, the nature of labor markets has changed dramatically in the past one hundred years, and perhaps even further in the last fifty years since Harry Braverman wrote about deskilling in *Labor and Monopoly Capital*. While many employers continue attempts to deskill, they also have cut back their workforce and require workers to cover multiple tasks at once. Today, US union members are more likely to have completed at least some college. Even workers in precarious minimum wage jobs may be required to understand complicated technology, speak multiple languages, or know how to multitask.

Anticapitalist activists within the labor movement can work to organize collective agents around shared values and connect those values to multiple interests, particularly those aimed at emancipation. My examples may be overly optimistic. I have selected them not because they are representative of most campaigns, or because they are sure to succeed. The odds are still strongly in the favor of capital. But

36   Allen J. Smith, "Nominee for Labor Secretary Advances through Confirmation Hearing." SHRM, February 5, 2021, shrm.org.

37   Max Roser and Esteban Ortiz-Ospina, "Literacy" and "Tertiary Education," Our World in Data, 2013, ourworldindata.org.

Wright's framework provides a way to rethink the conundrum faced by historical debates that suggest only one specific strategy for anti-capitalist movements and one main identity (class) around which to organize. No one strategy will succeed: organizers must be ecumenical in their approach.

Contributors

Rina Agarwala is professor of sociology at Johns Hopkins University. She teaches and researches labor, migration, gender, and the Global South. She is the author of *Migration-Development Regime: How Class Shapes Indian Emigration* (2022) and *Informal Labor, Formal Politics and Dignified Discontent in India* (2013), and coeditor of *Whatever Happened to Class? Reflections from South Asia* (2016).

Gianpaolo Baiocchi earned his PhD from Wisconsin in 2001 and is a professor at New York University, where he directs the Urban Democracy Lab. A political sociologist of utopian bent, he has worked on participatory budgeting, the civic imagination, popular sovereignty, and most recently, with Jake Carlson, on social housing.

Ruy Braga is a full professor at the Department of Sociology at the University of São Paulo (USP) and former director of the Center for Studies on Citizenship Rights (Cenedic-USP). Specializing in labor studies, he has published, among other books, *The Anguish of the Precariat: Labor and Solidarity in Racial Capitalism* (2023).

Harry Brighouse is Mildred Fish Harnack professor of philosophy of education, Carol Dickson Bascom professor of humanities, affiliate professor of education policy studies, and director of the Center for Ethics and Education at the University of Wisconsin–Madison.

Michael Burawoy is professor emeritus at the University of California, Berkeley. Most recently, he is the author of *Public Sociology: Between Utopia and Anti-Utopia* (2021).

H. Jacob Carlson is an assistant professor of sociology at Kean University. His research focuses on democracy, housing, and changing cities. He was previously a postdoctoral research associate at Brown University's Population Studies and Training Center and was a dissertation fellow at University of Wisconsin's Institute for Research on Poverty.

Rodolfo Elbert is a researcher at the National Scientific Research Council (CONICET) at the Gino Germani Institute, and professor at the Sociology Department, University of Buenos Aires. He researches labor, class and informality and has published articles in international journals such as *Current Sociology, Critical Sociology,* and *Latin American Perspectives.*

Greta R. Krippner is associate professor of sociology at the University of Michigan. She is a historical sociologist who writes on the sociology of credit and finance. Her current book project explores the individualization of risk in American capitalism over the course of the long twentieth century.

Stephanie Luce is professor of labor studies at the School of Labor and Urban Studies, City University of New York (CUNY). She received her PhD in sociology from the University of Wisconsin–Madison. Her books include *Fighting for a Living Wage* and *Practical Radicals: Seven Strategies to Change the World.*

João Alexandre Peschanski serves as the executive director of the Wikimedia affiliate in Brazil and as a board member of Wikipedia and Education. He earned his PhD in sociology from the University of Wisconsin–Madison. Currently, he leads the Digital Communications Research team at the São Paulo Research Foundation NeuroMat Center.

Peter Ramand is a graduate student at the University of Wisconsin–Madison. He is the author of *Yes: The Radical Case for Scottish*

Independence (2014) and the editor of *Old Nations, Auld Enemies, New Times: The Selected Works of Tom Nairn* (2014).

Gay Seidman is a professor of sociology at the University of Wisconsin–Madison. Her research focuses mainly on labor and social movements in the global South. Her books include *Manufacturing Militance: Workers' Movements in South Africa and Brazil, 1970–1985* and *Beyond the Boycott: Labor Rights, Human Rights, and Transnational Activism.*

Kwang-Yeong Shin is a CAU fellow at Chung-Ang University in Seoul, Korea, and currently president of the East Asian Sociological Association. He has been researching class, labor, and comparative political economy. Recently, he published *Precarious Asia: Global Capitalism and Work in Japan, South Korea, and Indonesia* (with Arne L. Kalleberg and Kevin Hewison).

Marta Soler-Gallart, professor at the University of Barcelona, is vice-president of the International Sociological Association and former president of the European Sociological Association. She is the director of CREA, Community of Research on Excellence for All, and is among the ten top researchers worldwide on social impact, according to Google Scholar.